First World War

and Army of Occupation

War Diary

France, Belgium and Germany

21 DIVISION
110 Infantry Brigade
Leicestershire Regiment
7th Battalion
29 June 1916 - 29 March 1919

WO95/2164/2

The Naval & Military Press Ltd
www.nmarchive.com
Published in association with The National Archives

Published by

The Naval & Military Press Ltd

Unit 10 Ridgewood Industrial Park,

Uckfield, East Sussex,

TN22 5QE England

Tel: +44 (0) 1825 749494

www.naval-military-press.com

www.nmarchive.com

This diary has been reprinted in facsimile from the original. Any imperfections are inevitably reproduced and the quality may fall short of modern type and cartographic standards.

Contents

Document type	Place/Title	Date From	Date To
Heading	WO95/2164-2		
Heading	7th Bn Leicester Regt Jly 1916-Apr 1919		
Heading	7th Battn. The Leicestershire Regiment. July 1916		
Miscellaneous	21st Division	07/08/1916	07/08/1916
Miscellaneous	7th Battn. Leicestershire Regt.		
War Diary	Bailleul Mont	29/06/1916	01/07/1916
War Diary	Souastre	02/07/1916	03/07/1916
War Diary	Wallincourt	04/07/1916	06/07/1916
War Diary	Talmas	07/07/1916	07/07/1916
War Diary	Hangest	08/07/1916	09/07/1916
War Diary	Hangest Sur Somme	10/07/1916	10/07/1916
War Diary	Bottom Wood	11/07/1916	13/07/1916
War Diary	Mametz Wood	14/07/1916	14/07/1916
War Diary	Bazantin Le Petit Wood	14/07/1916	14/07/1916
War Diary	Bazantin Le Petit	14/07/1916	14/07/1916
War Diary	Bazantin Le Petit Wood	14/07/1916	16/07/1916
War Diary	Fricourt	17/07/1916	17/07/1916
War Diary	Ribbemont	18/07/1916	22/07/1916
War Diary	Moncheaux	23/07/1916	28/07/1916
Heading	1/7th Battalion Leicestershire Regiment August. 1916.		
War Diary	Beaufort	28/07/1916	28/07/1916
War Diary	Agnez Les Duisans	29/07/1916	06/08/1916
War Diary	Trenches	07/08/1916	28/08/1916
Heading	1/7th Battalion Leicestershire Regiment September 1916.		
War Diary	Arras	01/09/1916	04/09/1916
War Diary	Denier	04/09/1916	13/09/1916
War Diary	Dernancourt	13/09/1916	15/09/1916
War Diary	Montruban	16/09/1916	25/09/1916
War Diary	Gueudecourt	25/09/1916	01/10/1916
Miscellaneous	War Diary Of 7th Battn Leicestershire Regt. Oct. 1-Oct 31st 1916		
War Diary		01/10/1916	31/10/1916
Heading	War Diary Of 7th Battn Leicestershire Regt. November 1st to 30th 1916		
War Diary	Hoenzollern Sector	01/11/1916	12/11/1916
War Diary	La Bourse	15/12/1916	19/12/1916
War Diary	Cauchy-A-La-Tour	20/12/1916	27/01/1917
War Diary	Houtkerque	28/01/1917	13/02/1917
War Diary	Bethune	14/02/1917	14/02/1917
War Diary	Trenches Hohenzollern Sector.	15/02/1917	26/02/1917
War Diary	Noyelles	27/02/1917	28/02/1917
Heading	7th (Service) Battalion The Leicestershire Regiment. 1-31 March 1917		
War Diary	Noyelles	01/03/1917	04/03/1917
War Diary	Hohenzollern Right Sub Sector	05/03/1917	31/03/1917
Heading	7th (Sec) Battn The Leicestershire Regiment War Diary From 1st to 30th April 1917		
War Diary	Lacauchie	01/02/1917	04/02/1917
War Diary	Mayenneville	03/04/1917	03/04/1917

War Diary	St Leger & Croisilles	04/04/1917	04/04/1917
War Diary	Cruisilles	05/04/1917	07/04/1917
War Diary	Moyenville	08/04/1917	15/04/1917
War Diary	Moyenville to Baillevlval	15/04/1917	25/04/1917
War Diary	Croisilles	25/04/1917	29/04/1917
War Diary	Boiry Becquerelle	30/04/1917	30/04/1917
Heading	War Diary of 7th (Sec) Battalion The Leicestershire Regt.1-31 May 1917		
War Diary	Boiry Becquerelle	01/05/1917	26/05/1917
Miscellaneous	Report on Operation by 7th Battn Leicestershire Regiment.	03/05/1917	03/05/1917
Heading	War Diary Of The 7th (Service) Battn The Leicestershire Regiment. for June 1917		
War Diary	Bienvillers	01/06/1917	01/06/1917
War Diary	Moyeneville	02/06/1917	28/07/1917
War Diary	War Diary Of the 7th (Service) Battalion The Leicestershire Regt. For July 1917		
War Diary	Adinfer Wood	01/07/1917	20/07/1917
War Diary	Trenches	20/07/1917	31/07/1917
Heading	War Diary of the 7th (Service) Battalion The Leicestershire Regiment. From 1st to 31st August 1917		
War Diary	Moyenneville	01/08/1917	06/08/1917
War Diary	Left Bde Sector	09/08/1917	17/08/1917
War Diary	Hamelincourt	18/08/1917	25/08/1917
War Diary	Gouy-En-Artois	26/08/1917	31/08/1917
War Diary	Beaufort	01/09/1917	03/09/1917
War Diary	Hauteville	04/09/1917	16/09/1917
War Diary	Caestre	17/09/1917	22/09/1917
War Diary	Berthen	23/09/1917	25/09/1917
War Diary	Forward Area	26/09/1917	30/09/1917
War Diary	Polygon Wood	01/10/1917	03/10/1917
War Diary	Wiltshire Farm H.35a.	03/10/1917	03/10/1917
War Diary	Zillebeke Lake	04/10/1917	04/10/1917
War Diary	Polygon Wood	05/10/1917	06/10/1917
War Diary	Reutel	06/10/1917	10/10/1917
War Diary	Anzac Camp H.30	11/10/1917	11/10/1917
War Diary	La Carnois	12/10/1917	15/10/1917
War Diary	Railway Embankments I 20.a.	16/10/1917	23/10/1917
War Diary	B Camp Chateau Segard N.30.C	24/10/1917	26/10/1917
War Diary	Clapham Junction	01/11/1917	03/11/1917
War Diary	Chateau Segard "B" Camp	04/11/1917	07/11/1917
War Diary	Zillebeke Bund	08/11/1917	08/11/1917
War Diary	Front Line J5a 4.2	08/11/1917	11/11/1917
War Diary	Zillebeke Bund	12/11/1917	13/11/1917
War Diary	Chateau Segard "A" Camp	14/11/1917	16/11/1917
War Diary	Devonshire Camp G22b 8.7	17/11/1917	17/11/1917
War Diary	Noote Boom	18/11/1917	18/11/1917
War Diary	Caudescure	19/11/1917	19/11/1917
War Diary	Gonnehem	20/11/1917	20/11/1917
War Diary	Coupigny	21/11/1917	24/11/1917
War Diary	Frevillers	25/11/1917	30/11/1917
Heading	War Diary 7th Bn Leicestershire Regt. Dec. 31st 1917 Vol 27		
War Diary	Front Line X 26 a 6.1	01/12/1917	03/12/1917
War Diary	Epehy F1 d 8.9	04/12/1917	07/12/1917
War Diary	Front Line X 20.26	08/12/1917	12/12/1917

War Diary	Villers Faucon	13/12/1917	16/12/1917
War Diary	Front Line X 20c X 26a	16/12/1917	28/12/1917
War Diary	Saulcourt	29/12/1917	31/12/1917
War Diary	Map Ref. 57c SE 4 62c NE 2	01/01/1918	04/01/1918
War Diary	Lieramont 62c	04/01/1918	15/01/1918
War Diary	Haut Allaines 62c	16/01/1918	19/01/1918
War Diary	Epehy 62c NE 2	20/01/1918	20/01/1918
War Diary	Epehy	21/01/1918	23/01/1918
War Diary	Front Line B.H.Q. X. 25c 50.80	24/01/1918	28/01/1918
War Diary	Saulcourt E 9 d.	29/01/1918	31/01/1918
Miscellaneous	21st Division Special Order.	15/02/1918	15/02/1918
Heading	7th (Service) Battalion the Leicestershire Regiment. War Diary For February 1918		
War Diary	Saulcourt E 9 d	01/02/1918	01/02/1918
War Diary	Front Line X 25 a 5.0	02/02/1918	04/02/1918
War Diary	Epehy	04/02/1918	07/02/1918
War Diary	Moislans	08/02/1918	17/02/1918
War Diary	'B' Camp Templeux La Fosse	18/02/1918	23/02/1918
War Diary	La Fosse	20/02/1918	20/02/1918
War Diary	Villers Faucon	23/02/1918	28/02/1918
Heading	7th Battn. The Leicestershire Regiment. March 1918		
Heading	7th (S) Bn Leicestershire Rgt. War Diary For March 1918		
War Diary			
War Diary		21/03/1918	31/03/1918
War Diary	Appendices		
Heading	Appendix "A"		
Miscellaneous		21/03/1918	21/03/1918
Miscellaneous	Killed in action		
Miscellaneous	Appendix 'A'		
Miscellaneous		21/03/1918	21/03/1918
Miscellaneous			
Miscellaneous		22/03/1918	22/03/1918
Miscellaneous			
Miscellaneous		22/03/1918	22/03/1918
Miscellaneous		23/03/1918	23/03/1918
Miscellaneous		21/03/1918	21/03/1918
Miscellaneous			
Miscellaneous	Appendix 'A'	21/03/1918	21/03/1918
Miscellaneous	Adjutant OAK	21/03/1918	21/03/1918
Miscellaneous		22/03/1918	22/03/1918
Miscellaneous	Adjt Oak		
Miscellaneous		22/03/1918	22/03/1918
Miscellaneous			
Miscellaneous	Appendix "B"		
Heading	1/7th Battalion Leicestershire Regiment April 1918		
Heading	War Diary for April 1918 7th (S) Battn Leicestershire Regt		
War Diary	Allonville	01/04/1918	02/04/1918
War Diary	Dranoutre	03/04/1918	04/04/1918
War Diary	Butterfly & Leeds Camps	05/04/1918	07/04/1918
War Diary	La Clytte	08/04/1918	08/04/1918
War Diary	Chippawa Camp	09/04/1918	09/04/1918
War Diary	Scottish Wood Camp	10/04/1918	10/04/1918
War Diary	Manawatu Camp	11/04/1918	16/04/1918
War Diary	Howe Camp	17/04/1918	30/04/1918

War Diary	Oak Operation Order No. 10 Appendix A		
Miscellaneous	Oak O O 10 Appendix B	15/04/1918	15/04/1918
Heading	Appendix B		
Miscellaneous	Appendix C		
Miscellaneous	Appendix D Operation Orders by Lt Col. Es. Chance Comdg Palm	29/04/1918	29/04/1918
Miscellaneous	Appendix D		
Operation(al) Order(s)	Operation Orders By Lt Col E.S. Chance Comdg Palm Appendix E	30/04/1918	30/04/1918
Miscellaneous	Appendix E		
Operation(al) Order(s)	Operation Orders No. 6 by Lt Col. N.M. Irwin. D.S.O., M.C. Commanding 8th Bn. Leicestershire Regt. Appendix F	30/04/1918	30/04/1918
Heading	Appendix F 7th Leics		
War Diary	Nr Cafe Belge	01/05/1918	02/05/1918
War Diary	Oost Houck	03/05/1918	04/05/1918
War Diary	In Trench	05/05/1918	06/05/1918
War Diary	Lagery	07/05/1918	13/05/1918
War Diary	Prouilly	14/05/1918	14/05/1918
War Diary	Trenches	15/05/1918	31/05/1918
Miscellaneous	Appendix A	26/05/1918	26/05/1918
Heading	War Diary of The 7th (S) Battalion The Leicestershire Regiment. June 1918		
War Diary	Etrechy	01/06/1918	03/06/1918
War Diary	Courjeonnet	04/06/1918	09/06/1918
War Diary	Moeurs	10/06/1918	14/06/1918
War Diary	Hangest Sur Somme	16/06/1918	16/06/1918
War Diary	Framicourt	17/06/1918	22/06/1918
War Diary	Monchy Sur Eu	24/06/1918	01/07/1918
War Diary	Puchvillers	02/07/1918	02/07/1918
War Diary	Arqueves	03/07/1918	16/07/1918
War Diary	Acheux Wood	17/07/1918	17/07/1918
War Diary	Arqueves	18/07/1918	18/07/1918
War Diary	Nr Acheux	19/07/1918	19/07/1918
War Diary	Acheux	20/07/1918	24/07/1918
War Diary	Englebelmer	25/07/1918	30/07/1918
War Diary	S.S.E. of Englebelmer	31/07/1918	31/08/1918
Heading	War Diary August 1918 7th Bn. Leicestershire Regt.		
War Diary	Englebelmer	01/08/1918	15/08/1918
War Diary	Forward Zone	15/08/1918	15/08/1918
War Diary	Barn Support	16/08/1918	17/08/1918
War Diary	Q 16 a 33	18/08/1918	22/08/1918
War Diary	Mailly Maillet	23/08/1918	24/08/1918
War Diary	R 16.c	24/08/1918	24/08/1918
War Diary	M 8 a	24/08/1918	25/08/1918
War Diary	M 22 b 9.5		
War Diary	M 22 b	26/08/1918	29/08/1918
War Diary	N 14 a	29/08/1918	31/08/1918
Operation(al) Order(s)	Jone Operation Order No. 28	02/08/1918	02/08/1918
Operation(al) Order(s)	Jone Operation Order No. 29	08/08/1918	08/08/1918
Operation(al) Order(s)	Jone Operation Order No. 30	09/08/1918	09/08/1918
Map			
Miscellaneous	Patrol Report		
Map			
Miscellaneous	Patrol Report		
Map			

Miscellaneous	Sketch Map No. 1		
Miscellaneous	Guides		
Miscellaneous	Joke Operation Order No. 31	10/08/1918	10/08/1918
Miscellaneous	O.C. "A" Coy.	09/08/1918	09/08/1918
Miscellaneous			
Miscellaneous	I.O.		
War Diary	W of Beaulencourt	01/09/1918	05/09/1918
War Diary	Sailly-Saillisel	06/09/1918	07/09/1918
War Diary	Manancourt	08/09/1918	09/09/1918
War Diary	Heudicourt	10/09/1918	10/09/1918
War Diary	N. Equancourt	16/09/1918	18/09/1918
War Diary	14 Willows R.	18/09/1918	19/09/1918
War Diary	Manancourt	20/09/1918	23/09/1918
War Diary	Sorel	24/09/1918	25/09/1918
War Diary	S. of Gouzeacourt	26/09/1918	30/09/1918
Heading	War Diary 7th Bn Leicestershire Regiment. October 1st-31st 1918		
War Diary		01/10/1918	31/10/1918
War Diary		01/10/1918	25/10/1918
Heading	War Diary of 7th Bn Leicestershire Regiment. From 1st November 1918 To 30th November 1918		
War Diary		01/11/1918	14/11/1918
War Diary	Beaufort	15/11/1918	30/11/1918
Heading	War Diary Of 7th Bn Leicestershire Regiment. From 1st December 1918 To 31st December 1918		
War Diary	Beaufort	01/12/1918	13/12/1918
War Diary	Berliamont	14/12/1918	14/12/1918
War Diary	Vendegies	15/12/1918	15/12/1918
War Diary	Inchy	16/12/1918	16/12/1918
War Diary	Ferrieres	17/12/1918	31/12/1918
Heading	War Diary of 7th Batt. Leicestershire Regiment. From 1st January 1919 To 31st January 1919		
Heading	War Diary 7th Battn Leicestershire Regiment. January 1919		
War Diary	Ferrieres	01/01/1919	31/01/1919
Heading	War Diary 7th Battn Leicestershire Regiment. February 1919		
War Diary	Ferrieres	01/02/1919	03/04/1919
War Diary	Bouchon	05/04/1919	27/04/1919
War Diary	Ferrieres	28/03/1919	29/03/1919

21ST DIVISION
110TH INFY BDE

7TH BN LEICESTER REGT

JLY 1916-APR 1919

From 37 DIV

110th Inf.Bde.
21st Div.

Battn. transferred with Bde. from 37th Div. 7.7.16.

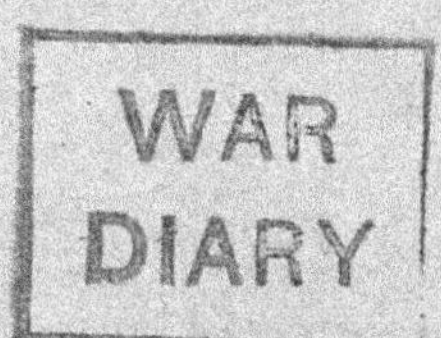

7th BATTN. THE LEICESTERSHIRE REGIMENT.

J U L Y

1 9 1 6

1
apr 19

21st Division.

Herewith War Diary of 7th Bn. Leic. Regt. for July.

110/21

7.8.16.

Brigadier-General,
Commanding 110th Infantry Brigade.

Confidential

110/21 Bde

Herewith War Diary
for July 1916

6/8/16

Capt & Adjt
for O.C. 7/ Leic Regt

Instructions regarding War Diaries and Intelligence Summaries are contained in F. S. Regs., Part II. and the Staff Manual respectively. Title Pages will be prepared in manuscript.

No 21 July

Army Form C. 2118.

7 Leicesters

WAR DIARY
or
~~INTELLIGENCE SUMMARY~~
(Erase heading not required.)

Place	Date	Hour	Summary of Events and Information	Remarks and references to Appendices
			7th Batt. Leicestershire Regt	Vol 10
			JULY 1916.	
				12.B 21 sheet

2449 Wt. W14957/M90 750,000 1/16 J.B.C. & A. Forms/C.2118/12.

Army Form C. 2118.

WAR DIARY
or
~~INTELLIGENCE SUMMARY~~
(Erase heading not required.)

Instructions regarding War Diaries and Intelligence Summaries are contained in F. S. Regs., Part II. and the Staff Manual respectively. Title Pages will be prepared in manuscript.

Place	Date	Hour	Summary of Events and Information	Remarks and references to Appendices
			(CONTD)	
BAILLEUL-MONT.	29/6/16	2.30 AM.	5. Operations. The Company moved from BIENVILLERS au BOIS at 2.30 am, and took up their position for the assault in slits dug in 87 Sector, south of BIENVILLERS – MONCHY Road.	
		4. AM	Gas and smoke were released from our front line trenches along the whole divisional front.	
		4.5 AM.	Gas turned off. Smoke continued.	
		4.10. AM	Artillery opened fire on enemy front line and known M.G. emplacements.	
		4.15 AM	Artillery lifted to supports. Raiding party emerged from trench No 87 through listening post saps, & formed up, walking to within 50 yards of enemy wire. Enemy M.G's opened fire but appeared to be firing high.	
		4.20 AM	Intensive bombardment of enemy's front line, by howitzers, 18 pdrs, 2" T.M. & Stokes guns.	
		4.25 AM	Company crawled up to enemy wire. Gap was found by marching on compass bearing of 90°.	
		4.30 AM.	Artillery lifted to supports. The enemy was seen to be lining his parapet in sentry boxes, and on seeing the first party advance rained upon firing rapidly & wildly. H.Q. Squad having rushed the portion allotted to them, A & B Squads commenced to file in with C in the rear. Communication by telephone was established with Lt. Horwill, the wire being cut immediately the "all in" was reported. All went well with B & C squads who went to the right on entering, B under 2nd Lt Pickering-Clarke along the fire trench, and C working up the communication trench to south end of the salient. 'A' Squad were held up immediately on entering enemy's trench, the first bayonet man being killed and 2Lt Mason badly wounded. The remainder of the Squad stayed on the parapet throwing bombs at the enemy who were firing from their sentry boxes. They rushed the trench and found a whole heap of German wounded & dead, bombing the remainder along until they reached their objective 40 yds from 'H.Q.' as their ranks were rather depleted they were ordered to block the trench at the point arranged, & hold on. No dugouts were found, and the R.E. sec were sent to reinforce B & C Squads.	
			(CONTD.)	

2449 Wt. W14957/M90 750,000 1/16 J.B.C. & A. Forms/C.2118/12.

Instructions regarding War Diaries and Intelligence Summaries are contained in F. S. Regs., Part II. and the Staff Manual respectively. Title Pages will be prepared in manuscript.

WAR DIARY
or
~~INTELLIGENCE SUMMARY~~
(Erase heading not required.)

Army Form C. 2118.

Place	Date	Hour	Summary of Events and Information	Remarks and references to Appendices
BAILLEUL MONT.	29/6/16	4.30 am.	The minor enterprise Company consisting of 4 officers - 70 men and 9 R.E. raided the enemys trenches, in conjunction with other companies from the division at 4.30 am.	
			1. Object of the raid. - To kill the enemy & bring back prisoners and identifications.	
			2. Composition & Equipment of the Company.	

H.Q. SQUAD.

	ARMS	BOMBS	AMM.	EXTRAS	REMARKS
O.C. Coy.	Revolver	4	10 rds	2 Lacrym. Bombs	Klaxon horn.
1st pair { Sniper	Rifle & bayonet	4	30.	4 Smoke bombs.	
Bomber	bayonet	8	–		
2nd " { Sniper	Rifle & bayonet	4	30	–	
Bomber	bayonet	8	–	wire cutters	
3rd " { Sniper	Rifle & bayonet	4	30	–	
Bomber	bayonets	8	–	wire cutters	
4th " { Sniper	Rifle & Bayonet	4	30	–	
Bomber	bayonet	8	–	wire cutters	
2 Stretcher bearers.	–	–	–	2 Stretchers.	
2 telephonists	Rifle.	–	30	2 telephones & wire.	

A SQUAD. (B & C SQUADS. Similar to A.)

ARMS	BOMBS	AMM.	EXTRAS	REMARKS		
Rifle & bay.	4	30.	–	–	2 Bayonet men.	
Revolver	2	12.	2 Lacrym. bombs.	wire cutters	O.C. SQUAD.	1 SEC.
Bayonets	8.	–	–	–	Throwers	
Revolver	4	12.	–	–	Leader	
Bayonets	12	–	–	–	Carriers	
					2 [illegible] guards	
Rifle & bayonets	4.	30.	2 ladders	–	2 do.	
					2 do.	
Rifle & Bayonets	4	30	–	–	Bayonet man	2 SEC.
Bayonets	8	–	–	–	Throwers	
Revolver	2	12	2 Lacrym. bombs.	–	Leader	
Bayonets	12	–	–	–	Carriers	
Revolver	4.	12.	Mallet	2 Lacrym. bombs.	1. N.C.O	BLOCKING PARTY.
Rifle & bayonets	4	30.	–	–	1 man	
Bayonets	8.	–	Wire &	Staples	1 do	
Bayonets	8	–	Wire &	Staples	1 do	
Bayonets	4	–	2 TORPEDOES.		2 R.E.	

(CONTD.)

2449 Wt. W14957/M90 750,000 1/16 J.B.C. & A. Forms/C.2118/12.

Army Form C. 2118.

Instructions regarding War Diaries and Intelligence Summaries are contained in F. S. Regs., Part II. and the Staff Manual respectively. Title Pages will be prepared in manuscript.

WAR DIARY
or
~~INTELLIGENCE SUMMARY~~

(Erase heading not required.)

Place	Date	Hour	Summary of Events and Information	Remarks and references to Appendices
			(CONTD).	
BAILLEUL-MONT	29/6/16.	4.30 a.m.	3. Training.	

The training of the company lasted about 6 weeks. The men were specially selected from C. & D. Coys. They were struck off all company duties & fatigues & attached to H.Q. The R.E. Sec were also attached to the Battn for a week before the raid took place.

Men were trained in Bayonet fighting, Physical Training (including running) and bombing.

A copy of the enemy trenches to be raided was obtained from photographs taken by aeroplanes,

Practice attacks were made on these trenches during night & day. They proved of good value to the company when the raid took place.

Special attention was paid to Bayonet fighting & gallows were erected & trenches dug.

4. Formation.

ENEMY 1st LINE.
GAP.
O.C. Coy.
Snipers & bombers
H.Q. SQUAD
A SQUAD
B SQUAD
Snipers & bombers
1st SECn
DUGOUT GUARDS.
2nd SECn
R.E.
BLOCKING PARTY.
SEARCHER
C. SQUAD.
1st SEC.
DUGOUT GUARDS.
2nd SEC.
R.E.
BLOCKING PARTY.
STRETCHER BEARERS
TELEPHONISTS.
TAPE MAN.

(CONTD)

2449 Wt. W14957/M90 750,000 1/16 J.B.C. & A. Forms/C.2118/12.

Instructions regarding War Diaries and Intelligence Summaries are contained in F. S. Regs., Part II. and the Staff Manual respectively. Title Pages will be prepared in manuscript.

WAR DIARY

or

~~INTELLIGENCE SUMMARY~~

(Erase heading not required.)

Army Form C. 2118.

Place	Date	Hour	Summary of Events and Information	Remarks and references to Appendices
BAILLEUL-MONT.	29/6/16.	4.30 AM.	5.(CONTD) Meanwhile B Squad had a great fight with, and worsted an enemy bombing party, who were all killed – our men picking up their grenades and throwing them back before they had time to explode. Excellent work was done with the bayonet and revolvers were very useful, as enemy's trench was found to be very narrow (about 2 ft wide) – B reached their objective, and blocked successfully with lacrymatory bombs and wire. The dugouts of which four were found were bombed, and afterwards torpedoed by the R.E. accounting for the occupants who were howling for mercy – These torpedoes consisted of a wooden box 9" x 12" x 12", charged with ammonal weighing about 30 lbs. A simple method of exploding was devised by a Nobel lighter, 9 sec fuse, and No 8 VII detonator, which was taken over all ready fixed in the charge. C Squad reached their objective with no resistance, and blocked the trench; they would have advanced further, but the trench was found to be muddy, & not much used, certainly no use for bombing. Two dugouts (one officers) were bombed & torpedoed, the occupants firing up the shaft. Meanwhile the snipers of HQ Squad were doing good work by picking off a party who were attempting to advance over the top to cut off C Squad. To do this they took up a position about 30 yds over the parados.	
		4.45 AM	The enemy by this time was bursting shrapnel over the point of entry, besides dropping rifle grenades and small T.M. bombs, so work being completed the order to withdraw was given, by sounding a "Klaxon" horn. The withdraw was done systematically, sections going first and then blocking parties. Gallantry was displayed by No 1 section B Squad, altho nearly all wounded continued to fight until their objective was reached – 2Lt Pickering Clarke. Sgt Jordan Cpl Toogood, Ptes Bennett Burns & Parker were especially good – Our total casualties were 1 officer died of wounds, 2 men killed (1 RE) 28 wounded (25 slightly) – all were brought in except the 2 men A Squad (killed). The total estimate of damage done to the enemy was 60 killed (including those in the dugouts) 30 of which were counted in the trench. The enemy kept up a continued bombardment on our lines & communications	

(CONTD)

2449 Wt. W14957/M90 750,000 1/16 J.B.C. & A. Forms/C.2118/12.

Instructions regarding War Diaries and Intelligence Summaries are contained in F. S. Regs., Part II. and the Staff Manual respectively. Title Pages will be prepared in manuscript.

WAR DIARY

or

~~INTELLIGENCE SUMMARY~~

(Erase heading not required.)

Army Form C. 2118.

Place	Date	Hour	Summary of Events and Information	Remarks and references to Appendices
			5 (contd) Starting from 4.4 AM when his alarm rockets were sent up.	
BAILLEULMONT	29/6/16.	5 AM.	The company having returned, the smoke was turned off.	[illegible]
do	30/6/16.		nil.	[illegible]
do	1/7/16.	5 AM	The Battalion left BAILLEULMONT for SOUASTRE marching via LA CAUCHIE - HUMBERCAMP. The 110th Inf Bde was Brigade in Corps reserve to the VII Corps, who attacked GOMMECOURT in the morning of 1st. The Battalion was not needed.	[illegible]
SOUASTRE.	2/7/16		Billets. Coy parades.	[illegible]
	3/7/16		The Battalion marched to WALLINCOURT via STAMAND. GAUDIEMPRE.	[illegible]
WALLINCOURT.	4/7/16.		Huts. Coy parades.	[illegible]
	5/7/16		do.	
	6/7/16.		110th Inf. Bde. transferred to 21st Division. The Battalion marched to TALMAS, falling in 2 AM and arriving 9 AM. The Corps commander wished us good bye and good luck at PAS.	[illegible]
TALMAS	7/7/16		Falling in at 9 AM we marched to HANGEST arriving 4.30 PM.	[illegible]
HANGEST	8/7/16.		Billets - resting.	[illegible]
do	9/7/16		Coy. parades.	[illegible]

2449 Wt. W14957/M90 750,000 1/16 J.B.C. & A. Forms/C.2118/12.

Army Form C. 2118.

Instructions regarding War Diaries and Intelligence Summaries are contained in F. S. Regs., Part II. and the Staff Manual respectively. Title Pages will be prepared in manuscript.

WAR DIARY
or
~~INTELLIGENCE~~ SUMMARY

(Erase heading not required.)

Place	Date	Hour	Summary of Events and Information	Remarks and references to Appendices
HANGEST SUR SOMME	10/7/16.		The Battn. left HANGEST at 1 am, and marched to AILLY entraining there for MERRICOURT which was reached about 11 am. Buses were provided to MEAULT where the rest of the day was spent resting, until 11 PM.	[illegible]
BOTTOM WOOD	11/7/16		The Battn having moved up – the 7th Bn Yorkshire Regt were relieved early in the morning. Guides were provided at Fricourt, but it was almost daylight before the relief was complete. The Quadrangle trench was occupied by C & D Coy with a platoon from B & D in the Quadrangle Support. H.Q. & A Coy & the remainder of B Coy were in BOTTOM WOOD. During the night previous & daytime, the enemy kept up a slow bombardment with 105 mm Schrapnel and 150 mm Howitzers.	[illegible]
do	12/7/16.		QUADRANGLE Trenches & BOTTOM WOOD. Intermittent bombardment all day. We suffered about 30 casualties including 2Lt A. Spencer D Coy killed.	[illegible]

2449 Wt. W14957/M90 750,000 1/16 J.B.C. & A. Forms/C.2118/12.

Army Form C. 2118.

Instructions regarding War Diaries and Intelligence Summaries are contained in F. S. Regs., Part II. and the Staff Manual respectively. Title Pages will be prepared in manuscript.

WAR DIARY
or
INTELLIGENCE SUMMARY

(Erase heading not required.)

Place	Date	Hour	Summary of Events and Information	Remarks and references to Appendices
BOTTOM WOOD.	13/7/16.		After a more or less slow bombardment all day including 77mm guns the Battn was relieved by the 10 K.O.Y.L.I. and marched back for rest to Fricourt.	
	~~14/7/16~~		The day was spent resting & preparing for the attack on the morrow.	[illegible]
MAMETZ WOOD	14/7/16.		ATTACK ON BAZANTIN LE PETIT Wood & village by the 110th Inf. Bde. The Battn was drawn up for the assault in four lines. The first three lines were in front of MAMETZ Wood & were to move forward in succession at Zero, the first line to take clear and hold the German first line, the remainder to push on capture and consolidate the FOREST trench (enemy support line). The fourth line were drawn up behind the North edge of MAMETZ Wood to move forward half an hour after Zero, and push forward through FOREST Trench ready to assault the German third line.	

2449 Wt. W14957/M90 750,000 1/16 J.B.C. & A. Forms/C.2118/12.

CONTD.

Army Form C. 2118.

Instructions regarding War Diaries and Intelligence Summaries are contained in F. S. Regs., Part II. and the Staff Manual respectively. Title Pages will be prepared in manuscript.

WAR DIARY
or
~~INTELLIGENCE SUMMARY~~

(Erase heading not required.)

Place	Date	Hour	Summary of Events and Information	Remarks and references to Appendices
MAMETZ WOOD	14/7/16		[CONTD.] By 2.55 AM all ~~xxx~~ dispositions were made each platoon being on its correct alignment. A number of casualties were suffered during this operation, one platoon of C Coy losing almost half its number. The men behaved admirably under trying conditions. At Zero 3.25 AM when the barrage lifted our first line trench was hardly close enough to it to rush the first line before the enemy could man it. As a result the advance was rather ragged. The right (A) Coy in conjunction with the 6th Battn had little difficulty in entering the trench: The left (D) Company were momentarily held up by machine gun fire but managed to keep up close to the parapet & rush the line. The two centre (B & C) Companies were held up for about 20 minutes by machine guns. The pressure was relieved by parties from the right working down a flank. [CONTD]	

2449 Wt. W14957/M90 750,000 1/16 J.B.C. & A. Forms/C.2118/12.

Instructions regarding War Diaries and Intelligence Summaries are contained in F. S. Regs., Part II. and the Staff Manual respectively. Title Pages will be prepared in manuscript.

WAR DIARY

or

~~INTELLIGENCE SUMMARY~~

(Erase heading not required.)

Army Form C. 2118.

Place	Date	Hour	Summary of Events and Information	Remarks and references to Appendices
BAZANTIN LE PETIT WOOD	14 7 16.		(CONTD) The centre companies were thus able to rush the trench. The second and third lines coming on swept the remainder of the first line with them and made for the Second Line [Forest Trench]. By this time of the officers of B Coy only 2nd Lieut EVANS was left, in C Coy only 2Lt REED, while in D Coy all the officers were out of action. The enemy in the first line trench at first made some resistance but many were caught in their dug outs, & the rest seeing that they could not stop our rush retreated into the Wood & made no resistance in the FOREST trench. By 4 AM our whole line was in occupation of FOREST trench and the work of consolidation was begun. Capt A.A. Clarke taking command. 2Lt Evans then sent back Coy. S.M. Geary to ensure	

Instructions regarding War Diaries and Intelligence Summaries are contained in F. S. Regs., Part II. and the Staff Manual respectively. Title Pages will be prepared in manuscript.

Army Form C. 2118.

WAR DIARY
or
~~INTELLIGENCE SUMMARY~~
(Erase heading not required.)

Place	Date	Hour	Summary of Events and Information	Remarks and references to Appendices
BAZANTIN LE PETIT.	14/7/16.		that the German front line was cleared of the enemy. This NCO with his party found a number of the enemy who had been passed over in the rush. In the meantime the left Coy (D) after pushing on too eagerly under our own barrage & being forced to retire turned towards the flank & established connection with the 8th Battn. At 4.25 AM. Capt A.A. Clarke, leaving 2Lt Evans in charge of the Front trench, went forward in charge of the party to capture the third objective. No resistance was met with on the right, but on the left considerable trouble was caused by a machine gun & by snipers and also by the observation post in the tree both Capt. CLARKE and Lieut WAKEFORD were hit. This left the assaulting line without an officer, but Sergt WALKER (A Coy) and L.Sgt SHERLOCK (C Coy) rallied their men and made good this line.	

2449 Wt. W14957/M90 750,000 1/16 J.B.C. & A. Forms/C.2118/12.

Instructions regarding War Diaries and Intelligence Summaries are contained in F. S. Regs., Part II. and the Staff Manual respectively. Title Pages will be prepared in manuscript.

WAR DIARY
or
~~INTELLIGENCE SUMMARY~~
(Erase heading not required.)

Army Form C. 2118.

Place	Date	Hour	Summary of Events and Information	Remarks and references to Appendices
BAZANTIN LE PETIT.	14. 7. 16.		There was no German trench in this position & in some cases the men again pressed forward & came under fire from our own barrage. Meanwhile the left (D) Coy being checked by the M.G. on the west of the wood & being unable to make headway were rallied by L/Cpl BUSH. An attempt was made to get round the position on the right, with the result that this party lost direction in the wood & finally found itself among the 6th Battn. L/Cpl BUSH then placed himself under the orders of an officer of that Battn.	
			Almost before the barrage lifted, the party under Sergt WALKER rushed the German trench on the north side of the wood. The enemy made no resistance here & being caught between the barrage of shell fire & our advancing line gave	

Instructions regarding War Diaries and Intelligence Summaries are contained in F. S. Regs., Part II. and the Staff Manual respectively. Title Pages will be prepared in manuscript.

WAR DIARY
or
~~INTELLIGENCE SUMMARY~~

(Erase heading not required.)

Army Form C. 2118.

Place	Date	Hour	Summary of Events and Information	Remarks and references to Appendices
BAZANTIN LE PETIT WOOD	14 7 16.		themselves up. By 6.45 A.M. we were established in the line on N. edge of the wood. Subsequently officers of the 5th Battn, bringing up supports took over command of this sector. About 7.15 A.M. Capt ~~[illegible]~~ GWYTHER now commanding the Battn, ordered 2Lt EVANS to push forward from FOREST TRENCH in supports of the front line. On reaching the position selected for the strong point on the Railway, this party came under M.G. fire from the N.W. corner of the wood. 2nd Lt EVANS took up the line covering the strong point & prepared for reconnaissance. The position therefore at 8 A.M. was:- Northern edge of wood held by us. Possession of the N.W. corner doubtful. Line of Railway and strong point secured by us.	

2449 Wt. W14957/M90 750,000 1/16 J.B.C. & A. Forms/C.2118/12.

Army Form C. 2118.

WAR DIARY
or
~~INTELLIGENCE~~ SUMMARY
(Erase heading not required.)

Instructions regarding War Diaries and Intelligence Summaries are contained in F. S. Regs., Part II. and the Staff Manual respectively. Title Pages will be prepared in manuscript.

Place	Date	Hour	Summary of Events and Information	Remarks and references to Appendices
BAZANTIN LE PETIT WOOD.	14 7 16		Throughout the morning the enemy kept up an intermittent bombardment with 150 mm howitzers and a few 77 mms, which grew in intensity about midday and during the afternoon. About 1 PM it was believed that the Germans were still holding the extreme edge of the wood at the N.W. corner, & an assaulting party of the 7th ~~R~~ Bn was organized to clear them out. The bushes & trees were very thick round this part which necessarily made progress slow, the enemy evacuating and manning a trench about 30 yards from the wood, before our men could get through. We suffered several casualties from a Machine Gun in the above mentioned trench.	

2449 Wt. W14957/M90 750,000 1/16 J.B.C. & A. Forms/C.2118/12.

Instructions regarding War Diaries and Intelligence Summaries are contained in F. S. Regs., Part II. and the Staff Manual respectively. Title Pages will be prepared in manuscript.

Army Form C. 2118.

WAR DIARY
or
~~INTELLIGENCE~~ SUMMARY
(Erase heading not required.)

Place	Date	Hour	Summary of Events and Information	Remarks and references to Appendices
BAZANTIN LE PETIT WOOD	14 7 16.		An attempt was made about 9 o'clock to reorganise the Battn, as they were considerably mixed up most of the officers becoming casualties. Lt Col Drysdale was wounded whilst the Battn was marching to its position in front of MAMETZ Wood, Capt & Adj A.A. AADWORTH taking command. Captains Wright, Gifford & Lts Burnett, Hollis, Abbott & 2nd Lt Newton, Gulbridge & Bain being all killed before our troops reached the first line. 2nd Lt Pickering-Clarke, Simpson & Reed also Lt Wakeford were killed in the wood. The wounded officers were Capt A.A. Clarke, ~~2nd~~ Lt Houghton & 2nd Lt Thomas, Webb, omit ~~Dridge~~ Nichol. Our total casualties were 18 officers & 535 men killed & wounded.	

2449 Wt. W14957/M90 750,000 1/16 J.B.C. & A. Forms/C.2118/12.

Instructions regarding War Diaries and Intelligence Summaries are contained in F. S. Regs., Part II. and the Staff Manual respectively. Title Pages will be prepared in manuscript.

WAR DIARY
or
~~INTELLIGENCE~~ SUMMARY
(Erase heading not required.)

Army Form C. 2118.

Place	Date	Hour	Summary of Events and Information	Remarks and references to Appendices
BAZANTIN LE PETIT WOOD.	14/7/16.		~~[illegible]~~ Our men along with the 9th Bn remained the trenches at the edge of the wood and remainder there until next morning. The night was quiet.	
do	15/7/16		By next morning about 100 men answered the Roll. So they were sorted out and given a piece of trench about 150 yds along the N. side of BAZANTIN le PETIT Wood.	
			About 2 PM. 40 men were taken up to support the 8th & 9th Bns in a further attack on N.W. corner. The troops holding the corner had been obliged to withdraw a few yards as the bombing & rifle grenading from the enemy 20 yards away was becoming intense, & there being many casualties.	
			It was behind that the enemy had again entered the corner	

2449 Wt. W14957/M90 750,000 1/16 J.B.C. & A. Forms/C.2118/12.

Instructions regarding War Diaries and Intelligence Summaries are contained in F. S. Regs., Part II. and the Staff Manual respectively. Title Pages will be prepared in manuscript.

WAR DIARY
or
~~INTELLIGENCE SUMMARY~~

(Erase heading not required.)

Army Form C. 2118.

Place	Date	Hour	Summary of Events and Information	Remarks and references to Appendices
BAZANTIN LE PETIT WOOD	15/7/16.		but by the time our troops got through, he had retired again to his Redoubt. The 40 men were left in the Strong point under the 9th Bn until the Bn was relieved. Nothing more of importance happened during the day or night. Enemy guns were quieter.	[illegible]
do	16/7/16		The day was quiet, except a few shells on the Strong point during the afternoon and evening. The Bn was relieved by the 10th Yorkshires at 10.P.M. It was raining, and the route was very bad. The enemy was dropping gas shells into MAMETZ wood which had no effect except that gas helmets were put on. The Battn bivouaced for the night near Fricourt Wood.	[illegible]

2449 Wt. W14957/M90 750,000 1/16 J.B.C. & A. Forms/C.2118/12.

Army Form C. 2118.

Instructions regarding War Diaries and Intelligence Summaries are contained in F. S. Regs., Part II. and the Staff Manual respectively. Title Pages will be prepared in manuscript.

WAR DIARY
or
~~INTELLIGENCE~~ SUMMARY
(Erase heading not required.)

Place	Date	Hour	Summary of Events and Information	Remarks and references to Appendices
FRICOURT	17/7/16.		The day was spent resting, and at 6 P.M. the battn marched to RIBBEMONT arriving about 12 MIDNIGHT.	[illegible]
RIBBEMONT	18/7/16.		Billets resting. Weather fine.	[illegible]
	19/7/16.		Congratulatory address by Major General Donald Campbell	[illegible]
	20/7/16.		Entrained for SALEUX and marched 15 kilometres to HANGEST.	[illegible]
	21/7/16.		Left HANGEST at 8 P.M. in busses for LONGPRE.	[illegible]
	22/7/16.		Marched through the outskirts of AMIEN to LONGUEAUX where we entrained for PETIT-HOUVIN arrived about 8 P.M. and marched to billets at MONCHEAUX.	[illegible]

2449 Wt. W14957/M90 750,000 1/16 J.B.C. & A. Forms/C.2118/12.

Instructions regarding War Diaries and Intelligence Summaries are contained in F. S. Regs., Part II. and the Staff Manual respectively. Title Pages will be prepared in manuscript.

WAR DIARY

or

~~INTELLIGENCE SUMMARY~~

(Erase heading not required.)

Army Form C. 2118.

Place	Date	Hour	Summary of Events and Information	Remarks and references to Appendices
MONCHEAUX	23/7/16. to 24/7/16		Coys were reorganized and fresh kits indented for.	[illegible]
	25/7/16.		The Battn. marched to BEAUFORT to billets.	[illegible]
	26/7/16 to 28/7/16.		Company parades. Major [illegible] of 9th Bn Leicestershire Regt took over command of the Battn.	[illegible]

2449 Wt. W14957/M90 750,000 1/16 J.B.C. & A. Forms/C.2118/12.

110th Brigade.

21st Division.

1/7th BATTALION

LEICESTERSHIRE REGIMENT

AUGUST 1916.

Instructions regarding War Diaries and Intelligence Summaries are contained in F. S. Regs., Part II. and the Staff Manual respectively. Title Pages will be prepared in manuscript.

WAR DIARY
or
~~INTELLIGENCE SUMMARY~~
(Erase heading not required.)

Army Form C. 2118.

7th Bn Leicestershire Regiment

21/110

Vol 11

Place	Date	Hour	Summary of Events and Information	Remarks and references to Appendices
BEAUFORT.	28/7/16		The Battn left BEAFORT for AGNEZ les DUISANS marching via AVESNES le COMTE and HABARCQ, arriving 12 noon.	
AGNEZ les DUISANS.	29/7/16 to 6/8/16.		The eleven days were spent chiefly in Company training, bayonet fighting, & physical training. The Battn was reinforced by three drafts during the time totalling 300 men. 20 new officers also joined from the S. Staffs Reg. & Sherwood Foresters. On 4th & 5th inst the trenches to be taken over were reconnoitred by officers. The line to be occupied by the Battn was to the N.E. of ARRAS. ref. 51B G12 A & C. Front line trenches which were divided by ARRAS - BAILLEUL - SIRE - BERTHOULT Rd. were on an average 200 yds from enemy front line. On the left the sector was bounded by the crater, CLAUDE. There was another crater CLARENCE immediately on the road & 100 yds to the right in 94 trench the crater CUTHBERT. Each of these craters were about 60 yds in diameter and 60 feet deep. They were immediately in the front line.	

2449 Wt. W14957/M90 750,000 1/16 J.B.C. & A. Forms/C.2118/12.

18.B
5 sheets

Army Form C. 2118.

Instructions regarding War Diaries and Intelligence Summaries are contained in F. S. Regs., Part II. and the Staff Manual respectively. Title Pages will be prepared in manuscript.

WAR DIARY
or
INTELLIGENCE SUMMARY
(Erase heading not required.)

Place	Date	Hour	Summary of Events and Information	Remarks and references to Appendices
AGNEZ LES DUISANS.	29/7/16 – 6/8/16.	CONTD	The trenches which were not very good, having previously been heavily bombarded were composed of three lines namely. 1st DEFENCE, 2nd IMMEDIATE SUPPORT, 3rd SUPPORT, all of which were held by the Battn. The front line 94 to 96 inclusive was about 350 yds in length.	[initials]
TRENCHES.	7/8/16.		The Battn relieved the 9th Leic. Reg 11 P.M. A & C Coys occupying the DEFENCE & IMMEDIATE SUPPORTS of 94 – 96 & B & D the Supports. Everything was very quiet during the first night, and the relief completed without casualties.	[initials]
	8/8/16. – 12/8/16		Work was started on deepening the trenches to 9 feet. Both DEFENCE and SUPPORT lines were traversed, and trench boards were put down. There were 6 mine dugouts to be completed under the Supervision of the R.E. Most of the Shafts of which there were two to each dugout were about 20 feet down, when They were deepened to 30 feet before work on the chambers was commenced. During this period there was no shelling by the enemy on our lines, although our field guns fired a fair amount at their front lines.	[initials]

2449 Wt. W14957/M90 750,000 1/16 J.B.C. & A. Forms/C.2118/12.

Instructions regarding War Diaries and Intelligence Summaries are contained in F. S. Regs., Part II. and the Staff Manual respectively. Title Pages will be prepared in manuscript.

WAR DIARY
or
INTELLIGENCE SUMMARY
(Erase heading not required.)

Army Form C. 2118.

Place	Date	Hour	Summary of Events and Information	Remarks and references to Appendices
TRENCHES	8/8/16 – 12/8/16		On 11th the enemy fired about 15 Oolb TM Bombs on 95 & 96 trenches. A fair amount of damage was done to the IMMEDIATE SUPPORT & SUPPORT of 95 trench the shock of the explosion shaking the sides of the trenches. 3 men were killed in the support line. A good retaliation was done by our 2" TM and Stokes guns. Companies in support relieved those in front line at 8 P.M.	[illegible]
	13/8/16		Vry quiet except for small T.M. bombs fired on 94 trench; they were silenced by our Stokes.	
	14/8/16	10 P.M.	Enemy exploded a mine immediately under CLARENCE CRATER. The new crater was immediately occupied on both lips by A & B. Coy. Enemy did not attempt to leave his trenches. It is thought that he fired the mine in order to blow in our galleries which were then only about 30 feet away from him. Vry good work was done by Lt Howitt A Coy & 2nd Lt EVANS in consolidating the near lip of the crater and digging out the men who were buried. About 250 feet of the Defence line was obliterated entirely and also the top of AUGUST AVE. 2nd Lt Phillips was killed.	

2449 Wt. W14957/M90 750,000 1/16 J.B.C. & A. Forms/C.2118/12.

Instructions regarding War Diaries and Intelligence Summaries are contained in F. S. Regs., Part II. and the Staff Manual respectively. Title Pages will be prepared in manuscript.

WAR DIARY
or
INTELLIGENCE SUMMARY
(Erase heading not required.)

Army Form C. 2118.

Place	Date	Hour	Summary of Events and Information	Remarks and references to Appendices
TRENCHES	14/8/16	CONTD.	The two companies in the firing line suffered 8 casualties all of which were killed. The 14th Battn Northumberland Fusileers who were working on the DEFENCE LINE had 15 men buried all of which were killed. Many men who were buried were dug out after being under several hours. Good assistance was given by the N.Z. tunnelling company & a troop of the 17th Lancers. By the morning of 15th 96 trench & a part of 95 & AUGUST AVE were clear and the lip of the crater consolidated.	[illegible]
	15/8/16		Everything was very quiet, practically no shelling. A few small T.M. bombs were fired every evening about 6 PM to 7 PM.	
	16 17/8/16		Our patrols were active during the whole period in obtaining a knowledge of the front, enemys wire & our own. A great deal of wire was put out on our front, 2 or 3 parties being at work every night. Two men were killed by rifle fire.	[illegible]
	18/8/16.		The Battn took over fresh trenches on the right. A Coy moving up from the left and occupying 89 to 92 inclusive. C Coy extended further to the right to 93, D Coy took over supports 89 to 95 & B Coy were in BRITANNIA WORK.	[illegible]

2449 Wt. W14957/M90 750,000 1/16 J.B.C. & A. Forms/C.2118/12.

Army Form C. 2118.

Instructions regarding War Diaries and Intelligence Summaries are contained in F. S. Regs., Part II. and the Staff Manual respectively. Title Pages will be prepared in manuscript.

WAR DIARY
or
~~INTELLIGENCE~~ SUMMARY
(Erase heading not required.)

Place	Date	Hour	Summary of Events and Information	Remarks and references to Appendices
TRENCHES	19/8/16 to 22/8/16		Very quiet, only small TM Grenades were fired into D4 & D5 Sector & a few rifle Grenades into 90 & 91. Companies changed over on 22nd. B Coy coming back to Supports and A to BRITANNIA WORKS. On 22nd 2Lt NEALE & one man were slightly wounded by small T.M. bomb.	[illegible]
	23/8/16 to 28/8/16.		Everything very quiet except on 26th when our Supports were shelled by about 10. 105 mm shells. 3 men were killed. The Battn was relieved by 6th Bn Leic. Reg at 6 P.M. B & D Coys proceeded to Cen ARRAS to billets. C Coy to the Candle Factory & A Coy to the REDOUBT LINE.	[illegible]

110th Brigade.

21st Division.

1/7th BATTALION

LEICESTERSHIRE REGIMENT

SEPTEMBER 1916.

Army Form C. 2118.

Instructions regarding War Diaries and Intelligence Summaries are contained in F. S. Regs., Part II. and the Staff Manual respectively. Title Pages will be prepared in manuscript.

WAR DIARY

~~or~~

~~INTELLIGENCE SUMMARY~~

(Erase heading not required.)

Place	Date	Hour	Summary of Events and Information	Remarks and references to Appendices
ARRAS	1/9/16		The battalion in trenches in ARRAS Sector – half the battalion being in reserve in ARRAS itself, half in the Keep line. No incident of importance occurred. Casualties nil.	
	2/9/16		The battalion was relieved by a battalion of "Bantams" & on the night of the 2/3rd marched from ARRAS to MONTENESCOURT where it remained until 4/9/16.	
	4/9/16		Battalion left MONTENESCOURT & marched to DENIER & SARS-les-Bois	
DENIER	4/9/16 -13/9/16		During the period 4/9/16 – 13/9/16 the battalion was engaged in training, including Route marching, Physical training & Bayonet Fighting. Specialists (Lewis gunners, Bombers & Signallers) were particularly in need of further training owing to casualties which it had been impossible to replace with fully trained men.	
DERNANCOURT	13/9/16		Battalion marched to FREVENT & on the night of 13th-14th entrained there for DERNANCOURT, encamping on the 14th at EDGE HILL	

2449 Wt. W14957/M90 750,000 1/16 J.B.C. & A. Forms/C.2118/12.

Army Form C. 2118.

Instructions regarding War Diaries and Intelligence Summaries are contained in F. S. Regs., Part II. and the Staff Manual respectively. Title Pages will be prepared in manuscript.

WAR DIARY
or
~~INTELLIGENCE SUMMARY~~

(Erase heading not required.)

Place	Date	Hour	Summary of Events and Information	Remarks and references to Appendices
DERNAN-COURT	15/9/16		Battalion went into billets at DERNANCOURT in the morning & the evening left for encampment at BECORDEL	
MONTAUBAN.	16/9/16		On the morning of 16th Battalion moved to bivouac outside MONTAUBAN by BERNAFAY WOOD	
	17/9/16 - 25/9/16		The battalion remained in bivouac & was employed on finding working parties in connection with preparations for the attack on GUEUDECOURT The casualties during this period were - Officers :- 2/Lt [illegible] Capt C.N. St John DICKINSON (W. in A.) 23/9/16) - O.R. killed wounded These casualties were all caused by shell fire, the work consisting of digging trenches & repairing roads & much of this was necessarily carried out under shell fire. The weather during this period was uncertain & the state of the ground led to a postponement of operations	
GUEUDECOURT	25/9/16		The attack on GUEUDECOURT was launched in the afternoon. The battalion was in Brigade reserve & did not leave bivouac until 5 AM. that morning. Two companies then moved to BROWN TRENCH in front of (N. of) DELVILLE WOOD, two companies remained in bivouac.	

2449 Wt. W14957/M90 750,000 1/16 J.B.C. & A. Forms/C.2118/12.

Instructions regarding War Diaries and Intelligence Summaries are contained in F. S. Regs., Part II. and the Staff Manual respectively. Title Pages will be prepared in manuscript.

WAR DIARY
or
~~INTELLIGENCE SUMMARY~~
(Erase heading not required.)

Army Form C. 2118.

Place	Date	Hour	Summary of Events and Information	Remarks and references to Appendices
GUEUDECOURT	25/9/16		These were the dispositions at midday. Two companies were then sent forward from BROWN TRENCH to occupy trenches vacated by 6th Batt. immediately in rear of SWITCH Trench – the two companies being brought up to take their place in BROWN Trench. At 6.0 pm another advance was made & dispositions were then as follows: A Coy GAP Trench B Coy & Batt. H.Q. SWITCH trench (astride COCOA LANE. C & D Coy with battalion bombers in new trenches in rear of SWITCH Trench. We were at this time unable to ascertain the exact situation in front. At midnight from orders communicated it appeared that the 8th & 9th battalions had taken part of GIRD Trench before GUEUDECOURT but only on a frontage of about 80 yards by PILGRIM WAY. A bombing attack was therefore organised in conjunction with a TANK. This was to be carried out by the 7th battalion bombers supported by C & D Coy.	
	26/9/16		At 10-0 AM this party moved off via FLERS, where the TANK was stationed, & thence to GIRD trench. Each man carried 2 bombs, 2 sandbags & 2 extra bandoliers of ammunition in addition to his normal equipment, while a supply of 1000 was drawn from Bde H.Q. The whole party was under the command of Capt A.W.H. TYLER, the bombers being led by 2/Lt H.J. WALSH.	

WAR DIARY
or
~~INTELLIGENCE SUMMARY~~

(Erase heading not required.)

Army Form C. 2118.

Instructions regarding War Diaries and Intelligence Summaries are contained in F. S. Regs., Part II. and the Staff Manual respectively. Title Pages will be prepared in manuscript.

Place	Date	Hour	Summary of Events and Information	Remarks and references to Appendices
GUEUDE-COURT	26/9/16		The attack was launched at 7.15 A.M. The ~~Tank~~ TANK moving along the trench from PILGRIM WAY eastwards followed closely by the battalion bombers, who were kept supplied with bombs by C & D Coys. The attack was entirely successful. Many of the enemy were killed in the trench, all dug-outs were bombed with great effect, phosphorus bombs proving very useful for this purpose. In about 30 minutes the trench was cleared as far as WATLING ST. Here a break in the trench caused by the SUNKEN ROAD caused a temporary check, but 2/Lt WALSH rushed his men across the gap in sections & continued the advance without loss. Our men entirely outthrew the German bombers, & when 200 yards beyond WATLING ST the Tank left the trench & proceeded towards the village the bombers were able to carry on without a check. At this point a large number of the enemy left their trench & surrendered to the troops holding the trench to their front. By 9.45 A.M. our bombers effected a junction with the Guards Division from LES BOEUFS & the whole of GIRD Trench was in our hands. Our casualties during the actual attack were 2 killed & 2 wounded. ~~[illegible]~~ Lieut G J R SAUNDERS (commanding C Coy) was killed by a shell in FLERS before the attack started.	

Army Form C. 2118.

Instructions regarding War Diaries and Intelligence Summaries are contained in F. S. Regs., Part II. and the Staff Manual respectively. Title Pages will be prepared in manuscript.

WAR DIARY
or
~~INTELLIGENCE SUMMARY~~

(Erase heading not required.)

Place	Date	Hour	Summary of Events and Information	Remarks and references to Appendices
GUEUDE-COURT	26/9/16		During the day the battalion remained in SWITCH Trench, less 2 companies (C & D) which held the captured line (GIRD TRENCH). GIRD Trench was heavily shelled during the day. 2/Lt H. JONES was killed. 4 O.R. killed & 47 wounded. On the night 26/27th the 6th Battn having occupied the village of GUEUDECOURT, the ~~battalion~~ two companies in SWITCH TRENCH moved forward to BULL Rd Trench & PIONEER Trench. Battn HQ were in BULL Rd Trench. [initials]	
	27/9/16 -29/9/16		Battalion remained in same position. Nothing of importance occurred during this period. 48 casualties were sustained through shell fire.	
	29/9/16		On the night of 29/30th Sept. the battalion took over from 6th Battn the line established N.E. of GUEUDECOURT. On the morning of 29th during the preliminary reconnaissance the Commanding Officer, Lt-Col W. DRYSDALE D.S.O. was killed by a sniper. Major R.B. UNWIN again took command but was wounded while taking over from the 6th Battn at night.	
	29/9/16 -1/10/16		During the 2 days 29/9/15 – 1/10/16 the battalion held & consolidated the line in front of GUEUDECOURT. The enemy shelled the village without cessation but caused few casualties, as he did not appear to have.	

2449 Wt. W14957/M90 750,000 1/16 J.B.C. & A. Forms/C.2118/12.

Army Form C. 2118.

WAR DIARY
or
~~INTELLIGENCE SUMMARY~~

(Erase heading not required.)

Instructions regarding War Diaries and Intelligence Summaries are contained in F. S. Regs., Part II. and the Staff Manual respectively. Title Pages will be prepared in manuscript.

Place	Date	Hour	Summary of Events and Information	Remarks and references to Appendices
GUEUDE-COURT	29/9/16 – 1/10/16		located our line, which was a little in advance of the edge of the village itself. Our casualties were therefore slight – ~~2/Lt~~ 2/Lt H WILD – 30/9/16 & 2/Lt R.B CHAPMAN – 1/10/16. O.R. 36.	
	1/10/16		In afternoon of 1st patrol went out under 2/Lt HOLT in conjunction with patrols on either flank from other units. Under cover of heavy shell fire they reached the German trench – their object being to ascertain whether this line (which lay beyond a ridge) was still occupied. If not they were to occupy it & other stronger patrols were to join them & consolidate. They found it strongly held – but the enemy evidently scared & inclined to run until they discovered it to be only a small patrol. 2/Lt HOLT brought his patrol back without loss under heavy M.G. fire, after inflicting several casualties on the enemy ~~casualties~~. On the night of 1/2nd Oct. the battalion was relieved by a battalion of 12th Division – EAST. SURREY Regt. The relief was carried out with great ease, as the enemy's artillery was almost silent during the night. Only 2 casualties were sustained during the relief. Casualties during this day were as noted above.	

[signature] Lt Col. Comdg 1/Herts Regt

2449 Wt. W14957/M90 750,000 1/16 J.B.C. & A. Forms/C.2118/12.

Vol 13

CONFIDENTIAL

WAR DIARY

of

7th Batt. LEICESTERSHIRE Regt.

Oct 1st – Oct 31st 1916

15 B
Leicest

Army Form C. 2118.

WAR DIARY
or
~~INTELLIGENCE SUMMARY~~

(Erase heading not required.)

Instructions regarding War Diaries and Intelligence Summaries are contained in F. S. Regs., Part II. and the Staff Manual respectively. Title Pages will be prepared in manuscript.

Place	Date	Hour	Summary of Events and Information	Remarks and references to Appendices
	1/10/16		Battalion held front line at GUEUDECOURT. at 2.30 pm., when the line advanced on our left, a patrol of one officer and four OR went out to reconnoitre enemy lines and ascertain exact position of his lines. Patrol threw several bombs into enemy trench & returned to our lines. Battalion was relieved at 9 pm., by 9th Battalion, East Surrey Regiment, and marched to BERNAFAY WOOD ~~[illegible]~~ H.J.W.	
	2/10/16		Battalion left BERNAFAY WOOD at 10.30 am. and marched to DERNANCOURT. Remained in billets until morning of 4th. H.J.W.	
	4/10/16		Entrained at DERNANCOURT at 3 pm. Casualties: 1 man killed (accidentally) H.J.W.	
	5/10/16		Detrained at LONGPRE at 2.15 am. and marched to PONT REMY where battalion billeted until 7th. H.J.W.	

2449 Wt. W14957/M90 750,000 1/16 J.B.C. & A. Forms/C.2118/12.

Army Form C. 2118.

Instructions regarding War Diaries and Intelligence Summaries are contained in F. S. Regs., Part II. and the Staff Manual respectively. Title Pages will be prepared in manuscript.

WAR DIARY
or
~~INTELLIGENCE SUMMARY~~

(Erase heading not required.)

Place	Date	Hour	Summary of Events and Information	Remarks and references to Appendices
	7/10/16		Entrained at PONT REMY at 9.30 p.m. H.J.W.	
	8/10/16		Detrained at BETHUNE at 4 a.m. and marched to LA BOURSE, where battalion billeted until 10/10/16. H.J.W.	
	10/10/16		Battalion relieved ROYAL IRISH RIFLES in trenches (HOHENZOLLERN SECTION). Nothing of importance happened during tour of duty in front line. H.J.W.	
	11/10/16		One man killed	
	14/10/16		~~Two men~~ killed, four men wounded. H.J.W.	
	17/10/16		Battalion was relieved by 8th Battn. Leicestershire Regiment, & went into Reserve (LANCASHIRE TRENCH). H.J.W. Three men wounded, one man killed.	
	22/10/16		Battalion relieved 8th Battn. in front line. One man killed H.J.W. One man wounded H.J.W.	
	25/10/16		One man wounded. H.J.W.	
	26/10/16		Trenches were heavily bombarded by enemy TM's during day & night of	
	27/10/16		27/28. One man wounded. H.J.W.	

2449 Wt. W14957/M90 750,000 1/16 J.B.C. & A. Forms/C.2118/12.

Instructions regarding War Diaries and Intelligence Summaries are contained in F. S. Regs., Part II. and the Staff Manual respectively. Title Pages will be prepared in manuscript.

WAR DIARY
or
~~INTELLIGENCE SUMMARY~~

(Erase heading not required.)

Army Form C. 2118.

Place	Date	Hour	Summary of Events and Information	Remarks and references to Appendices
	28/10/16		Battalion was relieved by 8 L. "A" Coy proceeded to RAILWAY KEEP, "B" Coy. to CENTRAL KEEP, "C" Coy. to RAILWAY RESERVE TRENCH, and "D" Coy to JUNCTION KEEP. H.J.W.	
	30/10/16		One man wounded. H.J.W.	
	31/10/16		Battalion still in support H.J.W.	

[illegible]
Lt Col
Comdg 7/Leic Regt

2449 Wt. W14957/M90 750,000 1/16 J.B.C. & A. Forms/C.2118/12.

21

7th Leics Regt
Vol 14

Confidential.

War Diary
of
7th Battn. Leicestershire Regt.

November 1st to 30th, 1916.

16.B.
2 sheets

Instructions regarding War Diaries and Intelligence Summaries are contained in F. S. Regs., Part II. and the Staff Manual respectively. Title Pages will be prepared in manuscript.

WAR DIARY
or
~~INTELLIGENCE SUMMARY~~

(Erase heading not required.)

Army Form C. 2118.

Place	Date	Hour	Summary of Events and Information	Remarks and references to Appendices
HOENZOLLERN SECTOR	1/11/16		Battalion in Support Line. A Coy in RAILWAY KEEP, B Coy in CENTRAL KEEP, C Coy in RAILWAY RESERVE TRENCH, D Coy in JUNCTION KEEP	JAC
	2/11/16		Following N.C.O's & men granted Military Medals by XV Corps Commander:- 17093 Sergt. T. Atkinson, 12933 Pte R Nussey, 16081 L/Cpl T.S. Griffiths, 11425 L/Cpl S. Bastock, 13482 Pte J W Smith, 5015 Pte A. Wright	JAC
	3/11/16		2nd Lt H R HORNE joined Battn from 4th Bn Leic Regt & posted to B Coy.	JAC
	3/11/16 to 9/11/16		Battn relieved 8th Battn in Front line. Considerable sniping activity by enemy during this tour. 7/11/16 2nd Lt H.C McLAREN joined Battn & posted to B Coy. Capt A.A. ALDWORTH, 2nd Lt A.G. HOLT & 2nd Lt H.J. WALSH awarded Military Cross.	JAC
	9/11/16		Battn relieved by 8th Battn & went into Reserve (LANCASHIRE TRENCH)	JAC
	15/11/16 to 21/11/16		Battn relieved 8th Battn in Front Line. 16/11/16 Draft of twenty O.R joined Battn. Two men killed, 2nd Lt SCARFE & four O.R. wounded.	JAC
	21/11/16 to 27/11/16		Battn relieved by 8th & proceeded to Support Line. A Coy to RAILWAY KEEP, B Coy to CENTRAL KEEP, C Coy to RAILWAY RESERVE TRENCH, D Coy to JUNCTION KEEP. 25/11/16 Armourer Sergeant visited all Coys.	JAC
	27/11/16 to 30/11/16		Battn relieved 8th Battn in Front. Enemy attempted a raid about 5 a.m on 28th inst. 10 to 14 of the enemy succeeded in getting inside our wire. Leader was shot by Flying Patrol & remainder immediately fled. 2nd Lt HALES & Sergt Cross wounded by snipers on 27.11.16.	JAC

A A Aldworth Lt Col Cmdg 7/Leic R[illegible]

2449 Wt. W14957/M90 750,000 1/16 J.B.C. & A. Forms/C.2118/12.

OAK

Instructions regarding War Diaries and Intelligence Summaries are contained in F. S. Regs., Part II. and the Staff Manual respectively. Title Pages will be prepared in manuscript.

WAR DIARY
or
INTELLIGENCE SUMMARY
(Erase heading not required.)

Army Form C. 2118.

7th Leicester Regt
21/110
Vol 15

Place	Date	Hour	Summary of Events and Information	Remarks and references to Appendices
HOHENZOLLERN SECTOR	Dec 1st		In the Front line CORK ST. to CLIFFORD ST. both inclusive	
			Casualties 19255 a/cpl GIBBS J. (W in A 1.12.16) 43038 Pte MANCHET AG (W in A 1.12.16)	
	Dec 3rd		Moved into RESERVE AREA Two companies in billets in MAZINGARBE. One company in cellar billets in VERMELLES, H.Q and one company in LANCASHIRE TRENCH.	
	Dec 3rd to Dec 9th		Battalion bathed and on working parties for REs and carrying parties for M. G. Coy	
	Dec 5th		Received reinforcement of 41 ORs	
	Dec 9th		Moved back into front line, original sector extended from CLIFFORD ST. to HULLUCH ALLEY exclusive	
	Dec 9th to Dec 15th		Enemy Snipers + Rum Jars active, just a few aerial Darts	
			Casualties 28826 Pte Ives L (W in A 9.12.16) 23936 Pte BEADA CP (Killed 10.12.16) 17485 Pte HORLEY D. (W accidentally 10.12.16) 40072 Pte RICHARDSON J (Killed 12.12.16)	
	Dec 12th		Reinforcement of 20 ORs	
LA BOURSE	Dec 15th		Relieved by 1st BTN. EAST YORKS REGT. Moved out of line. Two Companies and two platoons billeted in PHILOSOPHE, Two Companies less two platoons billeted in MAZINGARBE. H.Q. in LA BOURSE. Battalion on working parties for REs	
	Dec 16th		Reinforcement of 2 officers and 3 ORs	
	Dec 19th		Reinforcement of 1 officer.	

17.1

OAK

Army Form C. 2118.

WAR DIARY
or
INTELLIGENCE SUMMARY
(Erase heading not required.)

Instructions regarding War Diaries and Intelligence Summaries are contained in F. S. Regs., Part II. and the Staff Manual respectively. Title Pages will be prepared in manuscript.

Place	Date	Hour	Summary of Events and Information	Remarks and references to Appendices
CAUCHY-A-LA-TOUR	Dec 20th		Battalion less 350 men and proportion of officers NCOs and Transport, left LABOURSE and marched to CAUCHY-A-LA-TOUR where it was billetted.	
	Dec 21st		Training commenced	
	Dec 24th		Remainder of Battalion who had meanwhile been on working parties for REs, were brought in motorbuses to CAUCHY ~~[illegible]~~ and rejoined the Battalion.	
	Dec 25th		Church Parade. No special festivities. General kit and personal inspections.	
	Dec 26th		Special fare given to NCOs and men finishing with a most excellent seasonable dinner in the early evening. A day of general rejoicing. Casualties - Nil.	J.J.
	Dec 27th to Dec 31st		Training continued including Squad Drill Arm Drill, Route marches, Musketry Physical Training, Bayonet fighting and Specialists Training.	
	Dec 27th		Reinforcement of 18 ORs	
	Dec 31st		Still at CAUCHY-A-LA-TOUR Major TC Howitt at present in Command of Bn	

2449 Wt. W14957/M90 750,000 1/16 J.B.C. & A. Forms/C.2118/12.

7th Leicester Regt Army Form C. 2118.

Instructions regarding War Diaries and Intelligence Summaries are contained in F. S. Regs., Part II. and the Staff Manual respectively. Title Pages will be prepared in manuscript.

WAR DIARY
or
~~INTELLIGENCE~~ SUMMARY
(Erase heading not required.)

Place	Date	Hour	Summary of Events and Information	Remarks and references to Appendices
CAUCHY-A-LA-TOUR	1st Jan		Battalion in Rest billets. General and specialists training continued.	
			Reinforcement – 4 ORs.	
	4th Jan		Temp. Lt Col. A. A. Aldworth M.C. left for Senior Officers Course at Aldershot.	
			Reinforcement – 56 ORs	
	5th Jan		Lt Col. C. E. Heathcote D.S.O. (KOYLI) arrived and assumed command of the Battalion	
	11th Jan		Reinforcement – 1 officer (2Lt J. Emerson) and 100 ORs	
	19th Jan		Reinforcement – 1 officer (2Lt G. Francis)	
	22nd Jan		Reinforcement – 2 officers (2Lt K. G. Stiven and 2Lt E. West)	
	27th Jan		Left CAUCHY and marched to LILLERS. Entrained at LILLERS	Operation orders attached
HOUTKERQUE	28th Jan		Detrained at PROVEN marched to billets near HOUTKERQUE	
	29th Jan		Training continued.	
	31st Jan		Still at HOUTKERQUE	

C. E. Heathcote
Lt Col. cmdg
7th Ser. Btn Leicestershire Regt.

18.B
5 sheets

2449 Wt. W14957/M90 750,000 1/16 J.B.C. & A. Forms/C.2118/12.

Instructions regarding War Diaries and Intelligence Summaries are contained in F. S. Regs., Part II. and the Staff Manual respectively. Title Pages will be prepared in manuscript.

WAR DIARY
or
~~INTELLIGENCE SUMMARY~~

(*Erase heading not required.*)

7th Leicester Regt

Army Form C. 2118.

7th Btn. Leic Regt 21/114

Vol 17

Place	Date	Hour	Summary of Events and Information	Remarks and references to Appendices
HOUTKERQUE. ~~1/2/17~~	1/2/17		Battn in billets near HOUTKERQUE.	
~~2/2/17.~~	2/2/17		Battn inspected by Lt. Gen. Sir Aylmer Hunter-Weston, K.C.B., D.S.O. Commanding VIII Corps.	
~~3/2/17.~~	3/2/17		In order to create an impression on the enemy that we were concentrating troops towards the North of the YPRES salient, route marches were carried out from the 3rd to the 5th inclusive. The Battn with pack animals etc. (echelon "" of transport) commenced marching early each afternoon and continued until it was dusk. It then turned about & marched back to billets. Route taken:- roads EAST of HOUTKERQUE. Through WATTAU to St JAN der BIEZEN.	
	6/2/17		Orders received from 110th Inf. Bde. for a (test) turn out at 10.24 am. Battn turned out complete with waggons packed ready to move off at 12.5 pm.	
	7/2/17		Usual training.	
	9/2/17.		The Battn was inspected at training by Maj. Genl Campbell the Divl Commander.	
	10th to 12/2/17.		Usual training.	
	13/2/17.		The Battn moved from the VIII Corps Area & returned to the 1st Corps Area. Marched from billets and entrained at Proven at 9 am. Arrived FOUQUERIEUL at 12.45 pm. and marched to BÈTHUNE where the Battn billeted (Tobacco factory.)	
BÈTHUNE.	14/2/17		Battn marched to LABOURSE and billeted there.	

19 B 8 sheets

2449 Wt. W14957/M90 750,000 1/16 J.B.C. & A. Forms/C.2118/12.

Army Form C. 2118.

Instructions regarding War Diaries and Intelligence Summaries are contained in F. S. Regs., Part II. and the Staff Manual respectively. Title Pages will be prepared in manuscript.

WAR DIARY

~~or~~

~~INTELLIGENCE SUMMARY~~

(Erase heading not required.)

Place	Date	Hour	Summary of Events and Information	Remarks and references to Appendices
TRENCHES. HOHENZOLLERN SECTOR.	15/2/17.		The Battn relieved the 2nd Bn. York & Lancs. Regt in the support line HOHENZOLLERN sector. Relief complete by 12.30pm. Received a visit from the Brig. Gen. & Bde. Major.	
	16/2/17.		"A" & "C" Coys relieved by 2 Coys of the 9th Bn. in RESERVE TRENCH and RAILWAY RESERVE TRCH. "A" & "C" Coys relieved one Coy of the 6th Bn. in LANCASHIRE TRENCH. Thaw begins.	
	17/2/17.		Water in trenches & sides falling in owing to thaw. The Battn less "Keep" Garrisons on working and carrying parties. Casualty. Pte Lindsell (W. in A.)	
	18/2/17 } 19/2/17 }		Usual trench routine, strong working parties reqd each night for clearing trenches.	
	20/2/17.		Draft of 2 offrs (2nd Lts Manners & Rowles) and 25 O.R. arrived.	
	21/2/17.		Moved into front line. Right sub-sector. EAST CUT to SAVILLE Row, taking over from the 8th Bn Leicestershire Regt. Relief very satisfactory considering the almost (in some parts, quite) impassible state of the C.Ts. Relief complete by 12 noon. Three Coys in front line, one in support. "A" Right, "B" Centre "D" Left.	
	22/2/17.		LINE very quiet. Little activity by Enemy. Owing to misty state of the atmosphere & quietness of the enemy, much work was possible on the top during the day (wiring etc.) C.Ts in a very sticky state; trenches still slipping in. Weather mild. By night one of our patrols encountered an enemy listening post and some of the enemy were believed wounded by a bomb. Casualty. Pte. Wood. C.E. Bullet wound accidentally self-inflicted.	

2449 Wt. W14957/M90 750,000 1/16 J.B.C. & A. Forms/C.2118/12.

Army Form C. 2118.

Instructions regarding War Diaries and Intelligence Summaries are contained in F. S. Regs., Part II. and the Staff Manual respectively. Title Pages will be prepared in manuscript.

WAR DIARY
or
INTELLIGENCE SUMMARY

(Erase heading not required.)

Place	Date	Hour	Summary of Events and Information	Remarks and references to Appendices
TRENCHES — HOHENZOLLERN SECTOR.	23/2/17		Very little activity. Weather improving, but trenches still falling in.	
	24/2/17		No excitement. Major T.C. Howitt rejoined Bn. after 1 month's special leave in England	
	25/2/17		Little doing during day. Bombardment of our lines by enemy commencing at 12.30 pm. lasting for 1½ hours 77 mm, 4.2 and 5.9 shells and heavy, light, and medium T.Ms. Bombardment due apparently to nervousness on the part of the enemy. Casualties 3 W. in A. Capt H.H. Humphrie returned from 1st Army School Infantry Course.	
	26/2/17		Usual activity.	
NOYELLES.	27/2/17		Relieved by the 8th Bn. Leic. Regt. and went into Reserve Billets. Hutment camp at NOYELLES. Successful relief; no casualties.	
	28/2/17		"A" & "C" Coys moved into trenches. "A" into Lancashire trench, "C" into RAILWAY RESERVE TRENCH.	

C.H. Haswell[?] Lt Col.
Cmdg 7th Bn Leicestershire Regt.

2449 Wt. W14957/M90 750,000 1/16 J.B.C. & A. Forms/C.2118/12.

Army Form C. 2118.

Instructions regarding War Diaries and Intelligence Summaries are contained in F. S. Regs., Part II. and the Staff Manual respectively. Title Pages will be prepared in manuscript.

WAR DIARY
or
INTELLIGENCE SUMMARY
(Erase heading not required.)

Place	Date	Hour	Summary of Events and Information	Remarks and references to Appendices
			Vol 18	
			7th (Service) Battalion The Leicestershire Regiment 1 – 31 March 21/110 1917.	

20 B
4 sheets

2449 Wt. W14957/M90 750,000 1/16 J.B.C. & A. Forms/C.2118/12.

Instructions regarding War Diaries and Intelligence Summaries are contained in F. S. Regs., Part II. and the Staff Manual respectively. Title Pages will be prepared in manuscript.

WAR DIARY
or
INTELLIGENCE SUMMARY
(Erase heading not required.)

Army Form C. 2118.

7th Bn Lancashire Regt

Place	Date	Hour	Summary of Events and Information	Remarks and references to Appendices
NOYELLES	March 1		Battalion in Reserve. H.Q. + two Companies in NOYELLES, One Company in RAILWAY RESERVE TRENCH + one Company in LANCASHIRE TRENCH. Casualties 1 O.R. W. in A.	H.J.W.
	1–4.		Battn. supplied R.E. Working parties + T.M. Carrying parties	H.J.W.
HOHENZOLLERN Right Sub Sector	5		Battn. moved into front line relieving 8th Battn. Linc. Regt. Front was extended from POST 8 to GORDON ALLEY. Three Coys. in the front line and one Coy in Support line. Battn. H.Q. at EXETER CASTLE. Casualties 1 O.R. killed + 1 O.R. wounded.	H.J.W.
	5–10.		Usual trench warfare. Enemy's T.M.'s very active. A number of gas shells ~~sent~~ over in various parts of our line. 7th March. Casualties: One O.R. K. in A. 9th " Casualties One O.R. K. in A. 10th " Casualties One O.R. W. in A.	H.J.W.
	11		Battn. moved into Support on relief by 8th Battn. Linc. Regt. H.Q. near HULLOCH ROAD One Coy CENTRAL KEEP, One Coy. JUNCTION KEEP, one Coy in RESERVE TRENCH + one Coy in CURLY CRESCENT. Casualties: 1 O.R. W in A.	H.J.W.
	12–16		Battn. supplied carrying parties for RE's, T.M's, + front line Battns. 15th March. Casualties 1 O.R. wounded (Self inflicted).	H.J.W.

2449 Wt. W14957/M90 750,000 1/16 J.B.C. & A. Forms/C.2118/12.

Army Form C. 2118.

Instructions regarding War Diaries and Intelligence Summaries are contained in F. S. Regs., Part II. and the Staff Manual respectively. Title Pages will be prepared in manuscript.

WAR DIARY
or
INTELLIGENCE SUMMARY

(Erase heading not required.)

Place	Date	Hour	Summary of Events and Information	Remarks and references to Appendices
HOHENZOLLERN Rt. Sub. Sector	15		Casualties: Captain James Thornburn Mitchell & 2/Lt. Kenneth Cumming Stinson accidentally wounded by explosion of a bomb.	A.J.W.
	16		The Battn. Raiding Platoon took part in a successful Brigade Raid organized by 2nd in Command of Battn. Major T.C. Howitt. Enemy trenches were raided at DIAMOND POINT (G5.c and G.5.d.) 7 prisoners were captured & 24 men were seen dead in enemy front line. 40 casualties estimated in dug outs & machine gun emplacements destroyed by our mobile charges. Casualties: 4 O.R. W in A Captain James Thornburn Mitchell died of Wounds.	A.J.W.
	17		Battn. moved into front line relieving 8th Battn. Leic. Regt. Three Coys in front line & one Coy. in support. HQ. at EXETER CASTLE. Casualties. 1 O.R. K in A. 1 O.R. acc. wounded.	A.J.W.
	17 – 22		Nothing of importance ~~happened~~. Trenches were deepened & repaired & new wire put out. Our patrols were very active. Enemy T.M.'s active but was continually silenced by our artillery. Casualties. 18th March. 2 O.R. W in A. " " " 1 O.R. Wounded (self inflicted.) " 20th – 1 O.R. W in A. 20th March: Draft of 3 O.R. joined the Battn.	A.J.W.

2449 Wt. W14957/M90 750,000 1/16 J.B.C. & A. Forms/C.2118/12.

Army Form C. 2118.

Instructions regarding War Diaries and Intelligence Summaries are contained in F. S. Regs., Part II. and the Staff Manual respectively. Title Pages will be prepared in manuscript.

WAR DIARY
or
INTELLIGENCE SUMMARY
(Erase heading not required.)

Place	Date	Hour	Summary of Events and Information	Remarks and references to Appendices
HOHENZOLLERN Right Sub. Sector	21		Casualties: 1 O.R. W. in A.	H.J.W.
	23		Battn. moved into Reserve on relief by 8th Battn. Leicestershire Regt. H.Q. A & C. Coys in NOYELLES, "B" Coy in LANCASHIRE TRENC & "D" Coy in RAILWAY RESERVE TRENCH.	H.J.W.
			Casualties: 1 O.R. accidentally wounded.	
	24–27		Battn. supplied R.E. Working Parties, Wiring & T.M. Carrying parties.	H.J.W.
	28.		Transport moved by road from LABOURSE to LA CAUCHY.	H.J.W.
	29.		Battn. entrained at 8 a.m. at NOYELLES and detrained at SAULTY-LARBRET at 5.0 p.m. Marched to LA CAUCHY & billeted there.	H.J.W.
	31.		Battn. still at LA CAUCHIE.	H.J.W.

[signature] Lieut. Col.
Comg. 7th (Ser) Battn. Leicestershire Regt.

2449 Wt. W14957/M90 750,000 1/16 J.B.C. & A. Forms/C.2118/12.

Instructions regarding War Diaries and Intelligence Summaries are contained in F. S. Regs., Part II. and the Staff Manual respectively. Title pages will be prepared in manuscript.

WAR DIARY
or
INTELLIGENCE SUMMARY.
(Erase heading not required.)

Army Form C. 2118.

7th Bn Leicester Regt.

Vol 19

Place	Date	Hour	Summary of Events and Information	Remarks and references to Appendices
			7th (Ser) Battn The Leicestershire Regiment War Diary from 1st to 30th April 1917.	

21.B
5 sheet

A5834 Wt. W4973/M687 750,000 8/16 D. D. & L. Ltd. Forms/C.2118/13.

Instructions regarding War Diaries and Intelligence Summaries are contained in F. S. Regs., Part II. and the Staff Manual respectively. Title pages will be prepared in manuscript.

WAR DIARY
or
INTELLIGENCE SUMMARY.
(*Erase heading not required.*)

Army Form C. 2118.

Place	Date	Hour	Summary of Events and Information	Remarks and references to Appendices
LA CAUCHIE	1-3/4		Battn training including Battle formation, close order drill, patrol work, Tactical exercises Bombing & Lewis Gun training.	
MOYENNEVILLE	3		Battn marched from LA CAUCHIE to MOYENNEVILLE	Map ref. FRANCE Sheet 51B S.W. Edition 4 A.
ST LEGER & CROISILLES	4		Battn moved to front line & relieved 22nd Battn MANCHESTER REGT & R. WELSH FUSILIERS.	
			Dispositions were as follows:-	
			"A" Coy on the right No. 1 Outpost Coy.	
			Picquet line T. 18. c. 7.4 – T. 18. d. 1.3 – T. 24. b. 4.9.	
			Supports & Reserve in CROISILLES VILLAGE.	
			On the night of 5/6th picquet line advanced to T 18 b. 7.3. – U. 13. c. 1.8. – U. 13. c. 7 5.	
			Supports & Reserve at T. 18. c. 7.4 – T. 18. d. 1.3. – T. 24 b. 4.9.	
			Coy. H.Q. in CROISILLES VILLAGE.	
			B. Coy. on the left. No 2 Outpost Coy.	
			Coy. in sunken road T. 17. d. 6 7 – T. 18. c. 20. 55	
			One section at T. 17. c. 6.1 } by night only	
			One section at T. 17. d. 7.9 } by night only	
			One double sentry groups T. 18 c. 45 30 } by night only	
			Picquet line was advanced to T. 17 b 6 4. one platoon; T. 18 b. 0.1. one platoon	
			One section by night at T. 11. d. 81.	
			One section by night at T. 18. a. 8.1.	
			C. Coy. was in SUPPORT at T. 23 c. 7.8. to T. 23. c. 10. 6	
			D Coy. was in RESERVE at T. 27. d. 4.7 to T. 27. d. 8. 10.	
			Battn H.Q. at T. 27. d. 6. 8. Moved on 6th to ST LEGER T. 28. c. 75. 60.	

N/W

A5834 Wt. W4973/M687 750,000 8/16 D. D. & L. Ltd. Forms/C.2118/13.

Instructions regarding War Diaries and Intelligence Summaries are contained in F. S. Regs., Part II. and the Staff Manual respectively. Title pages will be prepared in manuscript.

WAR DIARY
or
INTELLIGENCE SUMMARY.
(Erase heading not required.)

Army Form C. 2118.

Place	Date	Hour	Summary of Events and Information	Remarks and references to Appendices
CRUISILLES	5th/4		Casualties: 1 OR. W in A, 1 Officer (2/Lt. Judge) W. in A.	
	6		" 1 OR. Missing	
			Reinforcements: Major A.A. Aldworth (2nd i/c) rejoined from Senior Officers Course at ALDERSHOT.	
	7		" 1 Officer (2/Lt. Cecil Hubert Blenkley) W. in A.	
			1 OR. K. in A.	
	7/8th		Battn, on relief by 9th Battn. Leicestershire Regt, moved back to MOYENNEVILLE.	
MOYENNEVILLE	8-13/4		Battn remained at MOYENNEVILLE & carried on with usual training	
	13.		Battn. relieved 8th Battn. Leicestershire Regt.	
			C. Coy in sunken road from T.17.b.2.0 to T.11.c.10.15.	
			D. Coy on road from T.11.c.10.15 to T.10.a.80.95.	
			A. Coy in SUPPORT: Three platoons on road from T.17.c.8.1. to T.10.c.0.9. one platoon on road T.23.a1.25.70 to T.23.a.9.5	
			B. Coy in RESERVE on road T.21.d.8.3 to T.21.d.4.9.	
			Battn. H.Q. at T.22.a.2.5.	
			Casualties: 1 OR. W. in A.	
	14/15		Battn. on relief by 9th Battn. H.L.I. (Glasgow Highlanders) moved back to MOYENNEVILLE.	
MOYENNEVILLE TO BAILLEULVAL	15		Battn. marched to BAILLEULVAL.	
BAILLEULVAL	15-23		Battn. in training. Work carried out including Battle formations, close order drill, patrol work, tactical exercises, Bayonet training, Topography, bombing & Lewis gun.	
	23		Battn. moved in the afternoon to ADINFER	
	24		Battn. moved to MOYENNEVILLE.	
	25.		Battn. relieved 2nd Battn. Worcestershire Regt. (B Echelon remained at MOYENNEVILLE) Dispositions as follows:	A.J.W.

A5834 Wt. W4973/M687 750,000 8/16 D. D. & L. Ltd. Forms/C.2118/13.

Instructions regarding War Diaries and Intelligence Summaries are contained in F. S. Regs., Part II. and the Staff Manual respectively. Title pages will be prepared in manuscript.

WAR DIARY
or
INTELLIGENCE SUMMARY.
(Erase heading not required.)

Army Form C. 2118.

Place	Date	Hour	Summary of Events and Information	Remarks and references to Appendices
CROISILLES	25		C. Coy on the right: No 1 Outpost Coy.	
			Coy. H.Q. at T. 24.a. 4.6	
			Picquets at U. 13.a. 3.2. – T. 18.d 9.8 – T. 18.d 5.2 with Supports at T. 18. d. 6.0 – T. 18. d. 3.5 and T. 18. d. 1.7. RESERVE of one platoon at T. 18. c. 9.2.	
			D. Coy. on the left: No 2 Outpost Coy.	
			Coy. H.Q. and two platoons in Sunken road T. 17. d. 5.6. to T. 18. c. 1.5.	
			Picquets at T. 18. c. 7.5. and T. 17. b. 7.5.	
			A. Coy. in SUPPORT at T. 23. d. 0.7.	
			B. Coy in RESERVE at T. 27. d. 5.7.	
			Battn. HQ at T. 28. c. 8.5.	
			Casualties: 4 O.R. accidentally wounded.	H.G.W.
	26.		Casualties: 3 O.R. Wounded (Shell shock).	
			1 O.R. W. in A.	
	27/28		Our artillery carried out wire cutting on the HINDENBURG front & support lines from from U.14.c.1.9. to U.1.c.4.0. For the purposes of patrolling the front was divided into three sectors as follows:–	
			GREEN U. 14. c. 1.9. to U. 7. d. 2.0.	
			ORANGE U. 7. d. 2.0. to U. 7. b. 0.0.	
			BROWN U. 7. b. 0.0. to U. 1. c. 4.0.	
			Patrols were sent out to inspect wire & report on same as follows.	
			D. Coy. GREEN 12 midnight to 1 am.	
			D. " ORANGE 2 am. to 3 am.	
			C " BROWN 1 am. to 2 am.	

A5834 Wt. W4973/M687 750,000 8/16 D. D. & L. Ltd. Forms/C.2118/13.

Instructions regarding War Diaries and Intelligence Summaries are contained in F. S. Regs., Part II. and the Staff Manual respectively. Title pages will be prepared in manuscript.

WAR DIARY
or
INTELLIGENCE SUMMARY.

(Erase heading not required.)

Army Form C. 2118.

Place	Date	Hour	Summary of Events and Information	Remarks and references to Appendices
CROISILLES	27/28		Wire was found to be much damaged but no lanes cut	
	27		Casualties: 1 OR K in A, 3 OR's W in A.	
	28.		Casualties. 2 OR K in A. 5 OR's W in A.	
			The 64th Infy Bde attacked on our left at 3 am. Enemy shelled our lines heavily. Very little damage done.	
		4.25 am	First Army & the Corps on right of 7th Corps attacked. The 7th Corps assisted by putting down a barrage 200 yards in front of our front line along the whole front. Enemy retaliation on our front was very heavy but little damage was done. Inter company relief took place. "A" Coy relieved C. Coy who moved to RESERVE. B. Coy relieved D. Coy who moved to SUPPORT.	H.J.W.
	28/29		Patrols went out to inspect wire as on previous night. No lanes found in the wire.	
	29		Battn. on relief by 10th Battn. Yorkshire Regt. moved to BOIRY BECQUERELLE. B Echelon moved from MOYENNEVILLE to BOIRY BECQUERELLE.	
			Casualties 1 OR K in A. 9 OR's W in A.	
BOIRY BECQUERELLE.	30		Battn. at BOIRY BECQUERELLE. The following reinforcements arrived during the month:- 8.4.17. 30 OR's 16.4.17. 1 officer (Lieut S.J. Hodson). 17.4.17 2 officers (2/Lts. Wood & McLaren) 102 OR's 20.4.17 13 OR's 28.4.17. 4 OR's	

[signature]
Lieut Col.
Comy. 7th Battn. Leic. Regt.

A5834 Wt. W4973/M687 750,000 8/16 D. D. & L. Ltd. Forms/C.2118/13.

7th Bn Leicester Regt

7th Bn Leic Regt

Vol 20

Army Form C. 2118.

Instructions regarding War Diaries and Intelligence Summaries are contained in F. S. Regs., Part II. and the Staff Manual respectively. Title pages will be prepared in manuscript.

WAR DIARY
or
INTELLIGENCE SUMMARY.
(Erase heading not required.)

Place	Date	Hour	Summary of Events and Information	Remarks and references to Appendices
			WAR DIARY of 7th (Ser) Battalion The Leicestershire Regt. 1 – 31 May, 1917	

22.B
7 sheets

A5834 Wt. W4973/M687 750,000 8/16 D. D. & L. Ltd. Forms/C.2118/13.

Instructions regarding War Diaries and Intelligence Summaries are contained in F. S. Regs., Part II. and the Staff Manual respectively. Title pages will be prepared in manuscript.

WAR DIARY
or
INTELLIGENCE SUMMARY.
(Erase heading not required.)

Army Form C. 2118.

Place	Date	Hour	Summary of Events and Information	Remarks and references to Appendices
BOIRY BECQUERELLE	1/5/17		Battn. supplied parties consisting of:-	
			(i) 4 Officers & 100 ORs for work on Brigade Dumps at N 36. c. 5. 3. & N. 36. b 5. 4.	Ref map Sheet 51B SW Edition 4. A
			(ii) 1 Officer & 20 men for work under Divisional Bombing Officer	
			Casualties ORs 4 Killed, 1 Missing & 4 Wounded	
	2		Battn. less B Echelon moved into Brigade Reserve at N. 34. a. b & d. Battn. H.Q. at N 34. a. 2. 9	
			Carrying parties supplied as follows:-	
			1 platoon for 110th Machine Gun Company	
			1 platoon for 110th Trench M. Battery	
			2 platoon for 8th Battn. Leic. Regt	
			2 platoon for 9th Battn. Leic. Regt	
			These carrying parties ~~[illegible]~~ did not rejoin the Battn. until after the operation on FONTAINE les CROISIELLES	
	3.	3.45am	110th Infantry Bde. attacked FONTAINE les CROISILLES Zero 3.45 am	
			8th & 9th Battn. Leic. Regt. advanced from BROWN line (T 6. a. 4. 7 – O. 31 C. 2. 6)	
			6th Battn. Leic. Regt in Support at N. 35. a. 4. 4.	
			7th Battn. Leic. Regt in Reserve in area N. 34. b & d.	
		4.30am	Battn. moved up into position vacated by 6th Battn. in CONCRETE Trench from T. 6. a 1. 9. to N. 36. c. 9. 8	

A5834 Wt. W4973/M687 750,000 8/16 D. D. & L. Ltd. Forms/C.2118/13.

Instructions regarding War Diaries and Intelligence Summaries are contained in F. S. Regs., Part II. and the Staff Manual respectively. Title pages will be prepared in manuscript.

WAR DIARY
or
INTELLIGENCE SUMMARY.
(Erase heading not required.)

Army Form C. 2118.

Place	Date	Hour	Summary of Events and Information	Remarks and references to Appendices
	3/5/17	6.30am	Battn moved up to BROWN Line	
		6.15pm	Orders were received for Battn to occupy WOOD trench as far as U. 2. a. 3. 5 – to get in touch with any posts or parties of our troops on either flank & to consolidate to either flank with the point U. 2. a. 3. 5 as pivot	(See report attached)
			Casualties: Captain H.H. Hemphill W in A 2/Lieut. G.C. White " " J.C. Walley " " W.A. Chapman " " M.C. McLaren " " S. Wood " " a/W. J.M. Manners " Capt R.B. Wallace (RAMC) W. in A	
			15 O.R's K. in A 3 " Missing 90 " W. in A	
	4.	11.30pm	Battn withdrawn to HINDENBURG SUPPORT Line. T. 5. b to T. 6 a	
	4	9pm	Battn relieved 1st. Battn. Lincolnshire Regt. in Front Line from T. 5. b. 8 1 to T. 11. d. 8 3. A & D Coys in front line B & C in Support in LEICESTER Trench on line approx T. 5. c. 7. 8. to T. 10. b. 6. 6	
	6th		Casualties: 3 O.R's W. in A.	

A5834 Wt. W4973/M687 750,000 8/16 D. D. & L. Ltd. Forms/C.2118/13.

Army Form C. 2118.

Instructions regarding War Diaries and Intelligence Summaries are contained in F. S. Regs., Part II. and the Staff Manual respectively. Title pages will be prepared in manuscript.

WAR DIARY
or
INTELLIGENCE SUMMARY.
(*Erase heading not required.*)

Place	Date	Hour	Summary of Events and Information	Remarks and references to Appendices
	8th		'B' Coy relieved D. Coy on left	
			'C' Coy relieved A Coy on right	
	9th		Casualties. 2/Lt C Francis accidentally wounded	
			1 OR Wd A., 3 OR's Wd	
	4th – 11th		Enemy shelling was very heavy throughout this period. Battn suffered very few casualties owing to the fact that the enemy could not locate the position of front line posts.	
	11th		Battn on relief by 9th Battn H.L.I. (Glasgow Highlanders) marched to area T. 20. c + d. Relief complete by 12.45 am 12th/5/17	
	12		Casualties: 2 OR's W in A	
			Battn marched to BIENVILLERS	
	12th 6 31st		Battn training including: Field operations Battle drill + the attack, Battn drill, Coy drill, musketry (including firing on range) Bayonet + Physical Training	
	25th		Battn inspected by Divisional Commander. Decorations were presented to N.C.O's + men of the Battn as follows:-	
			Sgt. W. N. Sparks (Bar to Military Medal)	
			L/Cpl W. Aitcheock Military Medal	
			Pte. V. Hollis "	
			Pte. G. M. Williams "	
	28		Battn inspected by Corps Commander.	

A5834 Wt. W4973/M687 750,000 8/16 D. D. & L. Ltd. Forms/C.2118/13.

Army Form C. 2118.

WAR DIARY
or
INTELLIGENCE SUMMARY.
(Erase heading not required.)

Instructions regarding War Diaries and Intelligence Summaries are contained in F. S. Regs., Part II. and the Staff Manual respectively. Title pages will be prepared in manuscript.

Place	Date	Hour	Summary of Events and Information	Remarks and references to Appendices
			The following drafts arrived during the month:—	[illegible]
	14/4/17		18 O.R's	
	21		15 O.R's	
	26		1 Officer: 2 Lt F.B. Stevenson & 21 O.R's.	

C A Aldworth
Major
Cmdg 7th Leic Regt

A5834 Wt. W4973/M687 750,000 8/16 D. D. & L. Ltd. Forms/C.2118/13.

Report on Operations by
7th Battn Leicestershire Regiment,
May 3rd, 1917.

---

1. On the evening of May 3rd the Battalion was holding the BROWN LINE along the Brigade Front with 2½ Companies. The remainder of Battalion being employed on various carrying parties
At 6.15.p.m. orders were received to occupy WOOD Trench as far as U.2.a.3.5. to get in touch with any posts or parties of our troops on either flank, and to consolidate to either flank with the point U.2.a.3.5. as pivot.

2. The following dispositions were reported:-
(a) L.G. post 6th Battn established on ROTTEN ROW at U.1.b. central.
(b) L.G. post 9th Battn on WOOD Trench at U.1.b.8.7.
(c) Post 9th Battn established in front of FONTAINE trench at about U.32.c.2.2.
(d) Men of 8th and 6th Battalions Leicestershire Regiment believed to be in small detachments along line of YORK trench to N.W. of it
(e) Enemy believed to be holding YORK trench

3. Instructions for attack were issued as follows:-

"A" Coy 7th Leicestershire Regiment (Capt Vanner) to work down ROTTEN ROW to point U.1.b.5.5.
"C" Coy (2/Lieut White) to work simultaneously down WOOD trench to point U.3.b.8.7.
"B" Coy to work down WOOD trench in sup ort and carrying bombs. From these points "C" Coy to continue down WOOD trench to U.2.a.3.5., getting touch with parties of 9th and 6th on their left and to consolidate in a direction facing E.
"A" Coy keeping touch with "B" Coy to form a line from U.1.b.5.5 to U.2.a.3.5. facing S. - to get in touch with parties of our men reported to be in front of YORK trench and push forward right flanks as far as possible towards road from U.1.d.7.9. to U.2.a.3.5.

4. At 7.15.p.m. the advance commenced at the same moment our Artillery barrage started. The enemy at once brought a very heavy barrage of heavy howitzers to bear on ROTTEN ROW, and the area including WOOD trench. "A" Coy were able to push on down ROTTEN ROW as far as U.1.b.4.5.
"C" Coy had difficulty in tracing WOOD trench which was found to be merely a traced trench, but not dug, except where our men had consolidated small posts in it.
On finding WOOD trench the leaders of "C" Coy were shot from N.E. probably by M.G. Fire. This and the extremely heavy barrage made it impossible for "C" Coy to advance with no cover, and they became somewhat disorganized.
2/Lieut WHITE drew his Company back to ROTTEN ROW, and got it re-organized - "B" Coy conforming. They were unable to advance.
Captain VANNER on reaching front U.1.b.4.5. found the enemy advancing in force from RIVER Road, they were driven back by rifle and Lewis Gun Fire.
The existence of following dispositions was established by Captain VANNER by personal reconnaissance:-
U.1.b.4.5.-L.G. Post (6th Leicestershire Regt)
U.1.b.3.6.-1 gun and 10 men of 110th Trench Mortar Batty.
U.1.b.8.7.-L.G. Post (Lewis Gun but no team left)

He therefore established the line U.1.b.4.5. to U.1.b.8.7. with an intermediate post at U.1.b.6.5.
He then reconnoitred to his flanks, and on the right he found a N.C.O. and 4 men of the 6th Leicesters at about U.1.b.3.3. They knew nothing of other parties on their flanks, The enemy held YORK trench strongly. On his left he found a N.C.O. and 14 men of 6th Leicesters at about U.2.c.0.9.. He could find no other men on his flanks here

(contd)

The posts at U.1.b.3.3. and U.1.b.4.5. were strengthened and strong points dug at these places.

He accordingly reported at 10.p.m. that his flanks were unprotected, and that he was not in a position to repel a strong counter attack. On reference to Brigade H.Q. orders were then issued to withdraw all men to BROWN LINE. This was successfully accomplished, a number of wounded men of other battalions being brought in.

Instructions regarding War Diaries and Intelligence Summaries are contained in F. S. Regs., Part II. and the Staff Manual respectively. Title Pages will be prepared in manuscript.

WAR DIARY

or

~~INTELLIGENCE~~ SUMMARY

(Erase heading not required.)

Army Form C. 2118.

3

7th Leicester R

Vol 21

Place	Date	Hour	Summary of Events and Information	Remarks and references to Appendices
			WAR DIARY OF THE 7th (Service) Battn. The LEICESTERSHIRE REGIMENT for June, 1917	

23 B

Instructions regarding War Diaries and Intelligence Summaries are contained in F. S. Regs., Part II. and the Staff Manual respectively. Title pages will be prepared in manuscript.

WAR DIARY
or
~~INTELLIGENCE SUMMARY.~~
(Erase heading not required.)

Army Form C. 2118.

Place	Date	Hour	Summary of Events and Information	Remarks and references to Appendices
BIENVILLERS	June 1	6 am	Battalion marched to MOYENEUVILLE.	
MOYENEVILLE	2-6		Battn training, including Close order Drill, Physical & Bayonet Training, Bombing Musketry & Battn Drill.	Ref Map FRANCE Sheet 51 B S.W. Edition 4 a.
	7.		Battn relieved 10th Battn Yorkshire Regiment in Brigade Support. B C + D Coys in GUARDIAN TRENCH V. 13. a + c. A. Coy in trench at T. 18. d. 85. 70. Battn H.Q. in V. 13. c. 0. 7.	
	8.		Casualties: 2 O.R's. W in A.	
	11.		Battn relieved 9th Battn Leicestershire Regt in Right Subsector in BURG TRENCH. A. Coy Right Coy. B. Coy. Centre Coy C. Coy Left Coy. D. Coy in Support in LINCOLN TRENCH. Casualties:- 6 O.R's W in A.	
	12		6 O.R's. W in A.	
	13		2 O.R's W in A. 1 O.R. accidentally wounded.	
	14		13 O.R's W in A. 1 O.R. accidentally killed.	

A5834 Wt. W4973/M687 750,000 8/16 D. D. & L. Ltd. Forms/C.2118/13.

Army Form C. 2118.

Instructions regarding War Diaries and Intelligence Summaries are contained in F. S. Regs., Part II. and the Staff Manual respectively. Title pages will be prepared in manuscript.

WAR DIARY
or
~~INTELLIGENCE~~ SUMMARY.

(Erase heading not required.)

Place	Date	Hour	Summary of Events and Information	Remarks and references to Appendices
	June 15	3.10am	The 173rd Infy Bde. 58th Divn. on our right advanced + captured the HINDENBURG FRONT LINE from the MEBUS at U.20.b.52.15 to U.14.a.05.05. Our Right Coy (Capt. J.C. Vanner in Command) Co operated with Rifle + Lewis Gun fire + rendered valuable assistance in keeping down hostile machine Gun fire. Many parties were dispersed by our fire and a hostile bombing party completely wiped out. A Coy captured 5 prisoners Casualties: 2/Lt. RAWLES W in A. 12 O.R's W in A. 2 O.R K in A.	HJW.
	15/16		On the night of 15/16th Battn was relieved by 12th Battn Northumberland Fusiliers. Battn. moved into RESERVE at S.E. of CROISILLES at T.23.b.&D Battn. H.Q. at T.23.C.9.8. During the whole of the tour in the line the enemy artillery was very active. Heavy + medium T.M's + aerial darts caused much annoyance. Our patrols were very active. A considerable amount of work was done in Front + Support + Communication Trenches + a great deal of new wire put out.	

A5834 Wt. W4973/M687 750,000 8/16 D. D. & L. Ltd. Forms/C.2118/13.

Army Form C. 2118.

Instructions regarding War Diaries and Intelligence Summaries are contained in F. S. Regs., Part II. and the Staff Manual respectively. Title pages will be prepared in manuscript.

WAR DIARY
or
~~INTELLIGENCE SUMMARY.~~
(Erase heading not required.)

Place	Date	Hour	Summary of Events and Information	Remarks and references to Appendices
	June 16–18		Battn supplied working parties for work in front line.	N/W
	19		Casualties: 3 O.R's W in A.	
	19.		Battn on relief by 5th Battn Scottish Rifles moved to F. Camp at MOYENEVILLE Casualties: 1 OR. W in A.	
	20.		Battn on relief by 9th Battn H.L.I. marched to ADINFER.	
	21		Inspections & re organization.	
	22–30		Battn training including Close order drill, Physical & Bayonet Training, Battn Drill, Field firing, bombing, Marching on Compass bearings etc.	
			The following reinforcements joined during the month:–	
	3		12 O.R.'s	
	11.		13 O.R's	
	23		5 Officers: Lieut. Charles Arthur HINE 2/Lts John Ernest HOLLAND, Douglas Henry HOLLAND, John Clifford WALLEY, Captain Herbert William Henry TYLER. 5. O.R's.	
	28.		8 O.R's.	

[signature] Lieut Col
Comdg 7th Battn Leic. Regt.

A5834 Wt. W4973/M687 750,000 8/16 D. D. & L. Ltd. Forms/C.2118/13.

Instructions regarding War Diaries and Intelligence Summaries are contained in F. S. Regs., Part II. and the Staff Manual respectively. Title pages will be prepared in manuscript.

WAR DIARY
or
INTELLIGENCE SUMMARY.
(Erase heading not required.)

Army Form C. 2118.

Vol 22

Place	Date	Hour	Summary of Events and Information	Remarks and references to Appendices
			WAR DIARY of the 7th (Service) Battalion The Leicestershire Regt for July, 1917.	

24B

A5834 Wt. W4973/M687 750,000 8/16 D. D. & L. Ltd. Forms/C.2118/13.

Army Form C. 2118.

Instructions regarding War Diaries and Intelligence Summaries are contained in F. S. Regs., Part II. and the Staff Manual respectively. Title Pages will be prepared in manuscript.

WAR DIARY
or
INTELLIGENCE SUMMARY
(Erase heading not required.)

Place	Date	Hour	Summary of Events and Information	Remarks and references to Appendices
ADINFER WOOD	July 1	8.30am	Battn. marched to F Camp, MOYENNEVILLE. Brigade was in Divl. Reserve.	MAP REF. FRANCE. 51B S.W. Edn. 4 A.
	2-7		Battn. training including Battn, Coy, & Platoon drill, musketry, Bombing, sniping Guard duties & tactical exercises.	
	8.		Battn. relieved 9th Battn. K.O.Y.L.I. in right sub. sector. Relief complete by 1pm	
			A. Coy - Right Coy. B. Coy - Centre Coy. D. Coy - Left. Coy	
			C. Coy in Support in GUARDIAN TRENCH.	
			Battn. H.Q. in QUARRY T.18.b.8.3.	
	9		Casualties:-	
			1 O.R. W in A.	
	10		4 O.R's. K. in A. 5 O.R's. W in A.	M/10
	12		3 O.R's W in A.	
	13		1 O.R. W in A.	
	14.		Battn. on relief by 9th Battn. Leic. Regt. moved into SUPPORT at T.23.c.8.8.	
			Battn. H.Q. at T.23.c.1.9. C. Coy. remained in QUARRY at T.18.b.8.3.	
			Casualties:	
			1 O.R. K in A. 3 O.R's. W in A.	
	16.		1 O.R. W in A.	
	17		B. Coy relieved C. Coy in the QUARRY.	
			Casualties:-	
	18		1 O.R. K in A.	
	19		2 O.R's. W in A.	
	20		1 O.R. W in A.	

2449 Wt. W14957/M90 750,000 1/16 J.B.C. & A. Forms/C.2118/12.

Army Form C. 2118.

Instructions regarding War Diaries and Intelligence Summaries are contained in F. S. Regs., Part II. and the Staff Manual respectively. Title Pages will be prepared in manuscript.

WAR DIARY
or
INTELLIGENCE SUMMARY
(Erase heading not required.)

Place	Date	Hour	Summary of Events and Information	Remarks and references to Appendices
TRENCHES.	July 20		Battn. relieved 9th Battn. Leic. Regt. in front line. Dispositions:- A. Coy. - Right Coy.; C. Coy. - Centre Coy.; D. Coy. - Left Coy.; B. Coy. in Support in GUARDIAN Trench. Battn. H.Q. in QUARRY at T. 18. 6. 8. 3.	
	21		Casualties:- 1 O.R. W in A.	
	24/25		A raid was attempted by the Battn. on the night of 24/25th at 4 days notice Exhaustive training on specimen trenches for 3 days. The wire was partly cut by 2" T.M's. but on account of one party finding the wire not properly cut the raiders withdrew without the enemy being aware of our intentions. Captain	
	25		A.W.H. TYLER was O.C. party. Lieut. R. CARNLEY & 2/Lieut. P. H. SMITH were in charge of the 2 parties which went over. Casualties. Nil.	A.f.W.
	25–28.		Fighting patrols were out every night in order to catch the enemy mending the gaps in wire. Enemy was very quiet & did not attempt to come out	
	25		Casualties:- 1 O.R. K in A. 2 O.R's W in A.	
	26		Battn. on relief by 9th Battn. Leic. Regt. moved to Support at T. 23. c. 8. 8. D. Coy. remained in QUARRY at T. 18. 6. 8. 3. Casualties:- 1 O.R. W in A.	

Army Form C. 2118.

Instructions regarding War Diaries and Intelligence Summaries are contained in F. S. Regs., Part II. and the Staff Manual respectively. Title Pages will be prepared in manuscript.

WAR DIARY
or
INTELLIGENCE SUMMARY
(Erase heading not required.)

Place	Date	Hour	Summary of Events and Information	Remarks and references to Appendices
	July 28		'A' Coy relieved D. Coy. in QUARRY at T.18.b.8.3.	
			Casualties:-	
			1 O.R. K in A. 2 O.R's. W in A.	
			During tour in front line enemy very quiet. While in Support working parties were found by Battn. for work in Front Line, C.T's & tunnel in QUARRY. Our men were very active at Patrol Work. No enemy encountered.	
	31.		Battn. in Support	
			The following reinforcements joined during the month:-	A.J.W.
			2.7.17. 2 Lieut. Agar, P.F. & 1 O.R.	
			3.7.17. Major T.C. Howitt rejoined from Senior Officers School. Aldershot	
			9.7.17. 2/Lieut. Clarke, A.A.	
			" Dowell, W.J.	
			" Scarfe, G.S. and 3 O.R's.	
			14.7.17. 4 O.R's.	
			20.7.17. 2/Lieut. Downing, A.	
			" West, A.A.	
			" Miles, R.T.W. and 1 O.R.	

T C Howitt Major
Comy 7th Battn Leic. Regt

2449 Wt. W14957/M90 750,000 1/16 J.B.C. & A. Forms/C.2118/12.

Instructions regarding War Diaries and Intelligence Summaries are contained in F. S. Regs., Part II. and the Staff Manual respectively. Title pages will be prepared in manuscript.

WAR DIARY
or
INTELLIGENCE SUMMARY.
(Erase heading not required.)

Army Form C. 2118.

Vol 23

Place	Date	Hour	Summary of Events and Information	Remarks and references to Appendices
			21/180 WAR DIARY of the 7th (Service) Battalion The Leicestershire Regiment. FROM 1st to 31st August, 1917.	25B 4 sheet

A5834 Wt. W4973/M687 750,000 8/16 D. D. & L. Ltd. Forms/C.2118/13.

Instructions regarding War Diaries and Intelligence Summaries are contained in F. S. Regs., Part II. and the Staff Manual respectively. Title pages will be prepared in manuscript.

WAR DIARY
or
INTELLIGENCE SUMMARY.
(*Erase heading not required.*)

Army Form C. 2118.

Place	Date	Hour	Summary of Events and Information	Remarks and references to Appendices
MOYENNEVILLE	AUGUST 1st–8th		Battalion at F Camp.	Ref Map 57B SW edn 2a.
			Battalion training, including bayonet fighting, physical training, wiring, squad drill, musketry, gas drill, bombing & rifle grenades, Lewis gun, tactical exercises, & platoons & companies in the attack.	
	2nd–6th		"B" Company (Capt Evans) at "B" Camp ST LEGER, working under supervision of R.E.	
LEFT BDE SECTOR	9th		110th Infy Bde relieved 62nd Infy Bde in the left Bde sector.	
			7th Batt Leic Regt relieved 12th Batt Northumberland Fusiliers in left sub sector (Posts 1 – 11 inclusive).	
			Dispositions:	
			D Coy – Right company. Nos 1, 2, & 3 Posts in SHAFT TRENCH. Coy H.Q in tunnel U 1/7 c 9 1.	
			C Coy – Centre company. Posts 4 & 5 in SHAFT TRENCH; no 6 HORN TRENCH; no 7 HORN & CLAW TRENCH. Coy H.Q in tunnel T 6 d 95 50	
				[illegible]

A5834 Wt. W4973/M687 750,000 8/16 D. D. & L. Ltd. Forms/C.2118/13.

Army Form C. 2118.

Instructions regarding War Diaries and Intelligence Summaries are contained in F. S. Regs., Part II. and the Staff Manual respectively. Title pages will be prepared in manuscript.

WAR DIARY
or
INTELLIGENCE SUMMARY.
(*Erase heading not required.*)

Place	Date	Hour	Summary of Events and Information	Remarks and references to Appendices
LEFT BDE SECTOR	AUGUST 9th		A Coy - Left Company. Post 8 in CLAW TRENCH; post 9 in MEBU, CLAW TRENCH; post 11 in PUG LANE. post 10 abandoned for tactical reasons but being too isolated.	Ref map 57 B SW Edit 2 4a.
			Coy H.Q. in gun emplacement in PUG LANE.	
			B Coy - Support Company. HIND TRENCH from U7a58 to T6d25.	
			Batt. H.Q. in tunnel in SHAFT TRENCH T6d 4095.	
			Casualties: 1 O.R. W in A; 1 K in A.	
	13th		B Coy (support) relieved A Coy (left Coy); A Coy moved to support U7a58 to T6d25.	
	14th		Casualties: 2 O.R's accidentally wounded.	
	15th		2 OR's W in A.	
	16th		1 O.R W in A.	
	9th-17th		During the tour in the line, enemy was very quiet. Hostile TM + artillery activity practically nil. Our patrols were very active but encountered no enemy patrols	

A5834 Wt. W4973/M687 750,000 8/16 D. D. & L. Ltd. Forms/C.2118/13.

Instructions regarding War Diaries and Intelligence Summaries are contained in F. S. Regs., Part II. and the Staff Manual respectively. Title pages will be prepared in manuscript.

WAR DIARY
or
INTELLIGENCE SUMMARY.
(Erase heading not required.)

Army Form C. 2118.

Place	Date	Hour	Summary of Events and Information	Remarks and references to Appendices
LEFT BDE SECTOR	AUGUST 17th		On relief by 12th/13th N.Fs the battalion moved to huts in HAMELINCOURT.	
HAMELINCOURT	18th		Cleaning, kit inspections, paying out.	
	19th–24th		Battalion training as for period 1st – 8th above.	
			Battalion was inspected by Brig. Gen. Lord Loch C.M.G. M.V.O., D.S.O.	
	25th	10.30 AM	110th Infy Bde relieved by 47th Infy Bde. Battalion marched by companies at 100 yards interval to GOUY-EN-ARTOIS. Route ADINFER – RANSART – BAILLEULVAL – LEBAC DU SUD	G.M.
GOUY-EN-ARTOIS	26th	8.55 AM	Battalion marched by companies at 100 yards interval to BEAUFORT. Route FOSSEUX – BARLY – AVESNES-LE-COMTE	
	27th–31st		Battalion training as for period 1st – 8th above.	
			The following reinforcements joined during the month:	
			15th: 2nd Lt N. DARLING (from 13th N.F)	
			2nd Lt H. WATTS (" " ")	
			20th: Lt V.C. HALES (from 3rd Batt Leic Rgt)	
			22nd: 5 O.Rs	
			24th: 3 O.R's.	
			31st: 6 O.R's.	

[illegible] Lt Col
Cmdg 7th Batt Leic Rgt

A5834 Wt. W4973/M687 750,000 8/16 D. D. & L. Ltd. Forms/C.2118/13.

Instructions regarding War Diaries and Intelligence Summaries are contained in F. S. Regs., Part II. and the Staff Manual respectively. Title pages will be prepared in manuscript.

WAR DIARY
or
~~INTELLIGENCE SUMMARY.~~
(Erase heading not required.)

Army Form C. 2118.

21/40 110/21

7th Bn Leicester Regt

Vol 24

Place	Date	Hour	Summary of Events and Information	Remarks and references to Appendices
BEAUFORT	1st	SEPT.	Church parade and baths.	
	2nd 3rd		Coy training, attack practice.	
HAUTEVILLE	4th		Wood fighting practice in the morning. Battalion moved to billets at HAUTEVILLE via AVESNES-LE-COMTE.	
	5th		Coy. training. Won 1st Round football cup beating 6th B. 4-1. A draft of 4 men joined the battalion.	
	6th		Coy. training. Won 2nd round of cup against 6th B (3-1). A draft of 4 men joined.	
	7th		Coy training. Battalion won the football cup presented by Brigadier General Lord Loch, beating the 9th Bn by 3-1. Final of the Bde boxing competition at AVESNES le COMTE. Bn won 2 events.	
	8th		Training. Bn played 6th Bn at Rugby football, lost (8-0).	
	9th		Church parade at the Chateau.	
	10th		Brigade Military Tournament at HAUTEVILLE. Competitions Coy in the Attack, blindfold drill, compass march, mule races, transport turnout etc. 7th Bn came out first in points.	

26 B
3 sheets

A5834 Wt. W4973/M687 750,000 8/16 D. D. & L. Ltd. Forms/C.2118/13.

(CONTD)

Instructions regarding War Diaries and Intelligence Summaries are contained in F. S. Regs., Part II. and the Staff Manual respectively. Title pages will be prepared in manuscript.

WAR DIARY
or
INTELLIGENCE SUMMARY.
(Erase heading not required.)

Army Form C. 2118.

Place	Date	Hour	Summary of Events and Information	Remarks and references to Appendices
HAUTEVILLE	11TH	SEPT.	Brigade training. Brigade attack practice	
	12TH to 15TH		Coy training a draft of 1 officer 2nd Lt G. DRAPES rejoined, and two men rejoined from the base.	
	16TH		The Bn marched at 7.45 AM to SAVY STN and entrained for	
CAESTRE			BELGIUM detraining at CAESTRE at 5 P.M. Camp at CAESTRE.	
	17th to 22nd		Bn training. A draft of 69 OR joined the Bn. They were all men who had been out before and a fair portion had been in the 110th Inf Bde	
BERTHEN.	23RD		marched from CAESTRE to BERTHEN.	
	24th 25th		Coy training including night marching. a draft of 3 officers joined the Bn (Lieuts) PATRINGTON. 2Lts. W.L. STUBBS. A.J. KNIGHT and T. STANDLEY. 44 OR joined from the base.	
FORWARD AREA.	26th		Bn embussed for the forward area, and moved to SCOTTISH WOOD and then on to BEDFORD Ho. where the Bn was in reserve to the 33rd Bde.	
	27th 28th		Bn returned to MICMAC CAMP near OODERDOM. Resting at MICMAC.	

Instructions regarding War Diaries and Intelligence Summaries are contained in F. S. Regs., Part II. and the Staff Manual respectively. Title pages will be prepared in manuscript.

WAR DIARY
or
INTELLIGENCE SUMMARY.
(*Erase heading not required.*)

Army Form C. 2118.

Place	Date	Hour	Summary of Events and Information	Remarks and references to Appendices
FORWARD AREA.	29th	SEPT.	Bn moved No 2 area WILTSHIRE FARM. Officers went forward to reconnoitre POLYGON WOOD. Major T.C. HOWITT and CAPT & ADJ. H.H. WALSH, M.C. were wounded on the return journey.	
	30th		The Bn relieved the 31st AUSTRALIAN INF in POLYGON WOOD RT SECTOR. MAJOR T.C. HOWITT in command. 2 men of the nucleus party were wounded by bomb splinters.	Appx II.

T.C. Howitt Major.
for Lt Col Cdg
7th Bn Leic: Regt

A5834 Wt. W4973/M687 750,000 8/16 D. D. & L. Ltd. Forms/C.2118/13.

110/21 (1)

11th Bn Leicester Regt

Vol 25

Instructions regarding War Diaries and Intelligence Summaries are contained in F. S. Regs., Part II. and the Staff Manual respectively. Title pages will be prepared in manuscript.

WAR DIARY
or
~~INTELLIGENCE SUMMARY.~~
(Erase heading not required.)

Army Form C. 2118.

Place	Date	Hour	Summary of Events and Information	Remarks and references to Appendices
			Reference Maps: Belgium and France Ed 3. 1/40.000. ZILLEBEKE. Trench Map 1/10.000.	
POLYGON WOOD	Oct 1 1917		Relief. Last night the Battn under command of Major HOWITT with a strength of 19 Officers and 400 Other Ranks marched from SCOTTISH WOOD, via BEDFORD HOUSE, ZILLEBEKE, SANCTUARY WOOD and CLAPHAM JUNCTION to relieve the support positions originally held by the 31st Battn of the 8th Australian Infantry Bde. A long halt was taken immediately N of BEDFORD HOUSE for tea, and to issue special fighting stores. Relief was complete by 11.30 p.m.	HWM?
			Dispositions. The 9th Battn Leicestershire Regiment were holding the right front the 8th Battn Leicestershire Regiment the left front of the Brigade front. The 7th Battn Leicestershire Regiment in support and the 6th Battn Leicestershire Regiment in Reserve. The 7th Battalion was disposed as follows:-	

276
18 above

Instructions regarding War Diaries and Intelligence Summaries are contained in F. S. Regs., Part II. and the Staff Manual respectively. Title pages will be prepared in manuscript.

(2)

Army Form C. 2118.

WAR DIARY
or
~~INTELLIGENCE SUMMARY.~~
(Erase heading not required.)

Place	Date	Hour	Summary of Events and Information	Remarks and references to Appendices
			Right front Coy J 9 d 2 1 C Coy under Captain W. H. HENPHILL Left front Coy J 9 d 2 4 D Coy under Captain A. A. CLARKE M. C Support Coy J 9 c 9 1 B Coy under Captain W. A. EVANS Reserve Coy J 9 c 1 1 A Coy under Lieut H. R. HORNE plus 3 reserve Lewis Gun teams Battn H. Q. J. 14 b 4 8	
			Partly dug positions were available for C and B Coys, other Coys had to dig in in their own areas. The whole of the relief was completed, and digging in well started without a single casualty. The night was exceptionally quiet.	[illegible]
			__Hostile Attack__ About 4.45 A.M. the enemy put down a heavy barrage, and at 5.20 A.M. delivered a heavy counter attack, the main weight of this appearing to come from CAMERON COVERT. Under this heavy pressure the left Battn of the Bde on our right appeared to be suffering very heavy casualties, and getting pushed back. A platoon of C Coy under Lieut V. C. HALES was right formed and moved up to get in touch with the rear line of the 9th Battn Leicestershire Regiment to form a right defensive flank. This platoon got in position, but	

A5834 Wt. W4973/M687 750,000 8/16 D. D. & L. Ltd. Forms/C.2118/13.

Instructions regarding War Diaries and Intelligence Summaries are contained in F. S. Regs., Part II. and the Staff Manual respectively. Title pages will be prepared in manuscript.

(3)

Army Form C. 2118.

WAR DIARY
or
~~INTELLIGENCE SUMMARY~~.

(Erase heading not required.)

Place	Date	Hour	Summary of Events and Information	Remarks and references to Appendices
			Lieut HALES was wounded. The enemy barrage line was due N – S through J.9. central. Our Left front Coy were suffering heavy casualties, so they moved further E to clear the barrage. Captain A.A. CLARKE M.C. was killed, and 2/Lieut P.E. AGAR and 2/Lieut C.G. SCARFE wounded. The hostile barrage and counter attack still continued, and the Right front Coy, supported by 2 platoons of Support Coy; Left front Coy supported by 1 platoon of Support Coy were pushed forward through the barrage in section snakes, to again attack the enemy in any of our positions. These supports lost very heavily going through the barrage (approximately 50%). The left front Battn were still holding to their original positions, and our supports acted as reinforcements. The Right front Battn had made 3 counter attacks and recovered all with the exception of 2 or 3 small shell hole posts.	
			2/Lieut R.W.T. MILES who had gone forward to reconnoitre, assisted by 1 platoon of D Coy joined in the counter attacks, was killed and then Sergt MOSS who was wounded in the leg still led the platoon forward until practically all became casualties under hostile Machine Gun fire and Sergt MOSS was again wounded in the face.	

A5834 Wt. W4973/M687 750,000 8/16 D. D. & L. Ltd. Forms/C.2118/13.

Instructions regarding War Diaries and Intelligence Summaries are contained in F. S. Regs., Part II. and the Staff Manual respectively. Title pages will be prepared in manuscript.

WAR DIARY
or
~~INTELLIGENCE SUMMARY.~~
(*Erase heading not required.*)

Army Form C. 2118.

(4)

Place	Date	Hour	Summary of Events and Information	Remarks and references to Appendices
			There was a gap of 250 yards to the East of CAMERON HOUSE and from our Bde Boundary due S. Our right front Battn had pushed out 3 small posts in this area.	
			With this big extension, and owing to the very heavy casualties of the right front Battn the necessity of forming a deep defensive flank it was considered unsafe to push forward any further counter attack for the 2 or 3 shell hole posts. The remainder of our Supports were therefore pushed from the shell hole line along the Eastern end of POLYGON WOOD J.10.c and the Eastern front of CAMERON HOUSE J.16.a.	
			<u>Consolidation</u>	
			When the hostile barrage had died down the Reserve Coy came forward and formed a support switch NE-SW about 200 yards long and 150 yards N.W. of the SE corner of POLYGON WOOD J.10.c.	
			Lieut Colonel BENT, 9th Battn Leicestershire Regt was killed in the counter attack which regained our positions. Major T.C. HOWITT took over command of 9th Battn Leicestershire Regt in addition to 7th Battn about noon.	[illegible]

A5834 Wt. W4973/M687 750,000 8/16 D. D. & L. Ltd. Forms/C.2118/13.

Army Form C. 2118.

WAR DIARY
or
~~INTELLIGENCE SUMMARY.~~

(*Erase heading not required.*)

Instructions regarding War Diaries and Intelligence Summaries are contained in F. S. Regs., Part II. and the Staff Manual respectively. Title pages will be prepared in manuscript.

Place	Date	Hour	Summary of Events and Information	Remarks and references to Appendices
			From the reports of 4 different prisoners captured on the Right Bde front the enemy was expected to attack again at dusk. There had been considerable movement of troops in CAMERON COVERT all the afternoon. A slow barrage was kept up during the afternoon to strengthen our line, and at dusk when the hostile barrage came down and our guns replied magnificently. Any hostile counter attack was at once smashed by these, and only one prisoner leaked through.	
			<u>Reserve Battn</u>	
			2 Reserve Coys of the 6th Battn Leicestershire Regt moved from the S.E end of GLENCORSE WOOD and arrived at front line H Q about 9 P.M. One Coy was put in support just E of CAMERON HOUSE and the other formed into a switch NE - SW line behind the S. E angle of POLYGON WOOD. These Coys consolidated very quickly, and for the first time since 5. 30. A.M. the line was tactically sound. At midnight Lieut Col STEWART and one Coy of the 6th Battn Leicestershire Regt moved to the front line. This Coy was formed as support to left front Battn. During the night advanced posts were pushed out along the front helping our front line slightly forward.	
	Oct 2		At dawn the S. O. S was put up on the right flank Bde front. Our own and the enemy's barrage came on for about half an hour. The day was fairly quiet,	

A5834 Wt. W4973/M687 750,000 8/16 D. D. & L. Ltd. Forms/C.2118/13.

Instructions regarding War Diaries and Intelligence Summaries are contained in F. S. Regs., Part II. and the Staff Manual respectively. Title pages will be prepared in manuscript.

(6)

Army Form C. 2118.

WAR DIARY
or
~~INTELLIGENCE SUMMARY.~~
(Erase heading not required.)

Place	Date	Hour	Summary of Events and Information	Remarks and references to Appendices
			and we were able to evacuate all the wounded.	
			An enemy sniper at J 16. a 6. 6 in a concrete shelter caused a few casualties.	
			2/Lieut DOWELL crawled out and engaged this sniper, and was wounded through the shoulder whilst firing at him.	
			<u>Relief</u>	
			At 6.30 P.M. the enemy put down a heavy barrage, and ours came down as the S.O.S reached the ground. There was an intense artillery duel until 8.15 P.M. This gradually died away and the remainder of the evening was quiet.	
			About 8.30 P.M. a Battn of the East Surrey Regt (5th Division) relieved the whole of our men S of the Bde Boundary, and the 9th Battn K.O.Y.L.I (64th Brigade) relieved the remainder of our positions. This relief was complete by 11.15 P.M. and the Battn moved out along the same route that we entered the area, without any casualties.	
	Oct 3		A long halt was made S E of ZILLEBEKE LAKE to collect the Battn. After tea the Battn moved back into the WILTSHIRE FARM bivouac area H.35.a.	
			<u>Casualties</u>	
			During these 2 days the Battn had the following casualties:-	

A5834 Wt. W4973/M687 750,000 8/16 D. D. & L. Ltd. Forms/C.2118/13.

(1)

Army Form C. 2118.

Instructions regarding War Diaries and Intelligence Summaries are contained in F. S. Regs., Part II. and the Staff Manual respectively. Title pages will be prepared in manuscript.

WAR DIARY
or
~~INTELLIGENCE SUMMARY.~~
(Erase heading not required.)

Place	Date	Hour	Summary of Events and Information	Remarks and references to Appendices
			OFFICERS	
			Killed: Captain A. A. CLARKE, M.C.	
			2/Lieut R. W. T. MILES	
			Wounded: Lieut V. C. HALES	
			2/Lieut P. E. AGAR	
			2/Lieut C. G. SCARFE	
			2/Lieut G. DRAPES	
			2/Lieut W. T. DOWELL	
			O. RANKS	
			Killed 26	
			Wounded 115	
			Missing (believed wounded) 9	
			Gassed 4	
			Shell Shock 13	
			Communications	
			Signallers were useless, the Power Buzzer was not effective over 1500 yards. Pigeons were very good and got through quickly. The success of the whole operations was greatly due to the magnificent work of Battn and Coy runners.	

A5834 Wt. W4973/M687 750,000 8/16 D. D. & L. Ltd. Forms/C.2118/13.

Instructions regarding War Diaries and Intelligence Summaries are contained in F. S. Regs., Part II. and the Staff Manual respectively. Title pages will be prepared in manuscript.

WAR DIARY
or
~~INTELLIGENCE SUMMARY.~~
(Erase heading not required.)

Army Form C. 2118.

Place	Date	Hour	Summary of Events and Information	Remarks and references to Appendices
WILTSHIRE FARM H.35 D.			The Battn was re-organized, 2 platoons in each Coy plus one extra Lewis Gun team. 2 Officers and 8 Other Ranks were brought up from Nucleus to strengthen the organization.	
ZILLEBEKE LAKE	Oct 4		Z day of the Divl attack.	
		8.30 AM.	The Battn marched up to S of ZILLEBEKE LAKE, and bivouaced there for the day. Lieut Colonel A A ALDWORTH M.C. came up to take command and relieve Major T. C. HOWITT. Capt Emmerson replaced Capt Evans B Coy.	
POLYGON WOOD.	Oct 5th	3.45 PM	The Bn. moved up to the Support line W of POLYGON WOOD. J10c. relieving the 6th Bn in consolidated shell holes. There was intermittent shelling during the day and night. 2Lt Dorning was gassed. Capt Emmerson 2Lts Mangan + Raistrick were wounded.	
do	6th		The day was fairly quiet, from 5.30 to 7.30 PM heavy shelling. At 8 PM C and A Coys moved up to the front line at REUTEL J11c. relieving elements of 9th, 10th KOYLI, and 1st [illegible]. B. D Coys moved into local support J11c. The relief was quiet.	

Army Form C. 2118.

Instructions regarding War Diaries and Intelligence Summaries are contained in F. S. Regs., Part II. and the Staff Manual respectively. Title pages will be prepared in manuscript.

WAR DIARY
or
~~INTELLIGENCE SUMMARY.~~

(Erase heading not required.)

Place	Date	Hour	Summary of Events and Information	Remarks and references to Appendices
REUTEL	Oct 6th (Contd)		one Coy 8th Bn & one Coy 9th Bn moved into reserve at J11c. and came under orders of 7th Bn. 6th Bn were on left, & Cheshires (5th Div) on right	
do.	7th		The situation was fairly quiet, and the day was spent consolidating the line. Patrols were sent out during the night and reported the JUNIPER COTT: to be clear of the enemy. At 5 PM an SOS signal was put up on the left resulting in heavy firing by both sides. No infantry action developed.	
do	8th		The day was fairly quiet on the whole	
do	9th	4.45 AM	A. B Coys withdrew from their forward position to about 500 yds westward to allow 7th Div attack to pass through. At 8 AM the situation being vague in front A. B Coys moved back to the positions they had vacated. This movement was observed by the enemy and his shell fire caused us some casualties.	

2353 Wt. W2544/1454 700,000 5/15 D. D. & L. A.D.S.S./Forms/C. 2118.

Instructions regarding War Diaries and Intelligence Summaries are contained in F. S. Regs., Part II. and the Staff Manual respectively. Title pages will be prepared in manuscript.

WAR DIARY
or
INTELLIGENCE SUMMARY.
(*Erase heading not required.*)

(10) Army Form C. 2118.

Place	Date	Hour	Summary of Events and Information	Remarks and references to Appendices
	Oct.			
REUTEL	9th (contd)		During the night patrols were sent out to find the 2nd HAC who had attack in the morning. Only a few men were found, & there were many wounded about. They held no definite line.	
do	10th		The day was fairly quiet except for intermittent shelling. We had some casualties.	
do	do	5PM	The Bn commenced to withdraw from their forward position in accordance with Bde orders, in the order A C B D. A Coy was fired at by an enemy plane at close range, having a few casualties. The 2 attached Coys of 8th 9th remained in position until relieved by 10 Bn N.F. The Bn experienced a good deal of difficulty whilst coming out owing to hostile barrages; the last sections arriving at ANZAC CAMP at 9AM the following morning. Casualties whilst relieving were fairly severe, particularly in C Coy. 2Lt Standley C Coy was wounded.	App III

2353 Wt. W2544/1454 700,000 5/15 D. D. & L. A.D.S.S./Forms/C. 2118.

Instructions regarding War Diaries and Intelligence Summaries are contained in F. S. Regs., Part II. and the Staff Manual respectively. Title pages will be prepared in manuscript.

WAR DIARY

or

INTELLIGENCE SUMMARY.

(Erase heading not required.)

Army Form C. 2118.

(11)

Place	Date	Hour	Summary of Events and Information	Remarks and references to Appendices
ANZAC CAMP. H.30.	Oct 11th	12 Noon	The Bn marched from ANZAC to OODERDOM STN: where they entrained at 5PM for EBBLINGHEM arriving 9 P.M. Tea & rum were issued, and the Bn marched to billets and camp at LA CARNOIS.	

2353 Wt. W2544/1454 700,000 5/15 D. D. & L. A.D.S.S./Forms/C. 2118.

Instructions regarding War Diaries and Intelligence Summaries are contained in F. S. Regs., Part II. and the Staff Manual respectively. Title pages will be prepared in manuscript.

WAR DIARY

or

~~INTELLIGENCE SUMMARY.~~

(Erase heading not required.)

Army Form C. 2118.

Place	Date	Hour	Summary of Events and Information	Remarks and references to Appendices
LA CARNOIS	Oct 12th		Bn was paid out, and rested the remainder of the day.	
do	13th		The day was spent cleaning up & reorganizing. Coy commanders were arranged as A Coy. Capt Vanner MC. B. Capt Hodson C. Capt Hemphill. D Major Tyler MC.	
do.	14th		Church parade and address by commanding officer, who also read out appreciations from G.O.C. X Corps. XXI. Div. 110th Inf Bde. A warning order was received to be ready to move again.	
do.	15th		The Bn marched to LES CISEAUX, and embussed for SCHRAPNEL CORNER. I 20 a. being accommodated in dug outs in the railway embankment.	

2353 Wt. W2544/1454 700,000 5/15 D. D. & L. A.D.S.S./Forms/C. 2118.

Instructions regarding War Diaries and Intelligence Summaries are contained in F. S. Regs., Part II. and the Staff Manual respectively. Title pages will be prepared in manuscript.

WAR DIARY
or
~~INTELLIGENCE SUMMARY.~~
(Erase heading not required.)

(B) Army Form C. 2118.

Place	Date	Hour	Summary of Events and Information	Remarks and references to Appendices
RAILWAY EMBANKMENTS I 20.a.	Oct 16th to 23rd		A daily working party of 400 men carried logs for road making from BIRR X Rds to GLENCORSE WOOD TRACK. One log per man was carried daily. During the 8 days 12 OR were wounded by shell fire most of them slightly.	
"B" CAMP CHATEAU SEGARD. N.30.c.	24th		Brigadier General commdg 110th Inf Bde addressed the Bn and presented the Military Medal Ribbon to Pte Clements.	
	25th		The morning was spent reorganizing and training	
	26th		NOTE The remaining portion of the October diary will be forwarded when the Bn comes out of the line.	[initials]
			To be continued.	

2353 Wt. W2544/1454 700,000 5/15 D. D. & L. A.D.S.S./Forms/C. 2118.

Instructions regarding War Diaries and Intelligence Summaries are contained in F. S. Regs., Part II. and the Staff Manual respectively. Title pages will be prepared in manuscript.

(1.) 110/21

Army Form C. 2118.

WAR DIARY
or
INTELLIGENCE SUMMARY.
(Erase heading not required.)

7th Bn Leicestershire Regt

Vol 26

Place	Date	Hour	Summary of Events and Information	Remarks and references to Appendices
			Reference Maps:- Belgium and France Ed 3 1/40.000 ZILLEBEKE Trench Map 1/10.000 LENS XI HAZEBROUCK 5A.	
CLAPHAM JUNCTION.	Nov 1st 1917	to 3rd	Daily working parties of 90 men were sent to HOOGE CRATER digging cable trenches. During the three days hostile artillery was very active particularly with gas shells. On the night of Nov 1st/2nd respirators were worn almost continuously from 8 pm to 1 AM. Only one casualty was caused by gas, a shell bursting very close to a man and slightly gassing him. No other casualties were incurred.	ARH
do	3rd	9 P.M.	The Battalion was relieved by the 3/4th QUEENS, and moved via HOOGE CRATER, BIRR X ROADS and WARRINGTON ROAD to 'B' Camp CHATEAU SEGARD. While the relief was in progress hostile artillery remained inactive and no casualties were suffered. The 110th Infantry Brigade was now in reserve.	ARH.

28B
5 sheet

A7092). Wt. W12839/M1293. 750,000. 1/17. D. D & L., Ltd. Forms/C2118/14.

Army Form C. 2118.

(2.)

WAR DIARY

~~or~~

~~INTELLIGENCE SUMMARY~~.

(Erase heading not required.)

Instructions regarding War Diaries and Intelligence Summaries are contained in F. S. Regs., Part II. and the Staff Manual respectively. Title pages will be prepared in manuscript.

Place	Date	Hour	Summary of Events and Information	Remarks and references to Appendices
CHATEAU SEGARD. "B" CAMP	1917. NOV 4th to 6th		The days were spent in cleaning up, reorganizing and refitting. LT W.A.L. PRATLEY and 2nd LT W. STUBBS joined the Battalion.	HRH.
do	7th	10 AM	The G.O.C. 21st Division addressed the Battalion, and presented medals-ribbons won in the operations round POLYGON WOOD on October 1st 1917 to the following:- CAPT H.H. HEMPHILL. Military Cross No 17985 Pte JONES R. Military Medal " 10130 Pte WINTER S. Military Medal " 12113 Pte RYAN G. Distinguished Conduct Medal " 13728 Pte WALKER T.H. Military Medal.	HRH
do	"	2 P.M	The Battalion moved via SHRAPNEL CORNER to the dugouts, ZILLEBEKE BUND.	HRH
ZILLEBEKE BUND.	8th	3.30 P.M	The Battalion moved up to the front line, relieving the 1st EAST YORKS. C Coy was the right front Company at J 6 c; D Coy the left front Company at J 5 b; B Coy in support at J 5 central. A Coy in reserve at J 5 c 1.6. H.Q. at J 5 a 4.2.	HRH.

A7092). Wt. W12839/M1293 750,000. 1/17. D. D & L., Ltd. Forms/C2118/14.

Instructions regarding War Diaries and Intelligence Summaries are contained in F. S. Regs., Part II. and the Staff Manual respectively. Title pages will be prepared in manuscript.

WAR DIARY

~~or~~

~~INTELLIGENCE SUMMARY.~~

(Erase heading not required.)

(3)

Army Form C. 2118.

Place	Date	Hour	Summary of Events and Information	Remarks and references to Appendices
FRONT LINE J5a 4.2	1917 Nov 8th to Nov 11th		During this tour hostile activity very much decreased, especially artillery and sniping, and no enemy patrols were encountered. A great amount of work was done in repairing trenches which constantly fell in owing to wet weather. Casualties amounted to 11 other Ranks: 2 LT P.R. FOWLER, 2 LT J.H. BONSHOR and 2 LT A.E. GOODBODY joined the Battalion on the 10th Nov.	HRH.
ZILLEBEKE BUND	" 12th		On the night of Nov 11th/12th the battalion was relieved by 6th Batt Lin. Regt and moved to ZILLEBEKE BUND. A draft of 14 other Ranks joined the battalion.	HRH
do	13th	2 pm.	The Battalion ~~was~~ relieved by the 3rd Battalion Wellington Regt, and moved to "A" Camp. CHATEAU SEGARD	HRH.
CHATEAU SEGARD "A" CAMP	14th to 15th		The two days were spent in cleaning up, bathing and reorganizing. Drafts of 6 other Ranks joined the Battalion.	HRH.
	16th	8.30 AM	The Battalion marched via HALLEBAST CORNER and OUDERDOM to DEVONSHIRE CAMP G 22 b 8.7, in the RENINGHELST AREA.	HRH.

A7092). Wt. W12839/M1293 750,000. 1/17. D. D & L., Ltd. Forms/C2118/14.

Instructions regarding War Diaries and Intelligence Summaries are contained in F. S. Regs., Part II. and the Staff Manual respectively. Title pages will be prepared in manuscript.

WAR DIARY

~~or~~

~~INTELLIGENCE SUMMARY~~.

(Erase heading not required.)

(4.)

Army Form C. 2118.

Place	Date	Hour	Summary of Events and Information	Remarks and references to Appendices
DEVONSHIRE CAMP. G 22 b 8.7	1917 Nov 17		The morning was spent in cleaning up and training, and the afternoon in Company Inspections	HRH
NOOTE BOOM	18	10.10 AM	The Battalion marched to NOOTE BOOM via LOCRE and BAILLEUL; a halt for lunch was made 2 miles N.E of BAILLEUL, and the battalion arrived in billets at 4 p.m.	HRH
CAUDESCURE	19th	10.30 AM	The Battalion marched to CAUDESCURE via BLEU and LA COURONNE, arriving in billets at 1.15 p.m.	HRH
GONNEHEM	20th	9.25 AM	The Battalion marched to GONNEHEM via MERVILLE and Mt BERNENCHON; a long halt was made for dinners at 12 noon, and the battalion arrived in billets at 3 p.m.	HRH
COUPIGNY	21st	9.12 AM.	The Battalion marched to COUPIGNY via ANNEZIN, HAILLICOURT and BARLIN, arriving in camp at 2.30 p.m.	HRH
do	22nd to 24th		The three days were spent in cleaning up and training. A Draft of 40 Other Ranks joined the Battalion.	HRH.

A7092). Wt. W12839/M1293 750,000. 1/17. D. D & L., Ltd. Forms/C2118/14.

Instructions regarding War Diaries and Intelligence Summaries are contained in F. S. Regs., Part II. and the Staff Manual respectively. Title pages will be prepared in manuscript.

WAR DIARY

~~or~~

~~INTELLIGENCE~~ ~~SUMMARY~~.

(*Erase heading not required.*)

5

Army Form C. 2118.

Place	Date	Hour	Summary of Events and Information	Remarks and references to Appendices
FREVILLERS	1917 Nov 25	9.30 AM	The Battalion marched to FREVILLERS via VERDREL, FRESNICOURT and GAUCHIN LEGAL, arriving in billets at 1 pm. During the period Nov 16th to 25th, no men fell out on the march.	HRH
do	" 26th to 29th		The days were spent in training; the morning programme including Bayonet fighting, Physical training, Musketry and Arms Drill, and the afternoon, lectures and Tactical Exercises for Officers and N.C.O's. Baths were provided for the men on the 27th. Drafts of 94 other Ranks joined the Battalion.	HRH
	30th		Battalion received urgent orders to move and entrained at SAVY at 7.30pm for TINCOURT	[illegible]

[signature] Lieut Col
7th Leicester Regt

A7092). Wt. W12839/M1293. 750,000. 1/17. D. D & L., Ltd. Forms/C2118/14.

Vol 27

WAR DIARY.

4th Bn LEICESTERSHIRE Regt.

Decr 31st 1917.

29B
7 sheets

(1.)

Army Form C. 2118.

Instructions regarding War Diaries and Intelligence Summaries are contained in F. S. Regs., Part II. and the Staff Manual respectively. Title pages will be prepared in manuscript.

WAR DIARY
or
INTELLIGENCE SUMMARY.
(Erase heading not required.)

Place	Date	Hour	Summary of Events and Information	Remarks and references to Appendices
			Reference Maps:- LENS XI. FRANCE SHEET 57 C S.E. FRANCE SHEET 62 C N.E.	
FRONT LINE X 26 a 6·1	1917. Dec 1		The Battalion detrained at TINCOURT 7 am and marched to camp at COURCELLES. At 2. pm the Battalion left camp and marched via BUIRE, TINCOURT and LONGAVESNES to E 27 central, where a long halt was made for teas. The Battalion continued the march via VILLERS - FAUCON, ST EMILIE and EPEHY to X 26, where it took over the front line from detachments of the 1/4th and 1/5th KINGS OWN LIVERPOOL Regt. Dispositions after relief were as follows:- FRONT LINE X 26 b. RIGHT COY A. " " X 20 a and c LEFT COY B. IMM: SUPPORT. X 26 a and b RIGHT COY C. " " X 26 a and d LEFT COY D. BATTN H.Q X 26 a 6.1.	H.R.H.
	2 3		There was very ~~little~~ hostile activity, apart from intermittent shelling and sniping by machine guns at long range. The nights were spent in consolidation of our line; and the location of enemy posts by means of patrols. Sentry groups were located at PARRS BANK and at X 20 b 5·7.	H.R.H.

A5834 Wt. W4973/M687 750,000 8/16 D. D. & L. Ltd. Forms/C.2118/13.

Instructions regarding War Diaries and Intelligence Summaries are contained in F. S. Regs., Part II. and the Staff Manual respectively. Title pages will be prepared in manuscript.

WAR DIARY
or
INTELLIGENCE SUMMARY.
(Erase heading not required.)

(3)

Army Form C. 2118.

Place	Date	Hour	Summary of Events and Information	Remarks and references to Appendices
			No hostile patrols were seen, and no event of importance took place during this period. Casualties suffered 2 O.R. wounded in action.	ARH
EPEHY. F1 d 8·9	1917 Dec 4	6 pm	The Battalion was relieved by the 6th Battn LEICESTERSHIRE REGT, and moved into support in trenches running along in front of the railway just E of EPEHY. Companies were disposed in one line from right to left A. B. C. D. Battn HQ at F1 d 8·9. The enemy remained very quiet during the relief, and no casualties were suffered.	ARH
do	5	8 pm	D Company took over some of the trenches previously occupied by the 10th K.O.Y.L.I., and extended its line 200 yards further N.W.	HRH
do	7	5 pm	A Coy moved up into trenches about 500 yards in advance of their old position, to be in close support to the 8th Battn LEICS: Regt. During the period in support work consisted mainly in wiring in front of the support line, and in consolidation and improvement of the trenches. Casualties amounted to 1 O.R killed and 1 O.R wounded in action.	HRH.

A5834 Wt. W4973/M687 750,000 8/16 D. D. & L. Ltd. Forms/C.2118/13.

(3)

Instructions regarding War Diaries and Intelligence Summaries are contained in F. S. Regs., Part II. and the Staff Manual respectively. Title pages will be prepared in manuscript.

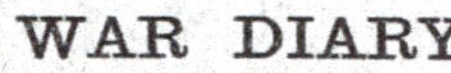

WAR DIARY
or
INTELLIGENCE SUMMARY.
(Erase heading not required.)

Army Form C. 2118.

Place	Date	Hour	Summary of Events and Information	Remarks and references to Appendices
FRONT LINE X 20. 26	1917 Dec 8th to 11th	5 pm.	The Battalion relieved the 6th Batth LEICS Regt in the front line. The Enemy remained quiet throughout the relief. Batth H.Q. were now at X 25 a 6.0.	
			Dispositions after relief were as follows:-	
			FRONT LINE — RIGHT COY — C	
			" " — LEFT COY — D.	
			IMMED. SUPPORT — RIGHT COY — A.	
			LEFT COY — B.	
			An inter company relief was carried out on the night of the 10th/11th, C Coy being relieved by A Coy, and D Coy by B Coy.	H.R.H.
			Hostile artillery was more active than during the preceding tour. Work consisted of wiring, improvement of existing trenches and the digging of a new front line trench in X 19 c and X 20 a. Casualties amounted to 1 O.R. wounded in action.	
	11th		A draft of 35 O.R's joined the Battalion.	H.R.H.
	12th	6 pm	The Battalion was relieved by the 6th Batth LEICS Regt and moved into Reserve at VILLERS FAUCON	H.R.H.

A5834 Wt. W4973/M687 750,000 8/16 D. D. & L. Ltd. Forms/C.2118/13.

Army Form C. 2118.

Instructions regarding War Diaries and Intelligence Summaries are contained in F. S. Regs., Part II. and the Staff Manual respectively. Title pages will be prepared in manuscript.

(L)

WAR DIARY
or
~~INTELLIGENCE SUMMARY~~.
(Erase heading not required.)

Place	Date	Hour	Summary of Events and Information	Remarks and references to Appendices
VILLERS FAUCON	1917 Dec 13		The day was spent in cleaning up, training and reorganising.	HRH.
"	Dec 14-16		Spent in training and reorganising	
FRONT LINE	16th	4.15 pm	The battalion relieved the 6th Batt. LEIC. Regt in the left subsector. Quiet relief.	
~~[illegible]~~	to		Dispositions after relief were	
X20c	19th		RIGHT FRONT coy C coy.	
X26a			LEFT " " D "	
			RIGHT SUPPT " A "	WH
			LEFT " " B " Batt H.Q. at X25 b 5 0	
			The dispositions remained the same throughought the tour. A patrol went out on the night of the 18th & dispersed a hostile working partys with rifle grenades. On the return journey they threw several bombs into an occupied dugout. Work was continued on the front line, & wiring the same. The new front line was dug to a depth of 7ft 6 & width of 7ft on the right post.	WH
			Casualties during tour – 3 O.R. wounded in action	

A5834 Wt. W4973/M687 750,000 8/16 D. D. & L. Ltd. Forms/C.2118/13.

5.

WAR DIARY

or

~~INTELLIGENCE SUMMARY.~~

(Erase heading not required.)

Army Form C. 2118.

Instructions regarding War Diaries and Intelligence Summaries are contained in F. S. Regs., Part II. and the Staff Manual respectively. Title pages will be prepared in manuscript.

Place	Date	Hour	Summary of Events and Information	Remarks and references to Appendices
FRONT LINE X20c 26a	1917 Dec 20	5.30 pm	The Batt. is relieved by the 6th Batt. LEIC Regt. On relief the batt. becomes Batt. in Support, & EPEHY GARRISON Dispositions as follows:- OUTER DEFENCES— B coy in railway ~~cutting~~ embankm't F1 b & d. D " " " cutting X25a Both companies garrison the trenches just East of the railway. INNER DEFENCES— C coy in cellars EPEHY F1a A " " " " " & E 6.b Both coys garrison posts on the outskirts of the village in X25.d F1 b, c, & d. Batt. H.Qs situated at F1 a 7.7, ~~[illegible]~~	WN
	23	11am	Batt. H.Qs moved to F1 a 8.2 in cellars.	
	24	5.30am	1 Killed and 2 wounded (gassed) by a gas shell ~~shell~~ (5.9") on a cellar.	WN
	24 to 27	9pm	The battalion relieves the 6th Batt. LEIC. Regt. in the front line. Dispositions A coy Right FRONT B " Left " C " Right SUPPORT D " Left " Bad weather hindered patrols, and work in general, but good progress was made on C.T. between posts in front line, approx 300x being dug. X20c	WN.

A7092). Wt. W12839/M1293 750,000. 1/17. D. D & L., Ltd. Forms/C2118/14.

Instructions regarding War Diaries and Intelligence Summaries are contained in F. S. Regs., Part II, and the Staff Manual respectively. Title pages will be prepared in manuscript.

(6)

Army Form C. 2118.

WAR DIARY
or
~~INTELLIGENCE SUMMARY.~~
(Erase heading not required.)

Place	Date	Hour	Summary of Events and Information	Remarks and references to Appendices
FRONT LINE X20c X26a	1917 Dec 28		Casualties during tour Nil	
		5.30 pm	The battalion was relieved by the 6th Batt LEIC Regt.	
			On relief the Batt. becomes Batt. in RESERVE at SAULCOURT	WM.
SAULCOURT	29		The day was spent in cleaning up, & with kit inspections etc	
	30		The men have their Xmas dinner at 12.30pm. Sergeants dinner at 5.30pm, and Officers at 7.30pm.	WM.
	31		Inspection of gas masks by Bde gas N.C.O.	
			Total casualties during the month	
			Kin-A 12 other Ranks. W-in-A 30 other Rks.	WM
			The following drafts joined the battalion during the latter half of the month:- 17th 5 OR. 19th 3 " 21st 1 " 26th 19 "	WM
			2/Lt MANGIN rejoined the batt. from hospital on Dec 11th	

A7092). Wt. W12839/M1293 750,000. 1/17. D. D & L., Ltd. Forms/C2118/14.

Instructions regarding War Diaries and Intelligence Summaries are contained in F. S. Regs., Part II. and the Staff Manual respectively. Title pages will be prepared in manuscript.

January 1918

WAR DIARY
or
~~INTELLIGENCE SUMMARY.~~
(Erase heading not required.)

Army Form C. 2118.

7th Bn Leicestershire Regt

Vol 28

Place	Date	Hour	Summary of Events and Information	Remarks and references to Appendices
Map ref. 57c SE 4 62c NE 2	1918 Jan 1	5.30 pm	The batt. relieved the 6th Batt. in the line. Dispositions of coys. on relief were as follows Right Front Coy. A coy. Centre " " C " Left " " 1 Plat + 1 L.G. B coy. Batt HQ X25 a 5.0 Support Coy. 2 Plats B coy. D coy. The relief was carried out by 7pm.	WR
		9pm	A patrol of 1 off. & 6 O.R. came into contact with a large party of enemy in the neighbourhood of the abandoned front line trench (X20.a). 2 of our patrol were killed in hand-to-hand fighting & 1 was wounded. Several casualties were inflicted on the enemy party.	WR
	2-3		Frosty weather prevented much digging being carried out. Work was continued on the wiring of both front & support lines.	
	4	7pm	The battalion was relieved by the 15 Durham L.I. Relief was complete by 7.30pm.	
LIERAMONT 62c			On relief the batt withdrew into Div^l Reserve at Lieramont. Casualties during the period 1st-4th amounted to 2 O.R. K-in-A and 1 O.R. W-in-A.	WR

30B

A7092). Wt. W12839/M1293 750,000. 1/17. D. D & L., Ltd. Forms/C2118/14.

Instructions regarding War Diaries and Intelligence Summaries are contained in F. S. Regs., Part II. and the Staff Manual respectively. Title pages will be prepared in manuscript.

WAR DIARY
or
~~INTELLIGENCE SUMMARY.~~
(Erase heading not required.)

(2)

Army Form C. 2118.

Place	Date	Hour	Summary of Events and Information	Remarks and references to Appendices
LIERAMONT 62 C	1916 Jany 5th to 14th		The days were spent in Training, Working Parties, and cleaning up and improving the camp area. Drafts of ~~officers~~ 22 O.R. joined the Battalion.	HRH
	15th	AM 9.30	The Battalion marched to 'B' Camp HAUT ALLAINES via AIZECOURT le BAS, TEMPLEUX la FOSSE and AIZECOURT le haut.	HRH
HAUT ALLAINES 62 c	16th to 19th		A training programme was carried out, consisting mainly of Physical Training, Bayonet fighting and firing on the Rifle Range. The following officers joined the Battalion – 2/Lt RAWLINGS 2/Lt WOOD, 2/Lt HOWITT W. and 2/Lt WATKINSON.	HRH
EPEHY 62 C NE 2.	20th	3 pm.	The Battalion entrained on the light railway at I 12 a 9.6, detrained at E 14 b 1.0. and relieved the 15th DURHAM LIGHT INFANTRY (as Support Battalion to the Brigade) in EPÉHY. On completion of relief Companies were disposed as follows:– D Coy. Right Front Company in Posts Eastern edge of EPEHY C " Left Front Company " " " A " Right Rear Company " cellars and [illegible] EPEHY B " Left Rear Company " " "	HRH

A7092). Wt. W12839/M1293 750,000. 1/17. D. D & L., Ltd. Forms/C2118/14.

Instructions regarding War Diaries and Intelligence Summaries are contained in F. S. Regs., Part II. and the Staff Manual respectively. Title pages will be prepared in manuscript.

WAR DIARY
or
~~INTELLIGENCE~~ SUMMARY.
(Erase heading not required.)

(3)

Army Form C. 2118.

Place	Date 1918	Hour	Summary of Events and Information	Remarks and references to Appendices
EPEHY	Jany 21st to Jany 23rd		During this period 6 hours work per day was carried out by Companies on the posts forming the village defences. Working parties of 130 men and O.R. were also found each night for work in the front line. EPEHY was shelled intermittently by hostile artillery with 5.9s and H.E. shells. Otherwise there was nothing of any interest to report. Casualties in the 4 days amounted to 2 O.R. slightly wounded remaining at duty. Drafts of 19 O.R. joined the Battalion.	F.R.H.
FRONT LINE B.H.Q. X 25 c 50.80	24th	6pm	The Battalion relieved the 6th Battn LEICESTERSHIRE REGT. in the LEFT SECTOR, LEFT BRIGADE. Dispositions on completion of relief were as follows:– RIGHT FRONT COY. D (½ Coy) PLANE TRENCH X 19 d X 20 c & X 26 a LEFT FRONT COY B (½ Coy) CRICKET TRENCH X 19 b and d. SUPPORT COY A (½ Coy) FIRE SUPPORT TRENCH X 25 b X 26 a RESERVE COY C Railway Cutting X 25 c A, B and D Coys each had ½ Coy in Railway Cutting X 25 c and carried out 1 Platoon reliefs every 24 hours owing to the bad condition of the trenches.	F.R.H.
		11pm	1 Platoon of C Coy moved into FIR SUPPORT on the left of A Coy	

A5834 Wt. W4973/M687 750,000 8/16 D. D. & L. Ltd. Forms/C.2118/13.

Instructions regarding War Diaries and Intelligence Summaries are contained in F. S. Regs., Part II. and the Staff Manual respectively. Title pages will be prepared in manuscript.

(4.)

Army Form C. 2118.

WAR DIARY ~~or~~ INTELLIGENCE SUMMARY.

(Erase heading not required.)

Place	Date	Hour	Summary of Events and Information	Remarks and references to Appendices
FRONT LINE BHQ X 25c 50·80	1918 JAN 25 to 27		Enemy were very quiet during this tour. Work was carried on in wiring, and improvement of Platoon Posts in front line and support line. Owing to the bright moonlight nights patrolling was confined to defensive measures. No hostile patrols were encountered. Casualties NIL. Drafts of 52 O.R joined the Battalion.	HRH.
do	28	6 pm.	The Battalion was relieved by the 6th Batt. LEICESTERSHIRE REGT and moved into Brigade Reserve at SAULCOURT	HRH.
SAULCOURT E 9 d.	29 to 31.		The days were spent in cleaning up, baths, and work on defences against aircraft. Carrying parties of 2 officers 60 O.R were found each night. A draft of 8 O.R joined the Battalion	HRH.

A5834 Wt. W4973/M687 750,000 8/16 D. D. & L. Ltd. Forms/C.2118/13.

21st DIVISION SPECIAL ORDER.

Friday, 15th February 1918.

Field-Marshal Sir DOUGLAS HAIG, KT. GCB. GCVO. KCIE. wishes me to express to all ranks of the 110th Infantry Brigade his appreciation of the smart manner in which the men turned out, handled their arms and marched past today. The Field-Marshal is quite confident, should the Germans attack on our front, that such men as he saw today will easily defeat any attack that may be launched against them, especially after the way the Brigade behaved on October 1st 1917. Of this performance the Field-Marshal spoke in the highest terms.

David Campbell

Major-General
Commanding 21st Division.

Army Form C. 2118

Instructions regarding War Diaries and Intelligence Summaries are contained in F. S. Regs., Part II. and the Staff Manual respectively. Title Pages will be prepared in manuscript.

WAR DIARY
or
INTELLIGENCE SUMMARY
(Erase heading not required.)

Vol 29

Place	Date	Hour	Summary of Events and Information	Remarks and references to Appendices
			7th (Service) Battalion The Leicestershire Regiment. WAR DIARY for FEBRUARY, 1918.	

31 B
Ealat

1875 Wt. W593/826 1,000,000 4/15 J.B.C. & A. A.D.S.S./Forms/C. 2118.

Instructions regarding War Diaries and Intelligence Summaries are contained in F. S. Regs., Part II. and the Staff Manual respectively. Title pages will be prepared in manuscript.

WAR DIARY

or

~~INTELLIGENCE SUMMARY~~.

(*Erase heading not required.*)

(1.)

Army Form C. 2118.

Place	Date	Hour	Summary of Events and Information	Remarks and references to Appendices
	1918		Reference Maps SHEETS 62C N.E.2 ; 57C S.E.4 ; 62C	
SAULCOURT Eqd.	Feby 1	4.15pm	The Battalion relieved the 6th Battalion LEICESTERSHIRE REGT in the LEFT FRONT LINE sector of the Brigade. Dispositions on completion of relief were as follows -	
			RIGHT FRONT COY - A X 20 c 2.1 to X 26 a 6.9	
			CENTRE " " - C X 20 c 2.1 to X 19 d 4.5	
			LEFT " - B X 19 d 1.8 to X 19 a 9.4	H.R.H.
			RESERVE COY - D Railway Cutting X 25 c	
			BATTN. HQ - X 25 a 5.0	
FRONT LINE X 25 a 5.0	"	7pm	Two Germans who had escaped from a prisoners of war camp MEAULTE were re-captured by a Sentry group of A Coy, while trying to get through the wire in front of our trenches. They were disguised as ROYAL ENGINEERS	
"	2nd to 4th		The enemy were very quiet during these days, and nothing of interest occurred. Work on improvement of trenches and wiring was carried on. Patrolling was confined to defensive measures, and no hostile patrols were seen. CASUALTIES during this period were NIL.	H.R.H.
			On the 2nd the Transport lines were moved from VILLERS FAUCON to LIERAMONT. Lt Col A.A. ALDWORTH M.C. proceeded to 7th Corps Reinforcement Camp and Major T.C. HOWITT D.S.O. assumed command of the Battalion	

T2134. Wt. W708—776. 500000. 4/15. Sir J. C. & S.

CH.

Army Form C. 2118

WAR DIARY
~~or~~
~~INTELLIGENCE SUMMARY~~

(Erase heading not required.)

Instructions regarding War Diaries and Intelligence Summaries are contained in F. S. Regs., Part II. and the Staff Manual respectively. Title Pages will be prepared in manuscript.

Place	Date	Hour	Summary of Events and Information	Remarks and references to Appendices
EPEHY	1918 Feby 4	6 pm	The Battalion was relieved by the 6th Battalion LEICESTERSHIRE REGIMENT, and on relief moved into Support in EPEHY.	HRH
"	5 6 7th		There was nothing of interest to report during this period, hostile artillery was inactive except for intermittent shelling of EPEHY on the 7th. CASUALTIES during this period were NIL.	HRH
"	7th	9 pm	The Battalion was relieved by 2 Companies of the 9th Battalion K.O.Y.L.I. and 1 Company of the 1st EAST YORKS, and on completion of relief moved by light railway to B Camp MOISLANS.	HRH
MOISLANS	8th 9th		The days were spent in cleaning up and reorganizing.	HRH
"	10th		Church Parade was held at 10 AM. The remainder of the day was spent in bathing and paying the men. "A" Company carried out musketry practice on the 500 yards range at HAUT ALLAINES.	HRH
"	11th to 16th		A programme of training was carried out by the Battalion. Morning work from 8.45 AM to 12.30 PM included Company Inspections, Battalion Parade and Drill, Demonstrations of Drill to Officers and N.C.O.s, Bayonet fighting, Physical Training and Games, Musketry Drill, Anti Gas training, Wiring and A Platoon in the Attack.	HRH

CH

1875 Wt. W593/826 1,000,000 4/15 J.B.C. & A. A.D.S.S./Forms/C. 2118.

Instructions regarding War Diaries and Intelligence Summaries are contained in F. S. Regs., Part II. and the Staff Manual respectively. Title pages will be prepared in manuscript.

WAR DIARY
or
~~INTELLIGENCE SUMMARY.~~
(Erase heading not required.)

(3)

Army Form C. 2118.

Place	Date 1918	Hour	Summary of Events and Information	Remarks and references to Appendices
MOISLANS	Feby 11 to 16	Contd	Each morning parade concluded with a March Past. In the afternoon 1 hour was devoted to Tactical Exercises for Officers and N.C.O's, and Demonstrations of Patrol Work. An average period of 2 hours daily was allotted to exclusive training of Specialists including Lewis Gunners, Signallers, Snipers & S.B's. Two days were spent on the 500 yds Range at HAUT ALLAINES. Firing practices carried out included (a) Grouping at 100 yds (b) Application at 300 yds (c) 1 Minute Rapid at 300 yds. Men failing in these tests received extra instruction on the 100 yds Range. All Box Respirators were tested in the Divisional Gas Chamber MOISLANS. An Inter-Platoon football competition was organised and completed. On the 15th the Battalion, with other units of the 110th Infantry Brigade, was inspected by the Commander in Chief, and after the inspection marched past in column of platoons (Special Order attached). A draft of 12 officers and 240 men joined the Battalion from the 9th Battalion LEICESTERSHIRE REGT. A fourth platoon for each Company was organised from these men. Capt and Adjt H. J. WALSH rejoined the Battalion from England.	JRH.

CM

A5834 Wt. W4973/M687 750,000 8/16 D. D. & L. Ltd. Forms/C.2118/13.

Instructions regarding War Diaries and Intelligence Summaries are contained in F. S. Regs., Part II. and the Staff Manual respectively. Title pages will be prepared in manuscript.

WAR DIARY

~~or~~

~~INTELLIGENCE SUMMARY.~~

(*Erase heading not required.*)

Army Form C. 2118.

(4)

Place	Date	Hour	Summary of Events and Information	Remarks and references to Appendices
	1918			
MOISLANS	Feb. 17	9.30am	Church of England Parade Service was held in the camp.	H.R.H.
		2.30pm	The final of the Inter Platoon Football Competition was played, the winner No 1 Platoon of A Coy being presented with Medals by Brigadier General Bayley DSO cmdg 110th Inf Bde.	
'B' Camp TEMPLEUX LA FOSSE	18	8am	The Battalion less A Coy, marched to B Camp TEMPLEUX LA FOSSE for work on the GREEN LINE, a shift of 4 hours from 10 Am to 2 Pm being carried out. 'A' Company after carrying out training in the Platoon in the Attack marched to TEMPLEUX LA FOSSE at noon. The Transport Lines moved to LONGAVESNES.	H.R.H. CH.
	Feb. 19/23		Three Coys worked on GREEN LINE Defences in the vicinity of TEMPLEUX LA FOSSE. One Coy worked on the railway at FLAMICOURT. Specialist training was carried out in the following: ~~subjects~~ Reserve Lewis Gunners, Stretcher Bearers, Snipers, Patrol Training, Tactical Exercises for Officers & N.C.Os.	A.W.

Instructions regarding War Diaries and Intelligence Summaries are contained in F. S. Regs., Part II. and the Staff Manual respectively. Title Pages will be prepared in manuscript.

WAR DIARY
or
INTELLIGENCE SUMMARY
(Erase heading not required.)

Army Form C. 2118

Place	Date	Hour	Summary of Events and Information	Remarks and references to Appendices
~~TEMPLEUX~~ LA FOSSE	Feb. 20		Lieut. Col. Guy Henry Sawyer, D.S.O., Royal Berkshire Regt. assumed command of the Battalion.	H.J.N.
VILLERS FAUCON.	" 23	2 pm	The Battalion moved to ADRIAN CAMP, VILLERS FAUCON and came under the orders of 16th Division for work in the forward area.	H.J.N.
"	24/27		Battn. turned out as strong as possible for work under the supervision of R.E. 16th Division. Three Coys. digging trenches and one Coy wiring. Coys marched off at 8.30 am daily and returned between 1.30 pm and 2.30 pm.	H.J.N.
"	" 27		Battn. turned out with the Brigade on a practice alarm. Orders received by wire at 5.23 pm. The Battn. turned out in fighting order with Lewis Gun limbers, Tool waggons, Grenade & S.A.A. limbers & maltese cart. The leading Coy. (A. Coy) moved off at 5.35 pm with the remainder at 5 minute interval and were in position at the rendezvous at E. 22. b. (Sheet 62 c. N.E) at 6 pm. Orders received from Brigade at 6.30 pm. for Battn. to move to RESERVE (about E. 24. c. [illegible]). Battn. was in position by 7.25 pm. Battn. then returned to ADRIAN CAMP.	H.J.N.

1875 Wt. W593/826 1,000,000 4/15 J.B.C. & A. A.D.S.S./Forms/C. 2118.

Instructions regarding War Diaries and Intelligence Summaries are contained in F. S. Regs., Part II. and the Staff Manual respectively. Title Pages will be prepared in manuscript.

WAR DIARY
or
INTELLIGENCE SUMMARY
(Erase heading not required.)

Army Form C. 2118

(6)

Place	Date	Hour	Summary of Events and Information	Remarks and references to Appendices
 VILLERS FAUCON	Feb. 28.		Work as for 27/2/18.	H/W
			The following reinforcements joined during the month:-	
			2nd Feb. 2 O.R's.	H/W
			8th " 2 O.R's.	
			10th " 1 O.R.	
			11th " 1 Officer 240 O.R's (from 9th Bn Leicestershire Regt)	
			19th " 3 O.R's.	
			26th " 8 O.R's.	

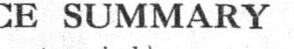

G. H. Sawyer Lt-Col.
Comdg 7th Bn Leicestershire Regt

1875 Wt. W593/826 1,000,000 4/15 J.B.C. & A. A.D.S.S./Forms/C. 2118.

110th Inf.Bde.
21st Div.

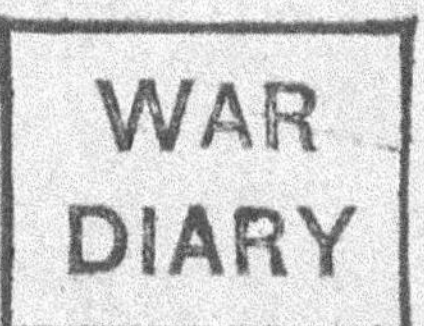

7th BATTN. THE LEICESTERSHIRE REGIMENT.

M A R C H

1 9 1 8

Attached:-

Appendices "A" & "B".

Army Form C. 2118.

110/21

Instructions regarding War Diaries and Intelligence Summaries are contained in F. S. Regs., Part II. and the Staff Manual respectively. Title Pages will be prepared in manuscript.

WAR DIARY
or
INTELLIGENCE SUMMARY
(Erase heading not required.)

Vol 30

Place	Date	Hour	Summary of Events and Information	Remarks and references to Appendices
			7th (S) Bn. Leicestershire Regt.	
			WAR DIARY	
			FOR	
			MARCH 1918	

32B

2449 Wt. W14957/M90 750,000 1/16 J.B.C. & A. Forms/C.2118/12.

Army Form C. 2118.

Instructions regarding War Diaries and Intelligence Summaries are contained in F. S. Regs., Part II. and the Staff Manual respectively. Title pages will be prepared in manuscript.

WAR DIARY
or
INTELLIGENCE SUMMARY.
(*Erase heading not required.*)

Place	Date	Hour	Summary of Events and Information	Remarks and references to Appendices
			The detailed War Diary for the month of March 1918 was destroyed by shell fire on March 23rd. All papers maps etc were sent down from the Bn Hd Qrs in the trenches on the evening of March 21st and were placed on a limber which was subsequently destroyed.	
			The following is a summary of the events of the month up to the commencement of the attack on March 21st from which date as full an account as possible is attached.–	
			The Bn occupied the left subsector of the right Brigade front on the evening of Feb 28th relieving the 2nd Bn Royal Irish Regt (16th Division)	
			The area ~~occupied~~ by the Bn was from BEECH AVENUE inclusive to just N of ANDREW STREET the 6th and 8th Bns Leicestershire Regt being alternatively on the right of the Bn and the 62nd Inf. Bde on the left after certain minor alterations the disposition of the Bn was as follows– Two Coys front line and support. One Coy garrisoning the five posts in PEIZIERE – One coy in reserve for counter attack purposes	
			The front line Coys were disposed as follows.– Right front Coy:– 1 Platoon in PLANE TRENCH (by night only – falling back to RED LINE before dawn) 1 Platoon in FIR SUPPORT and 2 PLATOONS in RED LINE	

2353 Wt. W2544/1454 700,000 5/15 D. D. & L. A.D.S.S./Forms/C. 2118.

2

Instructions regarding War Diaries and Intelligence Summaries are contained in F. S. Regs., Part II. and the Staff Manual respectively. Title pages will be prepared in manuscript.

WAR DIARY
or
INTELLIGENCE SUMMARY.
(*Erase heading not required.*)

Army Form C. 2118.

Place	Date	Hour	Summary of Events and Information	Remarks and references to Appendices
			Left front Coy:- 1 Platoon in CRICKET TRENCH - 1 Platoon in FIR SUPPORT - 2 Platoons in NEW. SQUASH and RED LINE - 2 sections (all from PEIZIERE garrison in RED LINE North of ANDREW. S^T^ The posts in PEIZIERE were garrisoned as follows:- PROCTOR POST - 1 Platoon - MACPHEE POST - 1 Platoon TOTTENHAM POST Coy H^d^ Q^rs^ and 2 sections - M^c^LEAN POST - 2 sections - MORGAN POST 2 sections The reserve (Counter attack) Coy was located in Railway cutting until about March 17th when it was moved into position near the new B^n^ ~~Batt~~ H^d^ Q^rs^ which were occupied the same day in W 30 a - west of northern end of PEIZIERE During the night 28th Feb/1st March and the following nights the enemy attempted several raids on the units on either flank. These raids were accompanied by considerable artillery fire but very little was directed on to the B^n^ front. After the first few days this raiding on the part of the enemy ceased and from then onwards to the commencement of the attack, his guns were remarkably quiet the hostile shelling being mainly confined	

2353 Wt. W2544/1454 700,000 5/15 D. D. & L. A.D.S.S./Forms/C. 2118.

3

Instructions regarding War Diaries and Intelligence Summaries are contained in F. S. Regs., Part II. and the Staff Manual respectively. Title pages will be prepared in manuscript.

Army Form C. 2118.

WAR DIARY
or
INTELLIGENCE SUMMARY.
(Erase heading not required.)

Place	Date	Hour	Summary of Events and Information	Remarks and references to Appendices

to a few gas shells mixed with H.E. fired during the night or early morning on CRICKET TRENCH and ANDREW St. On the morning of the 17th at about 6.20 am the enemy put down a light barrage on PLANE and CRICKET TRENCH. Except for this in spite of considerable harassing fire from our artillery and heavy concentration in connection with raids carried out by us the hostile artillery was almost completely silent

During the whole period active patrolling was carried out at night by the Bn protective patrols being put every night and strong fighting being sent out frequently. It was very seldom that any touch was obtained with the enemy. The following officers did well with fighting patrols. 2nd Lieut Dickinson. - 2nd Lt Facey, 2nd Lieut Carlile 2 Lieut Shackleton, 2 Lieut Godfrey and Lieut Watkinson

On the night 15th/16th March a patrol under 2nd Lieut Dickinson encountered the enemy in considerable force. Lieut Dickinson and 3 other Ranks were wounded and Lieut Dickinson was taken prisoner

The following casualties occurred during the period 28.2.18 - 20.3.18 the Bn was in the trenches

2353 Wt. W2544/1454 700,000 5/15 D. D. & L. A.D.S.S./Forms/C. 2118.

4

Army Form C. 2118.

WAR DIARY
or
INTELLIGENCE SUMMARY.
(Erase heading not required.)

Instructions regarding War Diaries and Intelligence Summaries are contained in F. S. Regs., Part II. and the Staff Manual respectively. Title pages will be prepared in manuscript.

Place	Date	Hour	Summary of Events and Information	Remarks and references to Appendices
			March 7th 1.O.R wounded (at duty)	
			" 11th 1.O.R " "	
			" 13th 1.O.R wounded	
			" 13th 1.O.R Killed	
			" 17 1 Officer (2nd Lieut Dickinson) wounded and missing	
			" 17 1.O.R. Killed	
			" 17 3.O.Rs Wounded.	
			During the same period the following drafts were received	
			March 6th 6 O.Rs	
			" 11th 4 O.Rs	
			" 14th 19 O.Rs	
			" 15th 8 O.Rs	
			During the period 28.2.18 – 20.3.18 the front line coys. were relieved every four days. The right front coy. becoming Bn Reserve (Counter Attack) Coy and the left front Coy forming garrison of PEIZIERE	
			On the morning of 21.3.18 the disposition of the Bn was as follows – A Coy front right coy, B Coy left front coy. C. Coy Bn Reserve (counter attack) coy, D. Coy Garrison of PEIZIERE – The 8th Bn Leic Regt were on our right and the 12th/13th Northumberland FUS (62nd Inf Bde) on our left	
			2 Tanks were in Reserve near Bn Hd Qrs	

2353 Wt. W2544/1454 700,000 5/15 D. D. & L. A.D.S.S./Forms/C. 2118.

5.

Instructions regarding War Diaries and Intelligence Summaries are contained in F. S. Regs., Part II. and the Staff Manual respectively. Title pages will be prepared in manuscript.

WAR DIARY
or
INTELLIGENCE SUMMARY.
(Erase heading not required.)

Army Form C. 2118.

Place	Date	Hour	Summary of Events and Information	Remarks and references to Appendices
			Diary of operations between 21st 3-18 inclusive	
	21-3-18	4-30 AM	At 4.30 am the enemy put down a heavy barrage gas shell bombardment of phosgene and mustard gas on the whole Bn area and on the positions in rear this gradually developed into heavy concentration of HE and shrapnel on the whole of our defences. The bombardment lasted till about 9.30 am. Most of the wire in front of our position front line was destroyed but the wire in front of FIR SUPPORT and the RED LINE was left nearly intact under cover of a very thick mist combined with smoke and dust from bursting shells the enemy was able to cross No Mans Land without being observed.	
		9.30 am	About 9.30 am the enemy entered PLANE TRENCH and 2nd Lt Darcy who was o/c of the observation party left in that trench had only just time to give the S.O.S. signal before the enemy reached him	
		10 am	The enemy had apparently broken through the front line of the Bn on our left and at this hour small parties attacked the Northern post of McPHEE in PEIZIERE and got into the railway cutting behind the RED LINE the detached position of McPHEE POST was captured and about 6 men taken prisoners	
		10 am	at about this hour C Coy and the tanks were ordered to counter attack and clear PEIZIERE up to the railway cutting The tanks proceeded round the Northern	

2353 Wt. W2544/1454 700,000 5/15 D. D. & L. A.D.S.S./Forms/C. 2118.

6

Instructions regarding War Diaries and Intelligence Summaries are contained in F. S. Regs., Part II. and the Staff Manual respectively. Title pages will be prepared in manuscript.

WAR DIARY
or
INTELLIGENCE SUMMARY.
(Erase heading not required.)

Army Form C. 2118.

Place	Date	Hour	Summary of Events and Information	Remarks and references to Appendices
			end of the village and C Coy by the two roads running NE and E from McLEAN POST The village was easily cleared, the enemy retiring from the village and cutting on the approach of the tanks. One of the men taken prisoner in McPHEE POST rejoined the Bn	
		11 am	On receipt of information that the village was clear C Coy and the tanks were withdrawn to their original positions	
			During the whole of the day the enemy made many futile attacks from the NE on the FIR SUPPORT and RED LINE attempting to bomb down the latter from New SQUASH TRENCH which he had entered early in the attack	
			The defence of FIR SUPPORT was conducted by 2nd Lt Wright with about 20 men against numerous bombing attacks in one of which flammenwerfers were used but these were stopped on our wire by rifle fire and the cylinders catching alight the enemy were burnt with their own weapons	
			Good work was done by the whole of this platoon and particularly by Pte HICKIN who on 2 or 3 occasions walked along the parapet firing a Lewis Gun from his hip at the enemy concentrating in the trenches on the flanks. Pte HICKIN was eventually killed in making one of these attacks	
			This platoon held out until dark when with only 6 men left it was ordered to fall back on the RED LINE	
			In the afternoon the enemy could be seen moving just S of VAUCHELLETTE	

2353 Wt. W2544/1454 700,000 5/15 D. D. & L. A.D.S.S./Forms/C. 2118.

7

Instructions regarding War Diaries and Intelligence Summaries are contained in F. S. Regs., Part II. and the Staff Manual respectively. Title pages will be prepared in manuscript.

WAR DIARY
or
INTELLIGENCE SUMMARY.
(*Erase heading not required.*)

Army Form C. 2118.

Place	Date	Hour	Summary of Events and Information	Remarks and references to Appendices
			FARM and in LINNET and THRUSH VALLEYS and large bodies were advancing up ANDREW ST and LEITH walk	
		5 pm	The two tanks were ordered up to the bridge and scattered the enemy massing in ANDREW ST	
		6 pm	The enemy continued to make progress southwards from VAUCELLETTE FARM and small parties were getting into PEIZIERE. The counter attack Coy and the two tanks were ordered to clear the village. The tanks and 2 platoons moving round the northern outskirts and 2 platoons by road running NE from	
		8 pm	McLEAN POST. The village was cleared by 8 pm and 5 prisoners sent back. As the left flank of the RED LINE seemed insecure 2 platoons from the counter attack Coy were ordered to make a defensive flank facing N from the railway cutting to McPHEE POST the flank was prolonged by a party of 1 officer and 14 O Rs from Bn Hd Qrs which occupied a trench at the junction of the sunken roads just N of Bn Hd Qrs the remainder of the counter attack Coy concentrated at McLEAN POST Bn Hd Qrs was established in the YELLOW LINE	
			The enemy did not attack during the night	
			Touch was kept the whole of the day with the 8th Lec on our right but there was a serious gap on the left until about 12 M.N. when connection was obtained with the 15th Durham L.I on our left in the YELLOW LINE	

T2134. Wt. W708—776. 500000. 4/15. Sir J. C. & S.

8

Instructions regarding War Diaries and Intelligence Summaries are contained in F. S. Regs., Part II. and the Staff Manual respectively. Title pages will be prepared in manuscript.

WAR DIARY
or
INTELLIGENCE SUMMARY.
(Erase heading not required.)

Army Form C. 2118.

Place	Date	Hour	Summary of Events and Information	Remarks and references to Appendices
	22nd		During the night the enemy rushed forward his field and heavy guns & in the early morning he opened an intense bombardment on the RED LINE PEIZIERE and the YELLOW LINE. Under a heavy barrage he attacked the RED LINE but was driven off	
		10 am	About this hour news was received that the enemy had captured St EMILIE and the southern end of EPEHY and the the 8th Bn Leic had been ordered to form a defensive on the EPEHY – SAULCOURT Rd. To combine with this and to cover the right rear of PEIZIERE a second defensive flank facing S. was made with every available man from Bn Hd Qrs between YELLOW SUPPORT LINE and CHAUFOURS WOOD	
		11 Am	As it was seen that the enemy were entering EPEHY in force from the south the two tanks were ordered forward to check his advance and if possible clear EPEHY. The enemy retired on seeing their approach and they report having inflicted heavy casualties. Unfortunately they were running short of petrol and as the engines required repair they were unable to proceed further and attempting to withdraw to SAULCOURT both were knocked out	
		12 noon	About this hour orders were received to withdraw the Bn behind to BROWN LINE and concentrate at LONGAVENES	

2353 Wt. W2544/1454 700,000 5/15 D. D. & L. A.D.S.S./Forms/C. 2118.

9

Instructions regarding War Diaries and Intelligence Summaries are contained in F. S. Regs., Part II. and the Staff Manual respectively. Title pages will be prepared in manuscript.

WAR DIARY
or
INTELLIGENCE SUMMARY.
(Erase heading not required.)

Army Form C. 2118.

Place	Date	Hour	Summary of Events and Information	Remarks and references to Appendices
	22nd	12-15 pm	Orders were issued for the withdrawal – up to this hour CAPT. VANNER. M.C. was still holding the RED LINE and driving off every attack made on it after the withdrawal of his Coy. he waited to superintend the demolition of both the bridges over the cutting. This was successfully carried out. The withdrawal of the Bn and the extrication of the posts in PEIZIERE was a matter of some difficulty as by the time of the receipt of the order by the Coys the enemy was in occupation of EPEHY and firing in from the N. The withdrawal was made under heavy M.G. fire from the SE and NE and a considerable number of casualties were incurred during it.	
		3-30 pm	Bn reorganized in valley just W of LONGAVESNES and received orders to march to AIZECOURT LE HAUT	
		6 pm	Bn arrived and went into camp. Men had a hot meal	
	23rd	12-MN	Orders received for Bn to occupy a position in GREEN LINE	
		1 AM	The Bn marched off and took up position in GREEN LINE. E + NE of EPINETTE WOOD. The Bn was in position by 4-30 am.	
		7 am	about this hour the enemy commenced a heavy bombardment of the	

2353 Wt. W2544/1454 700,000 5/15 D. D. & L. A.D.S.S./Forms/C. 2118.

10

Instructions regarding War Diaries and Intelligence Summaries are contained in F. S. Regs., Part II. and the Staff Manual respectively. Title pages will be prepared in manuscript.

WAR DIARY
or
INTELLIGENCE SUMMARY.
(Erase heading not required.)

Army Form C. 2118.

Place	Date	Hour	Summary of Events and Information	Remarks and references to Appendices
	23rd		position occupied by the Bn. our artillery also fired short dropping ~~shell~~ a considerable number of shells into the GREEN LINE. As this line was only 1 foot deep a good many casualties were caused by the bombardment	
		9am	The enemy attacked from the SE and penetrated between CURLU WOOD and EPINETTE WOOD. Our line was accordingly drawn back to the PERONNE – NURLU ROAD. This position was held for about two hours heavy casualties being inflicted on the enemy. at this time the left flank was in touch with the 9th DIVn along the road and the right flank with the N F Pioneers but with rather a large gap on this flank	
		10.30	Orders received to withdraw to the MIDENETTE LINE	
		11am	Withdrawal commenced from left flank which had the furthest distance to go. The line was occupied without serious interference by the enemy with right flank about 500 yds of the aerodrome sheds	
		1pm.	about this hour the enemy commenced working round the right flank & got several M.Gs in position W. of the aerodrome sheds which	

A7092). Wt. W12839/M1293 750,000. 1/17. D. D & L., Ltd. Forms/C2118/14.

11

Instructions regarding War Diaries and Intelligence Summaries are contained in F. S. Regs., Part II. and the Staff Manual respectively. Title pages will be prepared in manuscript.

WAR DIARY
or
INTELLIGENCE SUMMARY.

(*Erase heading not required.*)

Army Form C. 2118.

Place	Date	Hour	Summary of Events and Information	Remarks and references to Appendices
			which infiladed our line The line was withdrawn down the hill S. of MOISLAINS under heavy M G and rifle fire A short stand was made on the canal Bank and Continued to the high ground N W of HAUT ALLAINES. at this time there was a considerable gap on the left flank, touch being lost with the 9th Divn	
			The position above HAUT ALLAINES was held till dark without serious opposition	
		7pm	Order received to occupy the high ground WEST of BOIS-MARRIERS	
		8pm	New line occupied with N F Pioneers on the right and some of the south african Bde on left	
			The night passed without any attack by the enemy	
	24th		The early morning was quiet	
		9am	Large forces of the enemy was seen advancing up the valley between the position occupied by the Bde and CLERY. these were engaged by rifle and L. G fire and a considerable number of casualties inflicted as the enemy continued his advance on the high ground on	

A7092). Wt. W12839/M1293 750,000. 1/17. D. D & L., Ltd. Forms/C2118/14.

12

Instructions regarding War Diaries and Intelligence Summaries are contained in F. S. Regs., Part II. and the Staff Manual respectively. Title pages will be prepared in manuscript.

WAR DIARY
or
INTELLIGENCE SUMMARY.
(Erase heading not required.)

Army Form C. 2118.

Place	Date	Hour	Summary of Events and Information	Remarks and references to Appendices
	24th		our right flank the Bn was ordered to withdraw to the ridge S of LE FOREST WOOD and from there to the high ground S.E of MAUREPAS	
		1pm	Here orders were received from the G.O.C 35th Divn to cover with fire the advance of 2 Battn of reinforcements who were approaching from the S.W. This was done. Subsequently owing to a gap on the left flank the Bn was withdrawn to the high ground S.W of MAUREPAS	
		4pm	about this hour the line occupied by the Bn was taken over by the 15th Sherwood Foresters (35 Divn) and the Bn was withdrawn through MARICOURT to SUZANNE after reorganization the night of the 24/25th was spent in billets at SUZANNE	
	25	6AM	The Bn marched to BRAY-SUR-SOMME and bivouaced on the high ground just west of it. In the afternoon a composite Company 150 strong with 4 L Guns was formed in the Bn under command of Lieut Amley. This formed a part of a composite Bn organized in the Bde	
		6pm	The remainder of Bn marched to billets in BRAY	
		10pm	Bn details marched to Bde transport lines in wood just North of CHIPILLY	

A7092). Wt. W12839/M1293 750,000. 1/17. D. D & L., Ltd. Forms/C2118/14.

13

Instructions regarding War Diaries and Intelligence Summaries are contained in F. S. Regs., Part II. and the Staff Manual respectively. Title Pages will be prepared in manuscript.

WAR DIARY
or
INTELLIGENCE SUMMARY
(Erase heading not required.)

Army Form C. 2118

Place	Date	Hour	Summary of Events and Information	Remarks and references to Appendices
	25th	5pm	The composite Coy from the Bn forming part of a Composite Bde under Brig Gen Headlam marched into close support just W of MARICOURT	
	26	4am	Composite Coy moved back to take up position on the high ground just E of BRAY	
		10am	The enemy attacked from NE and the line was ordered to withdraw to the vicinity of VILLE. SUR. ANCRE. Composite Bns were then reorganized at RIBEMONT	
		7-am	Orders received at Bn Hd Qrs to organize a force 100 strong from Bn to form part of a composite coy formed from the Bde. This party marched off at 7.30 am and took up a defensive position just S of MORLANCOURT and fought a rear guard action due W towards MERICOURT	
		9am	The remainder of the Bn and Transport moved from CHIPILLY to BRESLE and BAIZIEUX	
			Remaining officers of the Bn detached for duty with Gen CUMMINGS force	
	27th		Lt CARNLEY'S Coy took up a position N.W. of RIBEMONT but were not attacked	
			Bn Hd Qrs moved to VADENCOURT and transport to BEAUCOURT	
	28th		Lt CARNLEY'S Coy were withdrawn to HEILLY in support of 3rd Australian Divn	

1875 Wt. W593/826 1,000,000 4/15 J.B.C. & A. A.D.S.S./Forms/C. 2118.

Instructions regarding War Diaries and Intelligence Summaries are contained in F. S. Regs., Part II. and the Staff Manual respectively. Title pages will be prepared in manuscript.

WAR DIARY
or
INTELLIGENCE SUMMARY.
(*Erase heading not required.*)

Army Form C. 2118.

Place	Date	Hour	Summary of Events and Information	Remarks and references to Appendices
			There they remained till the evening of the 30th when they were relieved by part of the 106th Bde and marched to FRECHENCOURT. On the 31st they marched to ALLONVILLE and rejoined the Bn	
	29th		Bn Hd Qrs moved to BEHENCOURT. A composite Coy was formed under Capt VANNER	
		6pm	This Coy and 2 other Coys from the other Bns of the Bde were formed into a Bn under command of Lt Col SAWYER and march to LA NEUVILLE in close support of the 3rd Australian Divn	
	30th		In the morning this composite Bn was relieved by Australians and marched to ALLONVILLE when the Bn went into billets and details of composite Bns rejoined their own units	
	31st		All scattered details of the Bn rejoined. Day spent in reorganising and resting. – Bde Church Parade	
			Total Casualties during period of operations were as follows	

	Officers	O Ranks
Killed	3	21
Wounded	10	128
Missing	8	286

Total Officers 21 } a List of Officers
O.Rs – 435 } Casualties is attached — appendix B

A7092). Wt. W12839/M1293 750,000. 1/17. D. D & L., Ltd. Forms/C2118/14.

Army Form C. 2118

Instructions regarding War Diaries and Intelligence Summaries are contained in F. S. Regs., Part II. and the Staff Manual respectively. Title Pages will be prepared in manuscript.

WAR DIARY
or
INTELLIGENCE SUMMARY
(Erase heding not required.)

Place	Date	Hour	Summary of Events and Information	Remarks and references to Appendices
			APPENDICES	
appendices		A	Certain messages received and sent during 21st and 22nd – These are very incomplete – certain of the more important messages received from Corp were sent on direct to 18th Hd Qrs	
appendices		B	List of officer casualties with dates (NB 2nd Lts NORTON and CARR were not serving with the 18th the former being with a detachment from the Divnl Signal School and the latter being employed on traffic Control)	

G Hawes [signature] Lt Col.
Commanding 7th 18th Leicestershire Regt

1875 Wt. W593/826 1,000,000 4/15 J.B.C. & A. A.D.S.S./Forms/C. 2118.

A P P E N D I X "A".

Prefix.......... Code.............m. Office of Origin and Service Instructions.	Words.	Charge.	This message is on a/c of:	Recd. at ....m.
	Sent		.... Service.	Date............
	At..............m.			From............
	To............			
	By............		(Signature of "Franking Officer.")	By............

TO { 2/Lt Boyton

Sender's Number.	Day of Month.	In reply to Number.	AAA
* AH 41	21		

Please take 2 men and
reconnoitre situation on left
flank [illegible] [illegible] to ascertain
whether the PEIZIERE – HEUDICOURT
railway is held by the enemy
and if so. in what force

Recd 6.45 pm
J.R.

From	OAK
Place	
Time	5 40 PM

The above may be forwarded as now corrected. (Z) H R Home

Censor. Signature of Addressor or person authorised to telegraph in his name.

* This line should be erased if not required.

(3796.) Wt. W492/M1647. 650,000 Pads. 5/17. H. W. & V., Ld. (E. 1187.)

	O. Ranks.
Killed in action	21
Wounded " "	128
Missing	286.
	435

APPENDIX 'A'

Prefix............Code...............m.	Words.	Charge.	This message is on a/c of:	Recd. at............m.
Office of Origin and Service Instructions.	Sent At...............m. To............... By...............		..........................Service. .... (Signature of "Franking Officer.")	Date............... From............... By...............

TO

Sender's Number.	Day of Month.	In reply to Number.	AAA
*			

From

Place

Time

The above may be forwarded as now corrected. (Z)

Censor. Signature of Addressor or person authorised to telegraph in his name.

*This line should be erased if not required.

(18965.) Wt. W12952/M1294, 187,500 Pads. 1/7 McC. & Co., Ltd. (E. 818.)

By........................

TO	AR [illegible]			

* Sender's Number.	Day of Month.	In reply to Number.	AAA
BM 47	2		

[illegible] Prisoners 123 Grenadier Regt captured N end of PEIZIERE [illegible] [illegible] [illegible] [illegible] [illegible] [illegible] PEIZIERE [illegible] [illegible]

From	[illegible]		
Place			
Time	9.15 PM		

The above may be forwarded as now corrected. **(Z)**

Censor. .... Signature of Addressor or person authorised to telegraph in his name.

Prefix.............Code.................m.	Words.	Charge.	This message is on a/c of:	Recd. at............m.
Office of Origin and Service Instructions.	Sent		............................Service.	Date....................
	At.................m.			From..................
	To.....................			
	By......................		.... (Signature of "Franking Officer.")	By.......................

TO

Sender's Number.	Day of Month.	In reply to Number.	AAA

From

Place

Time

The above may be forwarded as now corrected. (Z)

...ix..............Code..................m.	Words.	Charge.	*This message is on a/c of:*	Recd. at............m.
Office of Origin and Service Instructions.	Sent		..............................*Service.*	Date....................
	At....................m.			From....................
	To........................			
	By........................		(Signature of "Franking Officer.")	By........................

TO

Sender's Number.	Day of Month.	In reply to Number.	AAA
*			

From

Place

Time

The above may be forwarded as now corrected.

Censor.

(Z)

Signature of Addressor or person authorised to telegraph in his name.

Prefix..............Code..................m.	Words.	Charge.	*This message is on a/c of:*	Recd. at............m.
Office of Origin and Service Instructions.	Sent		..............................*Service.*	Date ....
	At....................m.			From ....
	To			
	By		(Signature of "Franking Officer.")	By ....

TO PRINCE

Sender's Number.	Day of Month.	In reply to Number.	AAA
* [illegible]	[illegible]		

[illegible] [illegible] [illegible] [illegible]
dispositions on N. flank

From
Place
Time

The above may be forwarded as now corrected. (Z)

Censor. Signature of Addressor or person authorised to telegraph in his name.

Prefix..............Code..................m.	Words.	Charge.	This message is on a/c of:	Recd. at............m.
Office of Origin and Service Instructions.	Sent		..............................Service.	Date.....................
	At....................m.			From..................
	To......................			
	By.......................		(Signature of "Franking Officer.")	By......................

TO

* Sender's Number.	Day of Month.	In reply to Number.	AAA

From

Place

Time

The above may be forwarded as now corrected. **(Z)**

.... *Censor.*

.... Signature of Addressor or person authorised to telegraph in his name.

Office of Origin and Service Instructions.	Sent	*This message is on a/c of:*	Recd. at............m.
....	At..................m.	..........................*Service.*	Date....................
....	To......................		From....................
....	By......................	(Signature of "Franking Officer.")	By.......................

TO

* Sender's Number.	Day of Month.	In reply to Number.	AAA
	22		

From			
Place			
Time 8.35 am			

The above may be forwarded as now corrected. .... *Censor.*

(Z) .... Signature of Addressor or person authorised to telegraph in his name.

Office of Origin and Service Instructions.

Sent

At..................m.

To....................

By....................

This message is on a/c of:

.............................*Service.*

(Signature of "Franking Officer.")

Recd. at............m.

Date....................

From..................

By......................

TO

Sender's Number.	Day of Month.	In reply to Number.	AAA
*			

From

Place

Time

The above may be forwarded as now corrected.

(Z)

Censor.

Signature of Addressor or person authorised to telegraph in his name.

*This line should be erased if not required.

Prefix..............Code..................m.	Words.	Charge.	*This message is on a/c of:*	Recd. at............m.
Office of Origin and Service Instructions.	Sent		..............................*Service.*	Date..................
	At...................m.			From..................
	To....................			
	By....................		(Signature of "Franking Officer.")	By....................

TO

Sender's Number.	Day of Month.	In reply to Number.	AAA
*			

From

Place

Time

The above may be forwarded as now corrected. **(Z)**

..................................*Censor.*

Signature of Addressor or person authorised to telegraph in his name.

* This line should be erased if not required.

(18965.) Wt. W12952/M1294. 187,500 Pads. 1/17 McC. & Co. Ltd. (**E. 818.**)

Prefix..............Code..................m.	Words.	Charge.	*This message is on a/c of:*	Recd. at............m.
Office of Origin and Service Instructions.	Sent At..................m. To..................... By.....................		............................*Service.* .... (Signature of "Franking Officer.")	Date.................... From.................... By....................

TO O/C PINE

Sender's Number.	Day of Month.	In reply to Number.	AAA
* HH 55	22		

My HQ are at E5 c 2 5 and I am holding RESERVE [illegible] LINE from E5 a 7 3 to E5 c 6 5 with right flank thrown back along Sunken road can you give me any information as to your present dispositions

From BAK
Place
Time 10.55 AM

The above may be forwarded as now corrected. (Z) H R Harm

Censor. Signature of Addressor or person authorised to telegraph in his name.

* This line should be erased if not required.

(E. 818.)

Prefix..............Code..................m.	Words.	Charge.	*This message is on a/c of:*	Recd. at.............m.
Office of Origin and Service Instructions.	Sent		..............................*Service.*	Date....................
	At..................m.			From....................
	To......................			
	By......................		(Signature of "Franking Officer.")	By......................

TO OC D Coy

Sender's Number.	Day of Month.	In reply to Number.	AAA
* AA 56	22		

Please inform me what posts are still held in PEIZIERE

From OMC
Place
Time 11 AM

The above may be forwarded as now corrected. (Z) HR Ross

.... *Censor.* Signature of Addressor or person authorised to telegraph in his name.

*This line should be erased if not required.

Prefix..............Code..................m.	Words.	Charge.	This message is on a/c of:	Recd. at............m.
Office of Origin and Service Instructions.	Sent At..................m. To.................. By..................		..............................Service. (Signature of "Franking Officer.")	Date.............. From.............. By..............

TO Capt VANNER

Sender's Number.	Day of Month.	In reply to Number.	AAA
* NH 57	22		

Hold	on	the	RED LINE
at	all	costs	aaa 8th Batt
are	making	defensive	flank
from	HIGH	STREET,	EPEHY
along	SAULCOURT	ROAD	aaa

From OAK
Place
Time 11. 30 AM

The above may be forwarded as now corrected. (Z) N R Horn

Censor. Signature of Addressor or person authorised to telegraph in his name.

*This line should be erased if not required.

Prefix..............Code..................m.	Words. Charge.	This message is on a/c of:	Recd. at............m.
Office of Origin and Service Instructions.	Sent At..................m. To.................... By....................	..............................Service. (Signature of "Franking Officer.")	Date.................... From.................... By....................

TO { H A by PALM

Sender's Number.	Day of Month.	In reply to Number.	AAA
* HH 58	22		

My RED LINE and posts in PEIZIERE are believed to be still holding aaa have established defensive flank with details in RESERVE YELLOW LINE in E 5 a and c aaa B.H.Q at E 5 c 2.5

From BAK
Place
Time 11.50 AM

The above may be forwarded as now corrected. (Z) W R [illegible]

.... *Censor.* Signature of Addressor or person authorised to telegraph in his name.

Prefix..............Code..................m. | Words. | Charge. | This message is on a/c of: | Recd. at.............m.

Office of Origin and Service Instructions.

Sent

At....................m.

To.......................

By.......................

..............................Service.

(Signature of "Franking Officer.")

Date.......................

From.....................

By.........................

TO PRINCE

Sender's Number.	Day of Month.	In reply to Number.	AAA
* HH 59	22		

Can I have two fresh TANKS aaa My TANKS are at present advancing towards S corner of EPEHY aaa Am informed that they will not be able to do another journey to-day aaa I consider those fresh TANKS would be most valuable

From OAK

Place 11.58 AM

Time

The above may be forwarded as now corrected. (Z) HR Hone

Censor. Signature of Addressor or person authorised to telegraph in his name.

Prefix..............Code..................m. | Words. | Charge. | *This message is on a/c of:* | Recd. at.............m.

Office of Origin and Service Instructions.

Sent

At....................m.

To......................

By......................

..............................*Service.*

(Signature of "Franking Officer.")

Date......................

From......................

By......................

TO ALL COYS and MO {OAK and B Coy BRASS PRINCE

Sender's Number. HHGo | Day of Month. 22 | In reply to Number. | AAA

BROWN LINE will become main line of resistance aaa Coys will withdraw in rear of BROWN LINE and concentrate at LONGAVESNES AERODROME and reorganize aaa A and B Coys will commence withdrawal on receipt of message covered by C and D Coys aaa C Coy will withdraw when A and B have passed through them. D Coy when C has passed through them aaa B Coy BRASS will withdraw when all OAK Coys have passed through, and will rejoin own unit in BROWN LINE aaa Each Coy will report commencement of withdrawal to present Batt HQ E 5 c 2 5 aaa Machine Guns will withdraw with Coys with which they are working and concentrate S of GUYENCOURT aaa Addressed ALL COYS, MO, B Coy BRASS repeated PRINCE

From OAK

Place

Time 12.35

The above may be forwarded as now corrected. (Z) H R H[illegible]

..............................*Censor.*

Signature of Addressor or person authorised to telegraph in his name.

Prefix............Code................m. | Words. | Charge. | *This message is on a/c of:* | Recd. at............m.

Office of Origin and Service Instructions.

Sent
At..................m.
To......................
By......................

..............................*Service.*

(Signature of "Franking Officer.")

Date......................
From......................
By......................

TO { OC | A. D. S | VIA | PRINCE

Sender's Number.	Day of Month.	In reply to Number.	AAA
* HH 61	22		

Cannot clear from here at present
barraged on Aid Post blown out
10 AM we will meet your man
as soon as possible

From M.O OAK
Place
Time 12.35 PM

The above may be forwarded as now corrected. (Z)

Censor.

Signature of Addressor or person authorised to telegraph in his name.

Prefix.............Code.................m. | Words. | Charge. | This message is on a/c of: | Recd. at............m.

Office of Origin and Service Instructions.

Sent

At.................m.

To........................

By........................

.............................Service.

(Signature of "Franking Officer.")

Date....................

From...................

By......................

TO PRINCE

Sender's Number.	Day of Month.	In reply to Number.	AAA
* H H 62	22		

Present Strength of Battalion in Camp

Officers	O R s
12	288.

From JAK

Place

Time 9.15 PM

The above may be forwarded as now corrected.

(Z) H R Horne Lt

Censor.

Signature of Addressor or person authorised to telegraph in his name.

*This line should be erased if not required.

(18965.) Wt. W12952/M1294. 187,500 Pads. 1/.7 McC. & Co., Ltd. (E. 818.)

TO PRINCE

Sender's Number.	Day of Month.	In reply to Number.	AAA
* RA63	22	GS 285	

Only have SAA available for average 100 rounds per man aaa Can you supply more in front of Transport lines for more to be brought up aaa Have only 3 Lewis Guns drums for these also required from Transport lines aaa the stretchers were battalion and Mortars but required aaa M.O requests information as regards evacuation aaa Tool cart also required if digging is necessary on GREEN LINE

From FAK

Place

Time 10.17 PM

The above may be forwarded as now corrected. (Z) H. R. [illegible] [illegible]

Censor. Signature of Addressor or person authorised to telegraph in his name.

*This line should be erased if not required.

(18965.) Wt. W12952/M1294. 187,500 Pads. 1/7 McC. & Co., Ltd. (E. 818.)

Office of Origin and Service Instructions.	Sent	This message is on a/c of:	Recd. at ....m.
	At ....m.	..........Service.	Date ....
	To		From ....
	By	(Signature of "Franking Officer.")	By ....

TO M. O OAK

Sender's Number.	Day of Month.	In reply to Number.	AAA
* AA 64	23		

Battalion will occupy GREEN LINE at once from N edge of EPINETTE WOOD Southwards moving by main NURLU RD and CAT COPSE aaa Order of march Advance Guard A Coy under Capt Vann, main Body Batt. HQ B. C. D Coys aaa Advance Guard will halt on reaching W edge of EPINETTE WOOD where orders as to occupation of front will be issued aaa Advance Guard will move at 1 AM main Body will be formed up ready to move at same hour

From Adjt OAK

Place

Time 12.30 AM

The above may be forwarded as now corrected. (Z) H R Horn

Censor. Signature of Addressor or person authorised to telegraph in his name.

*This line should be erased if not required.

Prefix............ Code..............m.	Words.	Charge.	This message is on a/c of:	Recd. at............m.
Office of Origin and Service Instructions.	Sent		...............................Service.	Date ....
	At..................m.			From ....
	To			
	By.......................		(Signature of "Franking Officer.")	By........................

TO PRINCE

Sender's Number.	Day of Month.	In reply to Number.	AAA
* HM 65	23		

Battalion has occupied its positions and touch has been obtained with unit on left rear Battn HQ at D 15 b 9 6

From HK
Place 4.30 Am
Time

The above may be forwarded as now corrected. (Z) H R [illegible]

Censor. Signature of Addressor or person authorised to telegraph in his name.

* This line should be erased if not required.

Prefix..............Code................m.	Words.	Charge.	This message is on a/c of:	Recd. at..........m.
Office of Origin and Service Instructions.	Sent		..........................Service.	Date..............
	At..............m.			From..............
	To..............			
	By..............		(Signature of "Franking Officer.")	By..............

TO PRINCE

Sender's Number.	Day of Month.	In reply to Number.	
* AH 16	23		AAA

Our shells are dropping in my front line near the [illegible] to [illegible] of CATS COPSE [illegible] place too [illegible]

AAR

From			
Place	7.25 AM		
Time			

The above may be forwarded as now corrected.

.... *Censor.*

(Z) AR [illegible]

Signature of Addressor or person authorised to telegraph in his name.

*This line should be erased if not required.

(1806?) Wt. W12952/M1294. 187,500 Pads. 1/17 McC. & Co., Ltd. (E. 818.)

Prefix..............Code..................m.	Words.	Charge.	*This message is on a/c of:*	Recd. at.............m.
Office of Origin and Service Instructions.	Sent		..............................*Service.*	Date ....
	At...................m.			From ....
	To			
	By		(Signature of "Franking Officer.")	By ....

TO 86 'B' Coy

Sender's Number.	Day of Month.	In reply to Number.	AAA
* HA 67	23		

Make	immediate	counter	attack
in S	direction	enemy	appear
to have	broken	through	[illegible]
Send	numbers		

From HAK
Place
Time 8 AM

The above may be forwarded as now corrected. (Z)

.... *Censor.*

H R [illegible]
Signature of Addressor or person authorised to telegraph in his name.

* This line should be erased if not required.

(18965.) Wt. W12952/M1294. 187,500 Pads. 1/.7 McC. & Co., Ltd. (**E. 818.**)

Prefix..............Code..................m. | Words. | Charge.

Office of Origin and Service Instructions.

Sent
At..................m.
To....................
By....................

This message is on a/c of:

..............................*Service.*

....
(Signature of "Franking Officer.")

Recd. at............m.
Date....................
From....................
By....................

TO PRINCE

Sender's Number.	Day of Month.	In reply to Number.	AAA
* HA 68	23		

Enemy	appear	to	have
broken	through	PALMS	front
aaa	I	am	counterattacking
towards	S	and	am forming
defensive	flank	on S	edge of
CAT	COPSE		

From OAK
Place
Time 8AM

The above may be forwarded as now corrected. (Z) [illegible]

Censor. Signature of Addressor or person authorised to telegraph in his name.

*This line should be erased if not required.

(18965.) Wt. W12952/M1294. 187,500 Pads. 1/.7 McC. & Co., Ltd. (E. 318.)

Prefix.............Code.................m.	Words. / Charge.	*This message is on a/c of:*	Recd. at............m.
Office of Origin and Service Instructions.	Sent At..................m. To..................... By.....................	..............................*Service.* (Signature of "Franking Officer.")	Date..................... From..................... By.....................

TO { PRINCE

Sender's Number.	Day of Month.	In reply to Number.	AAA
* AK 69	23		

Enemy broken through GREEN LINE aaa Parties of 7th and 8th Battns are holding the main NUREU RD behind CAT COPSE aaa Royal SCOTS on our left aaa S.A.A wanted urgently

From BAK
Place
Time 9.8 AM

The above may be forwarded as now corrected. (Z) [illegible signature]

Censor. Signature of Addressor or person authorised to telegraph in his name.

*This line should be erased if not required.

Prefix.............Code.................m.	Words.	Charge.	*This message is on a/c of:*	Recd. at..........m.
Office of Origin and Service Instructions.	Sent		............Service.	Date..............
	At.................m.			From..............
	To..................			By..................
	By..................		(Signature of "Franking Officer.")	

TO { PRINCE

Sender's Number.	Day of Month.	In reply to Number.	AAA
* AH 70	23		

The left sector of MIDINETTE TRENCH is now occupied with mixed detachments 6th 7th & 8th Lein Borders S Africans the majority of the latter being on my right flank aaa Only two Machine Guns in case of more could be set up we ought to be able to hold trench indefinitely aaa Batt H.Q. D 18 d 1·3

From OAK

Place

Time 11 AM

The above may be forwarded as now corrected. (Z) [illegible]

Censor. Signature of Addressor or person authorised to telegraph in his name.

* This line should be erased if not required.

(18965.) Wt. W12952/M1294. 187,500 Pads. 1/17 McC. & Co., Ltd. (E. 818.)

Prefix..............Code..................m. | Words. | Charge.

Office of Origin and Service Instructions.

Sent

At....................m.

To.......................

By.......................

This message is on a/c of:

...............................*Service.*

(Signature of "Franking Officer.")

Recd. at............m.

Date......................

From......................

By.........................

TO PRINCE

Sender's Number.	Day of Month.	In reply to Number.	AAA
* AH 71	23		

My right flank is being turned and I am commencing slow movement from the right please send me [illegible] [illegible] map next sheet 12 to 62 C N E

From OAK

Place

Time 12.50 PM

The above may be forwarded as now corrected. (Z)

Censor.

Signature of Addressor or person authorised to telegraph in his name. AR H

*This line should be erased if not required.

(18965.) Wt. W12952/M1294. 187,500 Pads. 1/7 McC. & Co., Ltd. (E. 818.)

Prefix..............Code..................m.	Words.	Charge.	This message is on a/c of:	Recd. at............m.
Office of Origin and Service Instructions.	Sent		..............................Service.	Date ....
	At..................m.			From ....
	To		....	
	By......................		(Signature of "Franking Officer.")	By......................

TO PRINCE

* Sender's Number.	Day of Month.	In reply to Number.	AAA
HA 72	23		

Am running very short SAA
can you send me some aaa
Enemy are advancing down slopes
of hill in D 25 Central aaa
I am just W of HAUT ALLAINS
old Arm camp aaa Have
no map of this area aaa
Where is Bde HQ

From BAK
Place
Time 1 40 PM

The above may be forwarded as now corrected. (Z) AR Hoare

Censor. Signature of Addressor or person authorised to telegra

* This line should be erased if not required.

(18965.) Wt. W12952 M1294. 187,500 Pads. 1/.7 McC. & Co., Ltd. (**E. 818.**)

Prefix.............Code..................m.	Words.	Charge.	*This message is on a/c of:*	Recd. at............m.
Office of Origin and Service Instructions.	Sent		..............................*Service.*	Date ....
	At...................m.			From ....
	To			
	By........................		(Signature of "Franking Officer.")	By......................

TO PRINCE

Sender's Number.	Day of Month.	In reply to Number.	AAA
* AA 73	23		

9th Bn located ½ mile to left rear behind ridge aaa [illegible] 2 [illegible] prisoners

From JAK

Place

Time 4 5 pm

The above may be forwarded as now corrected. (Z)

....

Censor. Signature of Addressor or person authorised to telegraph in his name.

*This line should be erased if not required.

(18965.) Wt. W12952/M1294. 187,500 Pads. 1/17 McC. & Co., Ltd. (E. 818.)

Prefix............Code..............m	Words.	Charge.	*This message is on a/c of:*	Recd. at.........m.
Office of Origin and Service Instructions.	Sent		........................*Service.*	Date..............
	At..............m.			From ....
	To..................			
	By..................		(Signature of "Franking Officer.")	By..............

TO 6C OAK

Sender's Number.	Day of Month.	In reply to Number.	AAA
* M/4	21.		

~~b~~ As far as known situation is as follows.

Enemy hold OAK, POPLAR and PLANE TRENCHES. Also reported that enemy are in FIR SUPPORT near ~~fall~~ FALLEN TREE ROAD, this is contradicted by a later report & situation is obscure

2/R Munster Fus. are hold RIDGE RESERVE and trenches in front of their Battn. H.Q. and Railway Cutting in F 2 c and F 1 b (VAUGHANS BANK)

6C MORGAN POST reports Railway Cutting clear of the enemy & RED LINE intact.

He informs us that he believes MC PHEE POST has fallen. No further information on this point.

From

Place

Time

The above may be forwarded as now corrected. **(Z)**

....

Censor. Signature of Addressor or person authorised to telegraph in his name.

Prefix............Code..............m | Words. | Charge. | This message is on a/c of: | Recd. at ....16.

Office of Origin and Service Instructions.

Sent At..............m. To.............. By..............

.... Service.

(Signature of "Franking Officer.")

Date............ From .... By............

TO Contd

Sender's Number. | Day of Month. | In reply to Number. | AAA

2 Companies PALM in this village not involved in the fighting all posts held by them intact.

[signature]
Lt for
OC
PINE

From

Place FISHER'S KEEP

Time 12.40 hrs

The above may be forwarded as now corrected. (Z)

Censor. Signature of Addressor or person authorised to telegraph in his name.

To OAKS

APPENDIX 'A'

All OK at MORGAN POST and PROCTOR POST AAA

Small party of enemy seen on left on EPEHY HIGH ST. but driven off AAA

MCPHEE POST reported fallen AAA

FINE POST enemy seen in CUTTING but absolutely no confirmation of this AAA

Tanks in action on left of PEZIERE AAA

OAK Counter attacking Coy. here & on left flank of village AAA

A M Field

Lieut

OC MORGAN POST

21 · III · 18

12.15 pm

To Adjutant
OAK.

12 Platoon have moved forward to edge of Railway Cutting by bridge. They are supported by 10 Platoon at the final objective v.g. road through X 30 B

Tanks have returned to starting point

Danger apparently coming from the left flank.

All posts still seem to be held.

[illegible]
Lieut
Comdt C Coy

21/3/18
1.0 pm
By runner.

O.A.K.

from B Coy.

I am holding RED line from the left (where it joins SQUASH Trench) to centre where I have joined up with A Coy. Have a strong Bombing post on my left which I still hold. 3 boxes of bombs left only. Am holding C.T. to PRINCE SUPPORT, also PRINCE to protect my flank & rear. Bodies of the enemy troops (approx 200 to 300) reported marching along ANDREW St. towards PEZIERE. I intend to hold on in my present position. Enemy seen to be massing at top end of Andrew St. near bridge. Casualties approx. 1/4 of Coy.

Wm J.C. [illegible] 2/Lt
O.C. B Coy.

21-3-18
1.30 pm

[illegible]

O.C. "D" Coy

PROCTOR — OK

Enemy massing on ANDREW & N of bridge

Appears a small body of cavalry [illegible] forward to about X 13 b, 14 a

2/Lt Godfrey is wounded. "C" Coy [illegible] don't know what to do & are occupying railway bank.

T. Cawley Lt.
PROCTOR POST

2.0 pm
21/3/18

Seen
J. Hubbard Capt

To. Adjutant
OAK.

Company now withdrawing to line W. of TOTTENHAM POST. Will report when withdrawal complete.

RED LINE appears secure at present.

[illegible]
Lieut
Comdg "C" Coy

21/3/18 2.40 pm [illegible]

To ADJT

[illegible]

The right platoon have established touch with "A" Coy & have arranged for a flying patrol to visit during the night. Position of Coy now Right Platoon resting on Railway Bridge. Left platoon [illegible] in trenches at McPHEE POST.

Vanner reports all correct on his immediate front but enemy holding RED LINE to left of ANDREW ST. Am therefore watching that flank particularly. One or both of the Reserve platoons will be sent to reinforce if necessary.

Both RED LINE & RAILWAY CUTTING have been blocked from left flank by Vanner.

22/3/18 3.10 am [illegible]

[illegible]
Comdg C Coy

Prefix SM Code HKAM Words 32	Received.	Sent, or sent out.	Office Stamp.
£ s. d.	From NES	At X m.	OX 57
Charges to Collect	By Pte Wellina	To	22/3/18
Service Instructions.		By	

Handed in at NES Office 12·50Am. Received 1·20A m

TO OX 57

*Sender's Number.	Day of Month.	In reply to Number.	AAA
GC262	22	—	

B Coy BRASS placed under your orders tonight aaa This coy not to move from YELLOW LINE without reference Brigade HQ aaa addressed OAK repeated B Coy BRASS

FROM
TIME & PLACE NES

Prefix S/m Code ALAM Words 108

£ s. d.

Charges to Collect

Service Instructions.

Received. From NES By Hickman

Sent, or sent out. At X m. To By

Office Stamp. OX57 22/3/18

Handed in at NES Office 1.50 p.m. Received 2.35 m.

TO OX57

*Sender's Number.	Day of Month.	In reply to Number.	AAA
GC266	22		

John ordered to hold from
level crossing E18B60 along
St EMILIE – Epehy road to
E12D81 aaa You are responsible
to form the defensive flank from
Yellow Line to connect with latter
point aaa 1 Coy Brass and Andrew
and 3 MGS at your disposal
as ordered GC260 aaa John
extending their flank along
Brown Line to include Caperon
Copse aaa WELD and MG Section at
Caperon Copse to revert to give [illegible]
div reserve on relief aaa Weld
to hold raw for MGS report Bde HQ aaa
report when relief complete Caperon Copse
and when in touch with John along

FROM

TIME & PLACE

Prefix........Code........Words........ | Received. From........ By........ | Sent, or sent out. At........m. To........ By........ | Office Stamp.

£ s. d.

Charges to Collect

Service Instructions.

Handed in at........Office........m. Received........m.

TO contd

*Sender's Number.	Day of Month.	In reply to Number.	AAA

Weld to hold camp
MGS report Bde HQ [illegible]
report when relief complete
Vaporer Copse and when in
Touch with John along St Emilie
– Epehy Road and [illegible] undefeated
Oak [illegible] weld

FROM
TIME & PLACE 0X57

A P P E N D I X "B".

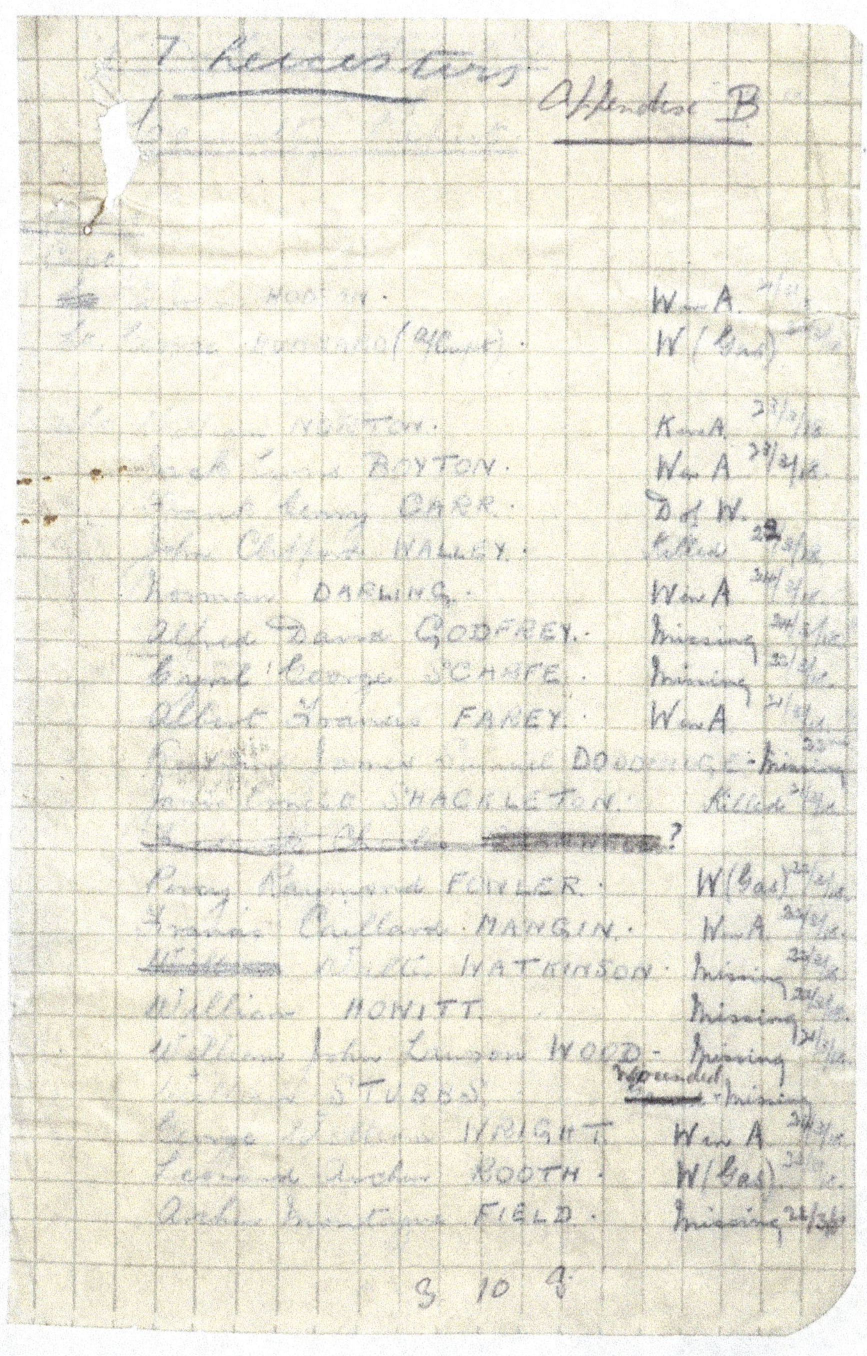

7 Leicesters

Appendix B

[illegible] HODSON. W. in A. [illegible]

[illegible] (2/Lieut.) W (Gas) [illegible]

[illegible] NORTON. K. in A. 23/3/18

[illegible] BOYTON. W. in A. 23/3/18

[illegible] CARR. D. of W.

John Clifford WALLEY. Killed 22/3/18

Norman DARLING. W. in A. 24/3/18

Alfred [illegible] GODFREY. Missing 24/3/18

Cyril George SCHAFE. Missing 22/3/18

Albert Thomas FAHEY. W. in A. 21/3/18

[illegible] DOODRIDGE. Missing 23/3/18

[illegible] SHACKLETON. Killed 21/3/18

~~[illegible]~~ ?

Percy Raymond FOWLER. W (Gas) 21/3/18

Francis [illegible] MANGIN. W. in A. 24/3/18

~~William~~ [illegible] WATKINSON. Missing 22/3/18

William HOWITT. Missing 22/3/18

William John [illegible] WOOD. Missing 21/3/18

[illegible] STUBBS. Wounded Missing

George William WRIGHT. W. in A. 24/3/18

Leonard Archer BOOTH. W (Gas) 22/3/18

Archie [illegible] FIELD. Missing 21/3/18

S 10 G

110th Brigade.

attcd. 21st Division

1/7th BATTALION

LEICESTERSHIRE REGIMENT

APRIL 1918.

Instructions regarding War Diaries and Intelligence Summaries are contained in F. S. Regs., Part II. and the Staff Manual respectively. Title pages will be prepared in manuscript.

WAR DIARY
or
~~INTELLIGENCE SUMMARY.~~
(Erase heading not required.)

Army Form C. 2118.

Vol 31

Place	Date	Hour	Summary of Events and Information	Remarks and references to Appendices
			WAR DIARY FOR APRIL 1918 7th (S) Battn LEICESTERSHIRE Regt	

33.B
31 Infantry

D. D. & L., London, E.C.
(A8004) Wt. W1771/M2-31 750,000 5/17 Sch. 52 Forms/C2118/14

Instructions regarding War Diaries and Intelligence Summaries are contained in F. S. Regs., Part II. and the Staff Manual respectively. Title Pages will be prepared in manuscript.

WAR DIARY
or
~~INTELLIGENCE SUMMARY~~
(Erase heading not required.)

Army Form C. 2118

Place	Date	Hour	Summary of Events and Information	Remarks and references to Appendices
ALLONVILLE	APRIL 1		The day was spent in reorganizing and cleaning up.	Reference MAP Sheet 28 1/40000
D°	2	1.20AM	The Battalion marched off en route for DRANOUTRE. Entrained at ST ROCH Station, AMIENS at 4.50AM. detrained at HOPOUTRE at 11.30 PM. & proceeded in Motor Lorries to MONMOUTHSHIRE CAMP Map Reference M35 b 3.3	
DRANOUTRE	3	11.30AM.	The Battalion was inspected by General Sir Herbert Plumer commanding the 2nd Army. The remainder of the day was spent in reorganizing and cleaning up.	
D°	4	9 OAM	Company inspections the remainder of the morning & the afternoon were spent in cleaning up.	
		5 PM	The Battalion moved A & B Companies to BUTTERFLY CAMP N19.a.8.0. C & D Companies to LEEDS CAMP M24 b.2.3	W.R.

1875 Wt. W593/826 1,000,000 4/15 J.B.C. & A. A.D.S.S./Forms/C. 2118.

Instructions regarding War Diaries and Intelligence Summaries are contained in F. S. Regs., Part II. and the Staff Manual respectively. Title Pages will be prepared in manuscript.

WAR DIARY
or
~~INTELLIGENCE SUMMARY~~
(Erase heading not required.)

Army Form C. 2118

Place	Date	Hour	Summary of Events and Information	Remarks and references to Appendices
BUTTERFLY & LEEDS CAMPS	APRIL 5		The day was spent in reorganizing and cleaning up. Companies bathed at the Divisional Baths at DRANOUTRE. B Company moved to LEEDS CAMP. A draft of 475 O.Rs joined the Battalion	WR
Do	6		A programme of training was carried out by the Battalion from 8.45 AM to 12.30 P.M including Company Inspections, Physical Training Games Musketry & close order drill. The Battalion was inspected by the M.O between 2 & 3.30 P.M. Tactical exercises for Junior Officers were carried out from 2.30 to 3.30 PM. A draft of 7 O.Rs joined the Battalion.	
Do	7	10 AM	The Battalion was addressed by General D. CAMPBELL commanding the 21st Division & congratulated on its success in the recent operations afterwards a Church Parade was held.	

Army Form C. 2118

Instructions regarding War Diaries and Intelligence Summaries are contained in F. S. Regs., Part II. and the Staff Manual respectively. Title Pages will be prepared in manuscript.

WAR DIARY
or
~~INTELLIGENCE SUMMARY~~
(Erase heading not required.)

Place	Date	Hour	Summary of Events and Information	Remarks and references to Appendices
BUTTERFLY & LEEDS CAMPS	APRIL 7	1.30PM	The Battalion moved, A Company to Babbington Camp M12 central B.C & D Companies to MORRUMBIDGEE CAMP N7.a.64 LA CLYTTE	
LA CLYTTE	8	10.30AM	The Battalion moved to CHIPPAWA CAMP M6a4b.	
		11.30AM	A programme of training was carried out including Company inspections & close order drill.	
		2.0PM	A conference was held by the Commanding Officer for all Officers of the Battalion.	
		5 PM	Companies were paid out. 2ND LIEUTS CARTER, FAULKES, FLINT & NUNN joined the Battalion from the 8th Battalion LEICESTERSHIRE REGT for temporary duty	WR
CHIPPAWA CAMP	9	9AM	A programme of training was carried out including company inspections, physical training & games & close order drill.	

1875 Wt. W593/826 1,000,000 4/15 J.B.C. & A. A.D.S.S./Forms/C. 2118.

Army Form C. 2118

Instructions regarding War Diaries and Intelligence Summaries are contained in F. S. Regs., Part II. and the Staff Manual respectively. Title Pages will be prepared in manuscript.

WAR DIARY
or
~~INTELLIGENCE SUMMARY~~
(Erase heading not required.)

Place	Date	Hour	Summary of Events and Information	Remarks and references to Appendices
CHIPPAWA CAMP	APRIL 9	2.30PM	The nucleus party marched to MALPLAQUET, DICKEBUSCH H34 a 91	
		3.30PM	The Battalion moved out, entrained at ZEVECOTEN siding and detrained at SCOTTISH WOOD CAMP, H35 b 60 in Reserve. Transport moved to DICKEBUSCH at H33 b	
SCOTTISH WOOD CAMP	10	5 AM	Under orders of the Brigade the Battalion moved into Support at MANAWATU CAMP, WARRINGTON ROAD I 20 b 79	
MANAWATU CAMP	11		The Battalion stood to in readiness to move up into the line in case of an enemy attack	
Do	12	7.30PM	The Battalion relieved the 22nd CORPS mounted Troops Composite Battalion in the line, RIGHT SUB-SECTOR, dispositions as follows:– C Company Front line Company D do Support do A do Right Reserve do B do Left Reserve do	Vide Appendix A.

WN

1875 Wt. W593/826 1,000,000 4/15 J.B.C. & A. A.D.S.S./Forms/C. 2118.

Army Form C. 2118

Instructions regarding War Diaries and Intelligence Summaries are contained in F. S. Regs., Part II. and the Staff Manual respectively. Title Pages will be prepared in manuscript.

WAR DIARY
or
~~INTELLIGENCE SUMMARY~~
(Erase heading not required.)

Place	Date	Hour	Summary of Events and Information	Remarks and references to Appendices
	APRIL		Front line. J25d 35.10 to J25b 92.20 with outposts at J32.a.74.90. J26c 93.04 & J25.c.78.30. J26 a.93.10. J26b 12.33	
			Support Line. The Glen Support Trenches, Image Avenue & Shrewsbury Support. The Nucleus moved to MANCHESTER CAMP N2 central	
			Reserve Line I 36b & I 35b	
			Battalion Headquarters at I30c. 35.00	
			1 O.R was wounded in action.	
	13		Battalion in the Line	WR
	14		Battalion in the Line. Nucleus moved back to MALPLAQUET CAMP H33b.	

1875 Wt. W593/826 1,000,000 4/15 J.B.C. & A. A.D.S.S./Forms/C. 2118.

Instructions regarding War Diaries and Intelligence Summaries are contained in F. S. Regs., Part II. and the Staff Manual respectively. Title Pages will be prepared in manuscript.

WAR DIARY

or

~~INTELLIGENCE SUMMARY~~

(Erase heading not required.)

Army Form C. 2118

Place	Date	Hour	Summary of Events and Information	Remarks and references to Appendices
	APRIL 15.		Battalion still in the line. The nucleus moved to No 21 Camp G 21 b 2 5	
	16		Under orders from the Brigade the Battalion withdrew from the positions held as follows:- A. Company commencing at 12 midnight (15/16 April) B Company " " 3.0 A.M. D Company " " 3.30 AM C Company " " 4.0 AM less two sections which remained in the front line to harass the advance of the enemy The Battalion took up a RESERVE position at HOWE CAMP. H24 central.	Vide appendix B.
		2 P.M.	The nucleus party moved to MONTREAL CAMP. H12 b 5 7 2 O.Rs were wounded in action.	

1875 Wt. W593/826 1,000,000 4/15 J.B.C. & A. A.D.S.S./Forms/C. 2118.

Instructions regarding War Diaries and Intelligence Summaries are contained in F. S. Regs., Part II. and the Staff Manual respectively. Title Pages will be prepared in manuscript.

WAR DIARY

or

~~INTELLIGENCE SUMMARY~~

(Erase heading not required.)

Army Form C. 2118

Place	Date	Hour	Summary of Events and Information	Remarks and references to Appendices
HOWE CAMP	APRIL 17		The Battalion relieved the 6th Battalion Leicestershire Regt in the new line I26 d.5.8 to I32 a.1.2 Dispositions as follows:—	
			A. Company Right Front Company	
			B. Company Left Front Company	
			C. Company Right Support 2 platoons	
			C do Right Reserve 2 do	
			D Company Left Support 2 platoon	
			D do Left Reserve 2 platoons	
			Battn H.Q at CHATEAU SEGARD H30.c.85 80	WL
			2ND LT F.B STEVENSON & 1 O.R. joined the Battalion	
			1 O.R. killed in action	
			6 O.Rs wounded do	
			The nucleus moved to No 21 CAMP BUSSEBOOM G22.b Transport moved to OUDERDOM H29 b	
	18		Battalion in the line. 3 O.Rs wounded in Action.	
			The nucleus moved to MONTREAL CAMP OUDERDOM H19 b.5.7	

1875 Wt. W593/826 1,000,000 4/15 J.B.C. & A. A.D.S.S./Forms/C. 2118.

Army Form C. 2118.

Instructions regarding War Diaries and Intelligence Summaries are contained in F. S. Regs., Part II. and the Staff Manual respectively. Title Pages will be prepared in manuscript.

WAR DIARY
or
~~INTELLIGENCE SUMMARY~~

(Erase heading not required.)

Place	Date	Hour	Summary of Events and Information	Remarks and references to Appendices
	APRIL 19		Battalion H.Q. moved to H 30 b 1 9 on account of heavy shelling at H.30.c.85.80. 1 OR killed & 5 O.R. wounded in action	W.R.
	20		Battalion holding the line 24 O.Rs. gassed & 4 wounded. 1 killed	
	21	7 PM	"C" Company relieved A Company in the right front line & D Company relieved B Company in the left front line. 14 O.Rs. gassed & 1 wounded in action	
	22	7 PM	The Battalion relieved the 6th Battalion LEICESTERSHIRE REGt in the CORPS POSTS LINE. Dispositions as follows:- Battn. H.Q. TORR TOP Tunnels I 24 d 64.27 A. Coy Right Company in POSTS at:- I 30 c 8 0 I 30 c 4 0 I 30 c 2 2	

2449 Wt. W14957/M90 750,000 1/16 J.B.C. & A. Forms/C.2118/12.

Army Form C. 2118.

Instructions regarding War Diaries and Intelligence Summaries are contained in F. S. Regs., Part II. and the Staff Manual respectively. Title Pages will be prepared in manuscript.

WAR DIARY
or
~~INTELLIGENCE~~ SUMMARY

(Erase heading not required.)

Place	Date	Hour	Summary of Events and Information	Remarks and references to Appendices
	APRIL 22		with standing Patrols at night at I30. c. 4 4 + I30. c. 3.5 Coy H.Q. at CANADA STREET 'B' Company 'Centre Company' at Posts I30/1A I30/1 + I30/2 H.Q. at HEDGE STREET 'C' Company. Left Company at POSTS I30/3, J19/1 J19/2 + J19/3 H.Q. at TORRTOP 'D' Company: Reserve Company at TORRTOP with 2 platoons at S.P. 1/2 – I24 d 2.2 6 O.Rs gassed + 2 wounded in action.	W.R.
	23.		Battalion in the line. 5 O.Rs joined the Battalion. The Transport moved to H19 a OUDERDOM	

2449 Wt. W14957/M90 750,000 1/16 J.B.C. & A. Forms/C.2118/12.

Army Form C. 2118.

Instructions regarding War Diaries and Intelligence Summaries are contained in F. S. Regs., Part II. and the Staff Manual respectively. Title pages will be prepared in manuscript.

WAR DIARY
or
~~INTELLIGENCE~~ ~~SUMMARY~~.
(Erase heading not required.)

Place	Date	Hour	Summary of Events and Information	Remarks and references to Appendices
	APRIL 24		A Company were relieved by a Company of the 1st Yorkshire Regt & went into SUPPORT at CANADA STREET. B Company took over POST I30/3 from C Company & handed over POST I30/1a to the 1st Yorkshire Regt. Posts now held as follows B Company I30/1, 30/2 & 30/3 with 1 platoon in SUPPORT at HEDGE STREET. C Company Posts J19/1 J19/2 & J19/3 1 Platoon in SUPPORT at TORR TOP. 1 O.R. wounded in action	[initials, bracketing 24–26 April]
	25		Battalion in the Line. 1 O.R. wounded in action	
	26		Under orders from the Brigade the Battalion withdrew from the CORPS POST LINE. The withdrawal commenced at 9 P.M. & was completed by 12 midnight. The Battalion took up	Appendix C.

D. D. & L., London, E.C.
(A8004) Wt. W1771/M1 31 750,000 5/17 Sch. 52 Forms/C2118/14

Army Form C. 2118.

WAR DIARY

or

~~INTELLIGENCE SUMMARY.~~

(Erase heading not required.)

Instructions regarding War Diaries and Intelligence Summaries are contained in F. S. Regs., Part II. and the Staff Manual respectively. Title pages will be prepared in manuscript.

Place	Date	Hour	Summary of Events and Information	Remarks and references to Appendices
	APRIL 26		a RESERVE Position at H 23 d 4.4 2 ORs wounded in action	
	27	7PM	A & D Company reinforced the 6th Battalion LEICESTERSHIRE REGT. in G.H.Q Line 2 A Company H 30.d 3.4 D Company H 24 d 7.7 The Enemy having captured LANKHOFF FARM D Company went forward to reconnoitre towards LOCK 8 & C Company took up a position in G.H.Q Line 2 at H 24 d 7.7 1 O.R. wounded 2 ORs missing	JWR.
	28		D Company went back into RESERVE at H 23 d 4.4 with the exception of 1 platoon which remained at IRON BRIDGE I 26 d 2.5. 1 O.R. wounded 2ND Lt ROLL was wounded in action	

D. D. & L., London, E.C. (A8004) Wt. W1771/M2-31 750,000 5/17 Sch. 52 Forms/C2118/14

Instructions regarding War Diaries and Intelligence Summaries are contained in F. S. Regs., Part II. and the Staff Manual respectively. Title pages will be prepared in manuscript.

WAR DIARY
or
~~INTELLIGENCE SUMMARY.~~
(Erase heading not required.)

Army Form C. 2118.

Place	Date	Hour	Summary of Events and Information	Remarks and references to Appendices
	APRIL 29		B Company relieved A Company 6th Battalion LEICESTERSHIRE REGT in G.H.Q Line I. 1 O.R. killed & 14 O.Rs wounded in action	Appendix D
				WR
	30		The Battalion was relieved as follows. B Company & 3 platoons of A Company by A Company 9th Royal Welsh Fusiliers	
			1 Platoon A Coy. by 1 platoon of B Coy. 9th R.W.F.	Appendices E & F
			C. Company by D Company 6th WILTSHIRE REGT	
			D Company by B Company 6th WILTSHIRE REGT with the exception of 1 platoon which was relieved by a platoon of D Coy. R.W.F.	WR.
			Companies marched independently to ~~H~~ 15.a.4.2 6 O.Rs killed 10 O.Rs wounded	

G. Hanger Lt Col.
Comdg 7th Leics Regt

D. D. & L., London, E.C. (A8004) Wt. W1771/M2 31 750,000 5/17 Sch. 52 Forms/C2118/14

Instructions regarding War Diaries and Intelligence Summaries are contained in F. S. Regs., Part II. and the Staff Manual respectively. Title pages will be prepared in manuscript.

WAR DIARY
or
~~INTELLIGENCE SUMMARY.~~
(Erase heading not required.)

Army Form C. 2118.

Place	Date	Hour	Summary of Events and Information	Remarks and references to Appendices
			The following Officers joined the Battalion during the month:–	
			Capt. W. O. Evans.	
			Lt. C. H. Lazarus	
			2/Lt. W. M. Acocks	
			– C. R. Berwick	
			– [illegible]	
			– J. Gresswell	
			– W. H. West	
			– F. W. Simmons	
			– J. Hughes	
			– J. Royle	
			Morgan	W. R.

D. D. & L., London, E.C.
(A8004) Wt. W1771/M2 31 750,000 5/17 Sch. 52 Forms/C2118/14

Appendix A

OAK Operation Order No 10

SECRET

Copy No. 8.

Ref MAP Belgium & France
Sheet 28 1/40,000

1/ The Battalion will relieve the 22nd Corps mounted Troops Composite Battalion in the RIGHT SUB SECTOR tomorrow 12th inst

STARTING POINT Battn Orderly Room

TIME. 7-15 pm

Order of March H.Q. D. A. B. C Coy

DRESS Fighting order.

Rations for the 13th inst will be carried on the man

Movement will be by platoons or posts at 200 yds interval

Guides for platoons and Battn HQ will meet parties at SHERWOOD DUMP I 29 D.3.5.

4/ The Intelligence officer and Signalling officer will report at NEW BATT^N H.Q at 10 a.m.

5/ All signal apparatus will be taken over on relief

6 RATION PARTY

O.C. A Coy will detail a party of one N.C.O and 5 men to take over duties at the Ration Dump I 35 a.2.7.

7 O.C. B Coy PUMPING PARTY will detail a party of 2 men to report at BATT^N HQ immediately after relief

8 Relief complete will be reported to Batt^n HQ by runner

[illegible]
Capt + Adjt
9th Batt^n [illegible] Regt

P.T.O

2 DISPOSITIONS AFTER RELIEF

C Coy ~~Front~~ line Coy
D Coy Support Coy
A Coy Right Reserve Coy
B Coy Left Reserve Coy

Battn HQ I 30. C. 4. 0.

3 ADVANCE PARTIES

advance parties consisting of one officer one N.C.O. and 2 Runners per Company and Sgt WILKINS for HQ I. 30. C. 40 at 3pm. all French stores Defence Schemes Maps SOS signals etc will be taken over The R.Q.M.S. and MASTER Cook They will accompany the advance Party and will take over all Rations regarding rations & water &c from the RQMS of Bn to be relieved

Guides will meet advance parties at SHERWOOD DUMP I 29.D.25

Appendix

SECRET. B OAK OO 10.

Ref: Map 1/40000 SHEET 28

1. A withdrawal is being made from the YPRES Salient to a general line East of YPRES.

Line to be occupied by the Brigade will be as follows:—

CONVENIT LANE I 32.a.5.0. to I 21.c.6.0. just NE of FRENCH FARM.

The Battalion on withdrawal will be in RESERVE at HOWE CAMP H.34 central.

2. Withdrawal will be carried out as follows:—

A Coy commencing at 12 MN
B Coy " " 3 am
D Coy " " 3-30am
C Coy " " 4 am

Front line posts of C Coy will be withdrawn commencing at 2-30am and join remainder of Coy in the Front Line.

The Right Flank Posts of D Coy will withdraw with C Coy under arrangements to be made by Coy. Commanders concerned.

The withdrawal will be covered by two Companies of PALM who will occupy posts in the Corps Line

3. Route of withdrawal

IMAGE AVENUE — KNOLL ROAD —
S. end of ZILLEBEKE Village —
VERBRANDEN ROAD +
SHRAPNEL CORNER to H.24.Central

One guide per Platoon will be at the S. end of ZILLEBEKE Village

4. O C C Coy will detail two sections to remain behind in the line after withdrawal, under an Officer. This party will do all they can to hinder the advance of the Enemy by Rifle fire, & when forced to withdraw will join Companies of PALM in the Corps Posts.

5. 2/Lieut BONSHOR & two sections of A Coy will report to Battn H.Q. at (for special employment. Instructions will be issued at Battn H.Q.

6. As much S.A.A. as possible will be carried out by the troops. Each man will be served out with two extra bandoliers

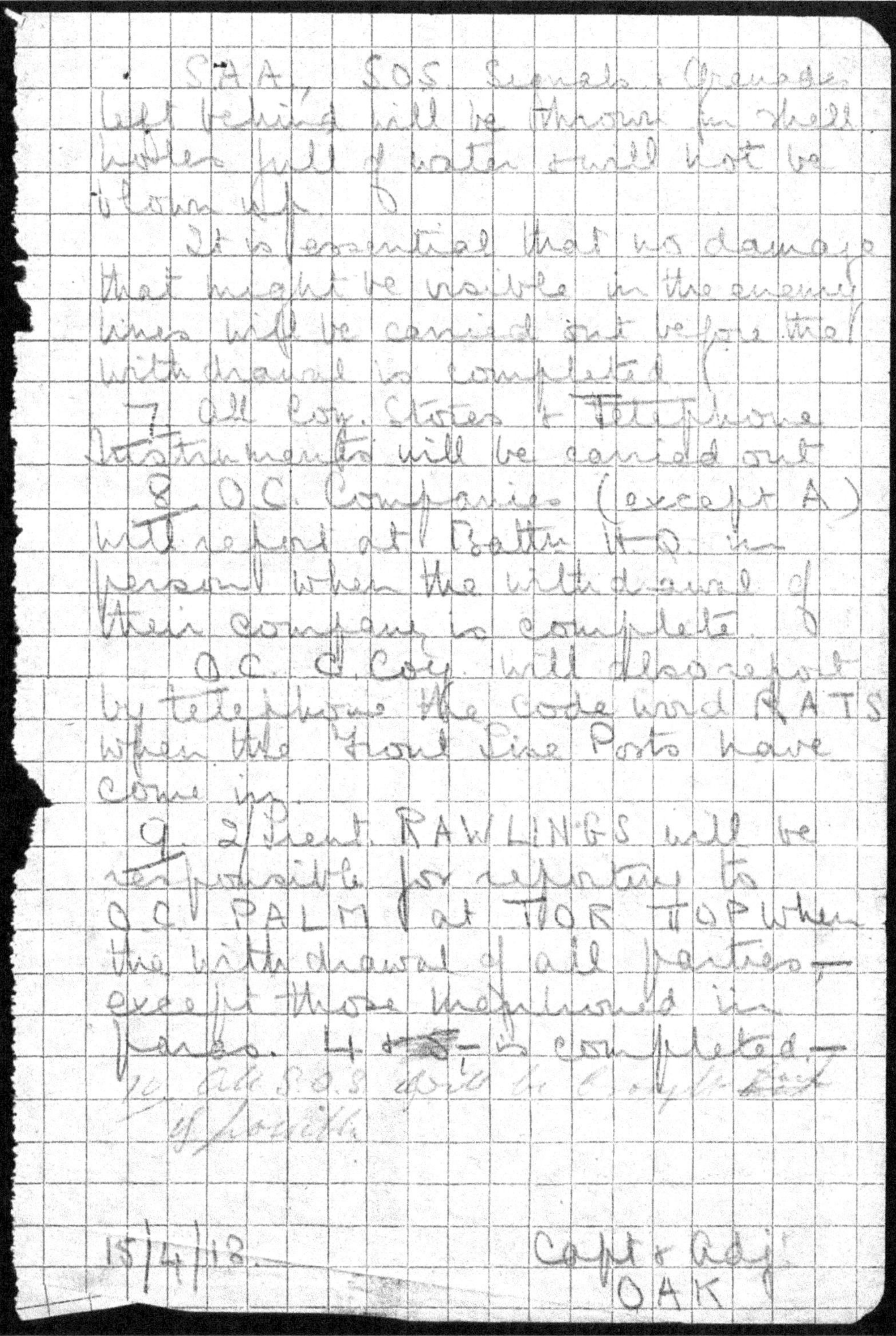

S.A.A., S.O.S. Signals & Grenades left behind will be thrown in shell holes full of water & will not be blown up.

It is essential that no damage that might be visible in the enemy lines will be carried out before the withdrawal is completed.

7. All Coy. Stores & Telephone Instruments will be carried out.

8. O.C. Companies (except A) will report at Battn. H.Q. in person when the withdrawal of their company is complete.

O.C. D Coy. will also report by telephone the code word RATS when the Front Line Posts have come in.

9. 2/Lieut. RAWLINGS will be responsible for reporting to O.C. PALM at TOR TOP when the withdrawal of all parties – except those mentioned in paras. 4 & 5 – is completed.

10. All S.O.S. will be [illegible] [illegible] if possible.

15/4/18.

Capt & Adjt.
OAK

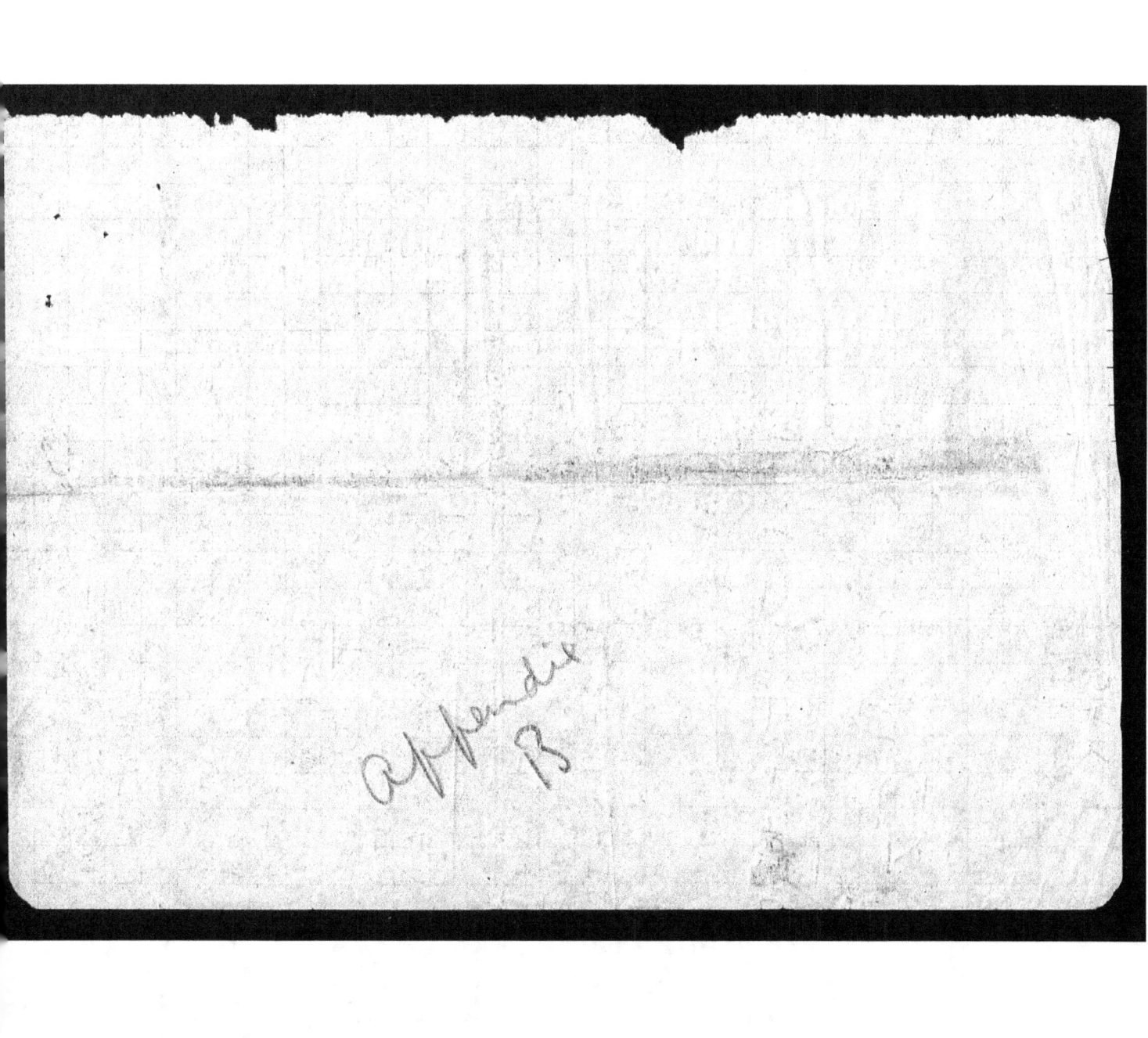

appendix B

SECRET. Appendix C

Copy No 9.

O.O/39.

Ref W.O. W/38.

1. 'A' Coy will commence to withdraw from CANADA ST. at ZERO.
D. Coy. will commence at the same hour.
B and C. Coys. will commence withdrawal from Posts at Z + 30 min. in the following order:-

B. Coy.
Posts I 30/3, I 30/2 I 30/1

C. Coy.
Posts J 19/3, J 19/2 J 19/1.

Support Platoons of Front Line Companies will form a rear guard for their respective Companies.

II. ROUTES.
A and B. Coys:- PLUMERS DRIVE SOUTH - VERBRANDEN ROAD - DERBY ROAD where guides will meet them.
C and D. Coys:- via PLUMERS DRIVE SOUTH - SANCTUARY TRACK - N end of ZILLEBEKE - WARRINGTON ROAD - DERBY Road where guides will meet them.

III. H.Q. Lewis Gun Platoon and 4 Vickers Guns will cover the withdrawal of the Battalion. 2 Lewis Guns of H.Q. Platoon will go to POST I 30/1 and 2 guns to I 30/3 at Z.

These guns and the Vickers Guns will not withdraw before Z + 3 hours and will maintain the normal rate of harassing fire.

Lewis Guns will come under the orders of O.C. Vickers Guns at Z.

O.C. Vickers guns will select the route for their withdrawal.

IV. Platoons will not move at less than 200 yards interval.

No transport will be available.

V. Dixies, S.O.S. Rockets and Telephone Instruments will be taken out by hand.

VI. Rations and tools will be drawn at H. 23. C. 95. 15 at 1 ~~pm~~ a.m.

VII. Battalion H.Q. will leave present position at Z. and will be established at the junction of PLUMERS DRIVE SOUTH and KNOLL ROAD at Z + 30 minutes where O.C. A and B. Coys. will report in person on completion of withdrawal.

2/Lieut. Rawlings will be at the junction of SANCTUARY TRACK and KNOLL ROAD N end of ZILLEBEKE. O.C. C and D. Coys. will report completion of withdrawal to 2/Lieut. Rawlings who will report immediately to Battn H.Q. at junction of PLUMERS DRIVE SOUTH and KNOLL ROAD.

VIII. The greatest care will be taken that no maps or secret documents are left behind.

IX. Pass Word LEICESTERS.

X. Acknowledge.

XI. Z will be notified later. 9 PM.

H J Dalby

Captain & Adjutant
O.A.R.

Distribution

O.C. A. Coy.	Copy No 1.
O.C. B. Coy.	" " 2
O.C. C. Coy.	" " 3
O.C. D. Coy.	" " 4
2nd D.L.I.	" " 5
Yorks Regt.	" " 6
O.C. M.G.C.	" " 7
Adjutant O.A.R.	" " 8
WAR DIARY	" " 9

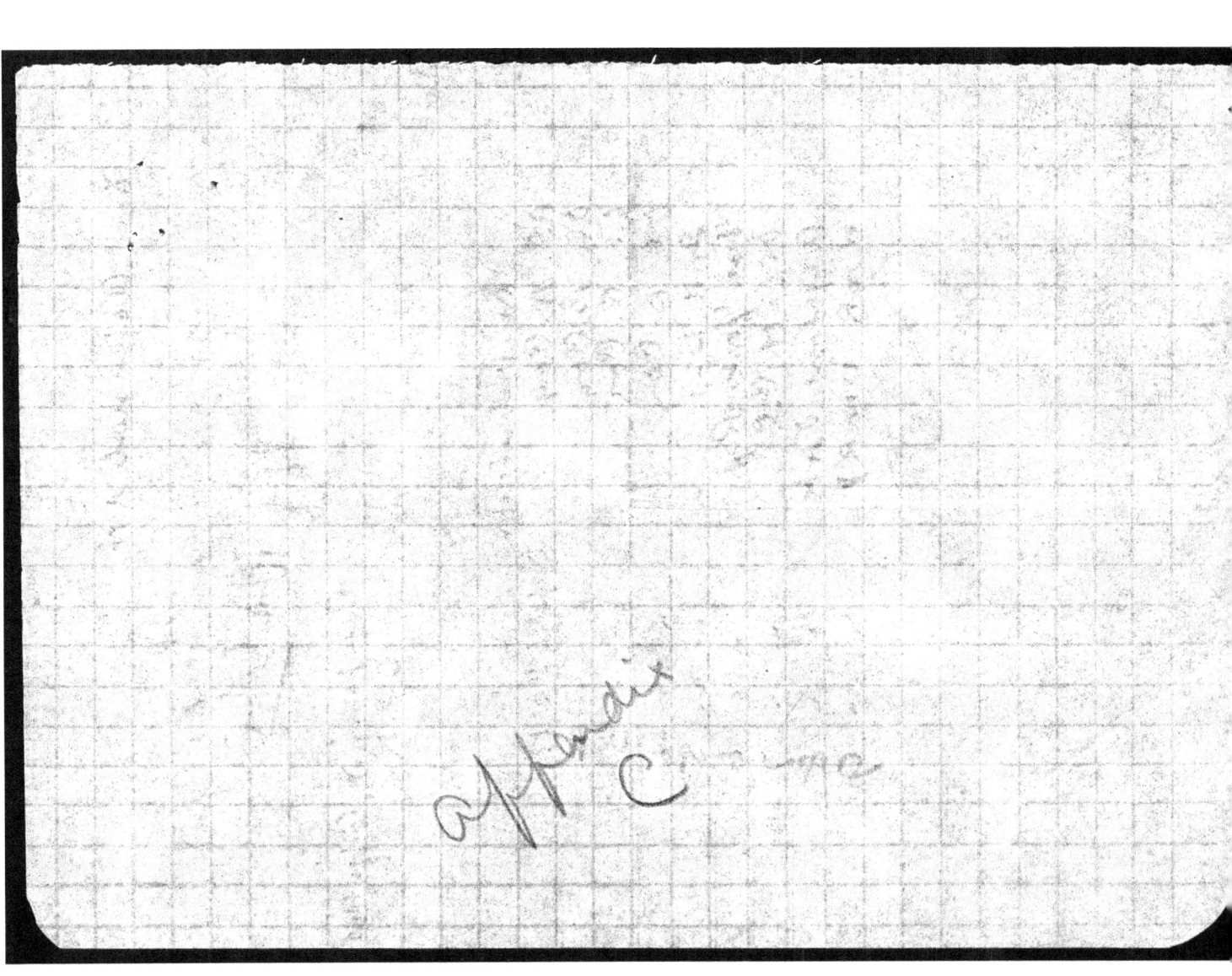

SECRET Appendix D.

Operation Orders by Lt Col: E.S. Clarke Cmdg PALM.

Copy No 3

1. A Coy PALM will be relieved by B Coy. OAK to-night 29/30th April, in G.H.Q. 1 Line.

2. No movement is to be made until after dusk.

3. On relief 'A' Coy PALM will occupy posts in G.H.Q. 2 Line vacated by 'B' Coy OAK.

4. All arrangements to be made between Coy. Cmdrs. concerned.

5. O.C. A Coy PALM will arrange for such details attached to his coy, as he considers advisable, to be relieved at the same time by B Coy. OAK.

6. Completion of relief to be notified to Bn. H.Q. by Codeword 'GOLD'

7. Acknowledge

DISTRIBUTION

Copy No 1. O.C. A Coy. PALM
2 " B Coy OAK
3 " OAK
4 " File.

[signature] Lieut
a/Adjt PALM.

29-4-18

Operation Orders by O.C. 'B' Coy [illegible]

1. 'B' Coy [illegible] will be relieved by [illegible] 'A' Coy [illegible] on the night [illegible]
CHQ & line

2. No movement is to be made until after dusk.

3. On relief 'A' Coy [illegible] will occupy posts & CHQ & line vacated by 'B' Coy CHQ.

4. All arrangements to be made between Coy Cmdrs concerned.

5. OC 'A' Coy [illegible] will [illegible] for guides [illegible] to the [illegible] at [illegible] of the same night by 'D' Coy [illegible]

6. Completion of relief will be notified to Bn HQ by codeword 'GOLD'

Appendix D

Distribution
Copy No 1 OC 'A' Coy [illegible]
2 'B' Coy [illegible]
3 [illegible]
4 File

[illegible]
20-11-18

Operation Orders by Lt Col. C.E.S. Clarke Cmdg PALM.
SECRET — Appendix E — Copy No 6

1. The Bn. will be relieved to-night by the 9th R.W.F. & 6th Wilts Regt as follows:—
A Coy R.W.F will relieve B Coy OAK & platoons of A Coy OAK on right & left of B Coy OAK.
B Coy R.W.F will relieve B Coy. PALM & platoon of A Coy OAK in the middle of B Coy PALM.
C Coy R.W.F will relieve the 2 platoons of D Coy. under Lt. CHART including advanced post at I.25.b.3.0 with 2 sections. This post will be occupied by Lt CHART by 9 p.m. to-night before relief. The R.E will dig a post to-night about I.25.b.2.4. which will be occupied by 1 Platoon C Coy. R.W.F. Two Sections C Coy R.W.F will be in support in CANAL.
D Coy. R.W.F will relieve CAPT GARNER's force at IRON BRIDGE & take over the whole defence of this Strong Point on both banks of CANAL. Capt GARNER will arrange relief of platoons of PINE attached, which will report to PINE H.Q. at SWAN CHATEAU on relief.

2 (a) Guides for A & B Coys R.W.F. will be at CAFE BELGE X roads at 8 p.m. under an officer. B Coy. PALM will arrange for an officer to take charge of these guides. There will be a guide for each platoon in the line.
(b) Guides from C & D Coys. PALM will be at Bn. H.Q. SWAN CHATEAU at 8 p.m. O.C. D Coy will arrange for a guide for each platoon or post. An officer will be in charge of the party.

O.C. D Coy. will arrange the relief of Lt CHART's 2 platoons.

3. An advanced party of 1 Officer & 4 men for Bn. H.Q. & 1 N.C.O & 4 men per Coy. will report at Bn. H.Q. at 6.30 p.m. to-night to take over billets to be occupied on relief.

4. A & C Coys. 6th WILTS Regt will relieve A Coy. PALM & 1 platoon A Coy OAK in G.H.Q. 2 line.

Guides – 1 Officer & 4 O.R. per platoon from A Coy PALM & platoon A Coy. OAK to be at OAK H.Q. at 9 p.m to night to meet relieving coys.

5. On relief OAK Coys. will rejoin OAK H.Q. (H.23.d.4.4.). Further orders will be sent as to where PALM Coys are to proceed on relief. All details of 17th KINGS will report on relief to 17th KINGS HQ. at H.30.c.5.5.

All details other than OAK, PINE, 17th KINGS will on relief remain with PALM Coys. until further orders.

6. All other arrangements will be made between Coy. Cmdrs. concerned.

7. All tools, S.A.A. & Trench Stores will be handed over to relieving Coys. & receipts obtained. Receipts will be forwarded to Bn. H.Q. as soon as possible after relief.

Very pistols will be taken out of the line.

8. 1 Officer & 1 N.C.O per Coy & 3 observers at Bn. H.Q. will remain behind in the line [illegible] for 24 hrs. They will proceed to rejoin the Bn under the senior officer on night

31st Apr / 1st May.

8. Relief complete will be notified to Bn HQ. by Codeword MAY.

9. Acknowledge.

DISTRIBUTION

Copy No 1. OC A Coy
2 " B "
3 " C & D "
4 T.O.
5 OC PINE
6 OC OAK
7 File.

B. B[illegible] Lieut
A/Adjt PALM.

30. 4. 18.

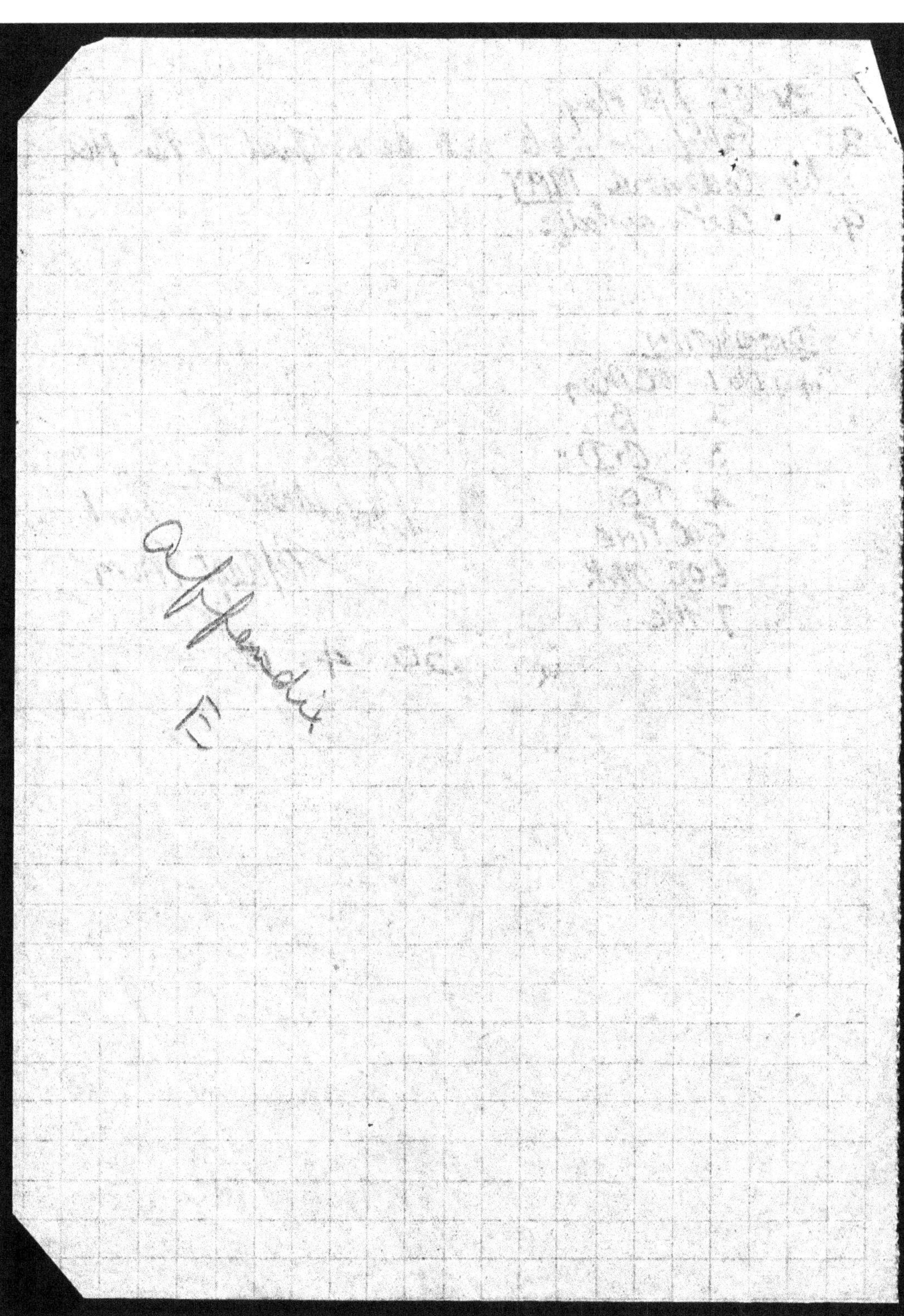
appendix
E

Appendix F Copy No. 6

SECRET

Operation Orders No. 6 by Lt Col. A.M.J. IRWIN, D.S.O. M.C., Commanding 8th Bn. LEICESTERSHIRE REGT

Ref Sheet 28 N.W. 1:20,000. 3/4 1916.

1. The Battn. less 1 Platoon B Coy at IRONGATE, will be relieved tonight by 9th WELSH.

2. Coys will be relieved as follows:-

A Coy	by	D Coy 9th WELSH
B " less 1 plat. at IRON BRIDGE	by	B " "
D "	by	A " "
C "	by	C " "

1 Plat. "B" Coy at IRON BRIDGE will be relieved by 9th R.W.F. under orders for O.C. "D" Coy 6th Leic Regt.

3. Guides will report to Battn. H.Q. at 7.45 pm to guide relieving Coys as follows:- (Orders already issued to O.C. "C" and "D" Coys)

Coy finding Guides.	Guides.	Where relieving party is met	Guided to.
A Coy	4 Guides (1 per platoon)	BELGIAN BATTERY CORNER.	Platoon positions
B "	8 " (2 per "A" Coys Platn)	"	WOODCOTE HO.
D "	4 " (1 per platoon)	"	Platoon posits.
D "	8 " (2 " platoon)	"	BEDFORD HO.

O.C. "A" and "B" Coys will arrange for post guides to meet relieving platoons at WOODCOTE HOUSE and BEDFORD HOUSE respectively.

First platoon of 9th WELSH are expected to arrive BELGIAN BATTERY CORNER at 8.35 pm.

4 The Relieved Coys will move back to billets in 6.15 a. by route Road and [illegible] [illegible]

just North of [illegible] Rd. just N. of SWAN
CHATEAU - BELGIAN BATTERY CORNER - Cross
Roads I.16.a.1.1. - Road Junction H.14 b.4.7
- Cross Roads H.19.b.4.6. - Road to
Bivouacs H.C.15.b. Guides will be at
H.19.b.4.6. to direct troops to bivouacs.
Platoons will close into companies near
BELGIAN BATTERY CORNER. O.C. Coys to use
own discretion as to above in event of shelling
at that point.

5 Transport will be in place road 200
yards W. of SWAN CHATEAU for Lewis guns
and mess kit at 11.0 pm and 2.0 a.m.
Coys will dump Lewis guns, drums, mess
kit at above point as they pass. A guide
will be on spot to show position of dump.
Coys will leave 2 Lewis Gunners to
look after Coy guns, load on to transport
and proceed back with transport.

6 Coys will hand over all tools, S.A.A.,
S.O.S. rockets, Very lights and [illegible]
[illegible], disposition maps, etc. to relief and
will obtain receipts which will be forwarded
to Battn H.Q. tomorrow.

7 Coys will leave one Officer and one
N.C.O. per company with the relieving
company until 6.0 pm tomorrow May
1st, at which time they will move back
to I.15.a.5.2., where they will receive
orders. Rations will be arranged.

8. 'C' Coy 7th Leic. Regt will be relieved by 'D' Coy 5th Leic. in GHQ 2 and will move back to C.T.C. on relief.

9. Companies will report relief complete by fullerphone and runner. Code word - HURRAH.

[illegible]
Capt & Adjt
5th L. Leic. Regt

Copy No. 1 A Coy
2 B "
3 C "
4 D "
5 C Coy 7th Leic.
6 7th [illegible] Regt
7 File.

appendix
F
OC
7th Leics

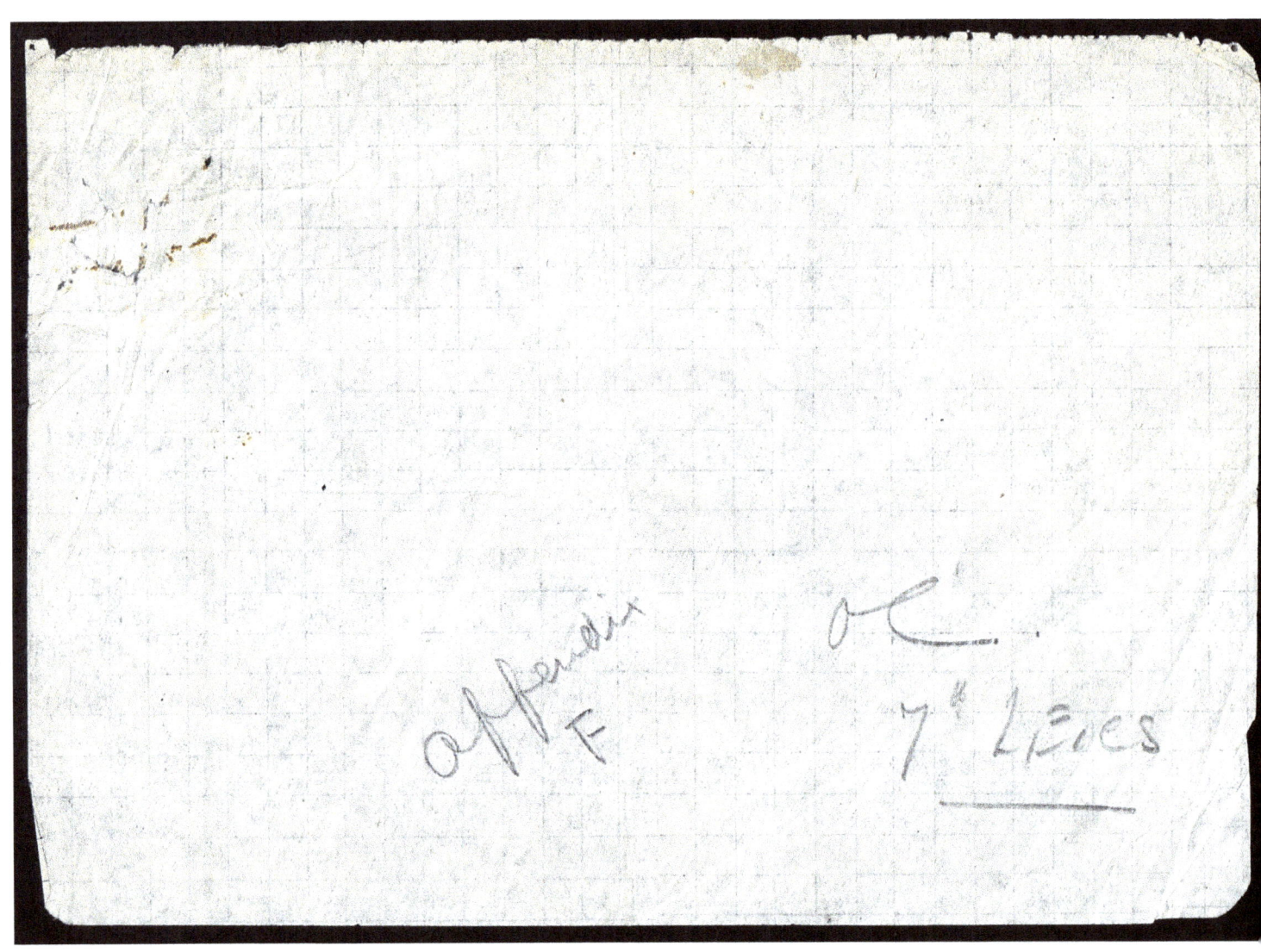

170/21

WAR DIARY
or
~~INTELLIGENCE SUMMARY.~~
(Erase heading not required.)

Army Form C. 2118.

Instructions regarding War Diaries and Intelligence Summaries are contained in F. S. Regs., Part II. and the Staff Manual respectively. Title pages will be prepared in manuscript.

May 1918

1st Bn Leicester Regt

Vol 3[illegible]

Place	Date	Hour	Summary of Events and Information	Remarks and references to Appendices
Nr CAFE BELGE	May 1st	3am	Bn relieved by 6th Bn Wilts: Regt. 19th DIVN. relief complete by 3am	Ref. Sheet 28 N.W.
		6am	Bn concentrated in camp about 1000 yds N.W. of BUSSEBOOM. - G15 a 5.2	
	...	3-0pm	Bn marched to wood on N.W. side of the POPERINGHE - STEENVOORDE Rd about 1½ miles N of ABEELE & bivouaced there for the night.	Ref. HAZEBROUCK Sheet 5A.
	2nd	9am	Bn marched via STEENVOORDE & CASSEL. Mid day halt about 1 mile W. of CASSEL for dinners for 1½ hours.	
		4pm	Bn reached OOST HOUCK & pitched camp in a field. Draft of O.Rs joined Bn.	
OOST HOUCK	3rd		Day spent in resting & reorganising.	
	4th	9am	Bn HdQrs & A. B & C Coys marched via St OMER to WIZERNES & entrained at 3pm. D Coy. under Major TYLER MC following by next train	
In Train	5th	1-30pm	Halt for 40 minutes at PONTOISE where hot water was provided for teas.	

D. D. & L., London, E.C. (A8c04) Wt W1771/M2031 750,000 5/17 Sch. 52 Forms/C2118/14

34 B
64

Instructions regarding War Diaries and Intelligence Summaries are contained in F. S. Regs., Part II. and the Staff Manual respectively. Title pages will be prepared in manuscript.

WAR DIARY
or
INTELLIGENCE SUMMARY.
(Erase heading not required.)

Army Form C. 2118.

Place	Date	Hour	Summary of Events and Information	Remarks and references to Appendices
	6th	2am	Bn HdQrs & A.B & C Coys detrained at SAVIGNY-SUR-ARDRE & marched to billets at LAGERY. arriving there about 5am.	Ref. SOISSONS Sheet 22.
LAGERY		8am	D Coy joined Bn	
— " —	7th	9 to 1pm	Training	
— " —	8th	— " —	— " —	
— " —	9th	— " —	— " —	
— " —	10th	— " —	— " —	
— " —	11th	— " —	— " — A party of officers went by bus to reconnoitre line to be taken over from the French	
— " —	12th	— " —	Further party reconnoitred line	
— " —	13th	9am	Bn marched via JONCHERY to PROUILLY	
		4pm	Arrived PROUILLY & went into camp.	
PROUILLY	14th	2am	Bn marched to reserve position in tunnels at CHAMPIGNONIERS due West of HERMONVILLE arriving there about 5-30 am. Nucleus party & transport moved to MARZILLY	
		9pm	Bn marched to the line in relief of 4th Bn 230th Rgt. French Army.	

D. D. & L., London, E.C.
(A8co4) Wt W1771/M2031 750,000 5/17 Sch. 52 Forms/C2118/14

Instructions regarding War Diaries and Intelligence Summaries are contained in F. S. Regs., Part II. and the Staff Manual respectively. Title pages will be prepared in manuscript.

WAR DIARY
or
INTELLIGENCE SUMMARY.
(*Erase heading not required.*)

Army Form C. 2118.

Place	Date	Hour	Summary of Events and Information	Remarks and references to Appendices
Trenches	15th	2am	Relief complete. Disposition of Bn. - Right front Coy A Coy with 2 platoons 'B' Coy attached Left front Coy D Coy - Garrison of 8 Posts - 'C' Coy Garrison of TENAILLE de GUISE - B Coy less 2 Platoons. Bn H.Qrs - P.C. ROUMANIE. The front held was from 2249-2938 to 2241-2951 with 6th Bn Leicestershire Regt. on right & 1st Lincolns (62nd Bde) on left. Very quiet day - no shelling by either side	Ref. Sheet BERRY-AU-BAC
	16th		Nothing special occurred.	
	17th		——— ——— One O.R killed by sniper.	
	18th		Inter-Coy relief carried out & following alterations made in disposition ~~Left~~ Right front Coy. B Coy. (2 extra platoons cease to be attached), left front Coy. 'C' Coy - Garrison of 4 Posts - Canal - Riga - HAUCHE & KLEBER 'D' Coy - Garrison of 2 Posts MARCEAU & LANNES & of TENAILLE de GUISE A Coy.	
	19th		Orders received to carry out raid before 26th. Point 2245-2945 selected & O.C. 'C' Coy. ordered to carry out reconnaissance of wire & make initial plans.	

D. D. & L., London, E.C.
(A8c04) Wt W1771/M2031 750,000 5/17 Sch. 52 Forms/C2118/14

Instructions regarding War Diaries and Intelligence Summaries are contained in F. S. Regs., Part II. and the Staff Manual respectively. Title pages will be prepared in manuscript.

WAR DIARY
or
INTELLIGENCE SUMMARY.
(*Erase heading not required.*)

Army Form C. 2118.

Place	Date	Hour	Summary of Events and Information	Remarks and references to Appendices
Trenches	20th		Nothing special to report.	
	21st		Decided to carry out raid with party of about 2 officers + 70 O Rs, to destroy enemy's wire with Bangalore torpedoes + to distract his attention by artillery fire directed on MT. SPIN + MT SAPIGNOL	
	22nd		Inter-Coy relief carried out A Coy relieving B - D Coy 'C' - C Coy relieving A + 'B' Coy relieving D	
	23rd		Date of raid fixed for night 25th/26th	
	24th		Nothing special to report - Orders received for relief of the Bn by the 6th Bn on night 26th/27th.	
	& 25th		Final preparations made during the day for the raid. The O C + Coy Cmdrs 6th Bn reconnoitred line during afternoon. Raiding party consisting of 2Lt. Bone + 2Lt. Hughes + 70 O Rs from the Bn + 12 Sappers under Lt Barnes by left TENAILLE de GUISE at about 10 pm to get into position. The R.E. were responsible for placing Bangalore Torpedoes in position prior to Zero hour	
	26th	1am	Zero hour for raid. 2 Torpedoes successfully blown + artillery opened on MT. SPIN + MT SAPIGNOL - Raiding party advanced through enemy's wire with no difficulty but found enemy's front line trench + ground behind	

D. D. & L., London, E.C.
(A8co4) Wt W1771/M2031 750,000 5/17 Sch. 52 Forms/C2118/14

Instructions regarding War Diaries and Intelligence Summaries are contained in F. S. Regs., Part II. and the Staff Manual respectively. Title pages will be prepared in manuscript.

WAR DIARY
or
INTELLIGENCE SUMMARY.
(*Erase heading not required.*)

Army Form C. 2118.

Place	Date	Hour	Summary of Events and Information	Remarks and references to Appendices
	26th		thick with wire which it was impossible to cut a way through. The left party under 2Lt. HUGHES got into the trench but were soon held up by wire. None of the enemy were met with. The raiding party were all back in our trenches by 2am. Casualties nil. Retaliation by enemy very slight.	
		6pm	Orders received that on completion of relief one Coy to remain in Bde Reserve at TENAILLE de GUISE, remainder of Bn to go into Divl Reserve at CHALONS LE VERGEUR	
		7pm	Orders for relief cancelled.	
		9pm	Information received from Bde that from information obtained from 2 prisoners it was expected that the enemy would attack at 3am on the 27th, the preliminary bombardment commencing at 1am.	Appendix 'A'
		11pm	A reserve Coy of 6th Bn Leic. Rgt arrived to strengthen defences. This Coy occupied TENAILLE de GUISE & the present garrison of two platoons was moved forward into main resistance line.	
	27th	12-30am	Bn H-Qrs moved to Battle H-Qrs - TENAILLE de GUISE.	

D. D. & L., London, E.C.
(A8004) Wt W1771/M2031 750,000 5/17 Sch. 52 Forms/C2118/14

Instructions regarding War Diaries and Intelligence Summaries are contained in F. S. Regs., Part II. and the Staff Manual respectively. Title pages will be prepared in manuscript.

WAR DIARY
or
INTELLIGENCE SUMMARY.
(Erase heading not required.)

Army Form C. 2118.

Place	Date	Hour	Summary of Events and Information	Remarks and references to Appendices
	27th	1am.	Hostile bombardment began - T.M. & field guns E of Canal. 10·5 & 15 cm. on main resistance line W. of Canal & on CORMICY - CAUROY road. Sneezing gas & then about 50 % Phosgene shells were used W. of CANAL. Smoke was greatly used E. of CANAL.	
		3-15am.	The enemy attacked our front system, the pressure being chiefly from the N. Old C.Ts were greatly used by the enemy. The 2 front Coys fought in their post blocks & fought their positions to the end.	
		6-15am.	Enemy penetrated into LA NEUVILLE. Shelling on area W. of Canal increased, gas shelling having then ceased.	
		7-20am.	Enemy crossed canal & pushed forward patrols in long grass towards main resistance line.	
		8·40am.	Enemy captured P.C. ROUMANIE & then continued bombing down the Boyau d'ECLUSE SUD until he reached TOURNAI trench. RIGA post was still holding out & heavy bombing was going on in the vicinity of it. The enemy twice attempted to attack the main resistance line ~~and~~ from the front with lines of waves but these were repulsed with rifle & L.G. fire, MARCEAU & HOCHE posts inflicted heavy casualties on the enemy during these attacks. He then started large bombing attacks assisted by L.T.M. on the posts along the C.Ts.	

D. D. & L., London, E.C.
(A8504) Wt W1771/M2031 750,000 5/17 Sch. 52 Forms/C2118/14

Army Form C. 2118.

Instructions regarding War Diaries and Intelligence Summaries are contained in F. S. Regs., Part II. and the Staff Manual respectively. Title pages will be prepared in manuscript.

WAR DIARY
or
INTELLIGENCE SUMMARY.
(Erase heading not required.)

Place	Date	Hour	Summary of Events and Information	Remarks and references to Appendices
	27th	6-15 am	HOCHE was captured & the line to the N.W had fallen to within 200 yds of CORMICY. A defensive flank was formed between CORMICY & MARCEAU facing N.W.	
		12-30pm	The garrison at MARCEAU held up all frontal & bombing attacks by enemy until 12-30pm when the post was captured by great superiority of numbers. Heavy concentration of artillery on TENAILLE de GUISE.	
		2-45pm	Many efforts by the enemy to take TENAILLE de GUISE from the front were all repulsed & he again developed heavy bombing attacks on the post. Heavy casualties were inflicted on these bombing parties.	
		3pm.	The small garrison that remained at the post was driven in & withdrew to the sunken road junction S.E of CORMICY	
		4pm	The enemy occupied the BOUFFIGNEREUX road N.W. of CORMICY & his patrols had reached the CAUROY road to the S.E. A frontage of about 700 yds was taken up on the high ground 300 yds S.W. of CORMICY & the details that remained organized into 5 small posts. The left was in touch with the 62nd Bde but on the right there was a big gap watched only by an officers patrol. This high ground was heavily shelled until about 7pm.	
		6-30pm	The enemy continued his attacks from the S.E. in the open, making excellent targets for L.G.s	

D. D. & L., London, E.C.
(A8c04) Wt W1771/M2031 750,000 5/17 Sch. 52 Forms/C2118/14

Army Form C. 2118.

Instructions regarding War Diaries and Intelligence Summaries are contained in F. S. Regs., Part II. and the Staff Manual respectively. Title pages will be prepared in manuscript.

WAR DIARY
or
INTELLIGENCE SUMMARY.
(Erase heading not required.)

Place	Date	Hour	Summary of Events and Information	Remarks and references to Appendices
	27th	7-45pm	The enemy penetrated our line on the left & worked round behind the small posts held by the Bn.	
		8pm	Report received from O.C 2nd LINCOLNS that the enemy were in the CHALONS-le-VERGEUR valley. The few H.Qrs details still remaining then withdrew with the 2nd LINCOLNS.	
		11pm	40 Stragglers arrived at VAUX VARENNES & these with 10 men of Bn H.Qrs were handed over to form a composite Bn from the Bde under command of the O.C 6th Leicestershire.	
	28th	3am	110th Bde was withdrawn to vicinity of LUTHERNAY FARM	
		8am	Orders received to withdraw to PEVY & form Divnl Reserve. On approaching PEVY, the village was found to be occupied by the enemy who had worked round the left flank. All details were in consequence diverted to high ground E of PROUILLY.	Ref. SOISSONS Sheet 22
		9-30am	Line formed on high ground above PROUILLY. Touch was obtained with 62nd Bde on left & eventually gap on right was filled by 64th Bde & the composite Bn from 110th Bde	
		4pm	Continual pressure from W & S.W. forced a further withdrawal to S. bank of VESLE. Here a further composite Bn was formed under O.C 7th Bn with orders to hold S bank of the VESLE from the [illegible] 1 mile W. of MUIZON for a	

D. D. & L., London, E.C. (A8c04) Wt W1771/M2031 750,000 5/17 Sch. 52 Forms/C2118/14

Army Form C. 2118.

Instructions regarding War Diaries and Intelligence Summaries are contained in F. S. Regs., Part II. and the Staff Manual respectively. Title pages will be prepared in manuscript.

WAR DIARY
or
INTELLIGENCE SUMMARY.
(Erase heading not required.)

Place	Date	Hour	Summary of Events and Information	Remarks and references to Appendices
			distance of about 800 yds.	
		6-30pm	Picquets established along river line & touch obtained with 62nd Bde on left & (considerably later) 64th Bde on right	
			Night passed quietly.	
	29th	6am	Small parties of enemy reported working through woods on North bank. These quickly withdrew when fired on. Except for the left which was continuously threatened by parties of the enemy who had crossed the river at JONCHERY, the morning passed without special incident.	
			During afternoon hostile shelling increased considerably	
		6-30pm	The 4th S. STAFFS (attd 62nd Bde) on our immediate left flank were driven back to the TILE WORKS – SAPICOURT road. The Bn Reserve was immediately ordered to withdraw to the line previously selected along the LES VAUTES – ROSNAY road. The Coy holding the S. bank of the river was ordered to hold on as long as possible & to conform to movements of troops on their left.	
		8pm	Information received that enemy was rapidly advancing through woods on W of LES VAUTES – ROSNAY road & as troops were rapidly falling back to high ground E.N.E of ROSNAY dispositions were altered to conform with them one picquet being posted at road junction 300 yds N. of ROSNAY in touch with French on left & 2 picquets on high ground NE of ROSNAY	

D. D. & L., London, E.C.
(A8cc4) Wt W1771/M2031 750,000 5/17 Sch. 52 Forms/C2118/14

Army Form C. 2118.

WAR DIARY
or
INTELLIGENCE SUMMARY.
(Erase heading not required.)

Instructions regarding War Diaries and Intelligence Summaries are contained in F. S. Regs., Part II. and the Staff Manual respectively. Title pages will be prepared in manuscript.

Place	Date	Hour	Summary of Events and Information	Remarks and references to Appendices
	30th	1am	Orders received from Bde that the French had taken over the line & that the Bn was to rejoin Bde at MERY PREMECY	
		2am	Party assembled & marched off.	
		3am	Arrived MERY PREMECY & received orders to continue march to POURCY	
		6-30am	Arrived POURCY.	
		11am	Orders received to continue march to ST MARTIN d'ABLOIS area	
		11-30am	Marched off.	
		3pm	Halted for an hour just N of DAMERY for teas.	
		7-30pm	Arrived at bivouac ground in FORÊT d'EPERNAY & bivouaced for night. The roads throughout the march were extremely congested by traffic of all kinds	
	31st	9-15am	Marched off	
		2pm	Arrived ETRECHY & went into billets.	
			Casualties during operations 27th to 30th - Officers. K.2 W.5 M.12 - Total - 19 - O.Rs. K.15 W.57 M.431 - Total 503.	
			All operation orders issued prior to May 27th were lost during the fighting	
			Copies of certain messages received & sent are attached as appendices	Appendix 'B' & 'C'
			G. Dawson Lt Col. Comdg 7th Bn Leic: Rgt	

D. D. & L., London, E.C.
(A8c04) Wt W1771/M2031 750,000 5/17 Sch. 52 Forms/C2118/14

War Diary 7th Leic Rgt Appendix 'A'

VERY URGENT SECRET

S.24/41.

From information received from two prisoners captured by the French Corps on the left of 9th Corps, the enemy will attack the CHEMIN DES DAMES to-morrow morning May 27th.

General FRANCHET D'ESPEREY considers it very probable that this attack will extend to our front.

In consequence of the above information the relief of 7th Bn. Leic. Regt. by 6th Bn. Leic. Regt. will not take place to-night May 26th/27th.

6th Bn. Leic. Regt. will send one Company to occupy TENAILLE DE GUISE as a reserve to-night, to be in position by 1 a.m. This Company will report its arrival to 7th Bn. Leic. Regt. and will be under the orders of O.C. 7th Bn. Leic. Regt. in case of necessity.

The remaining 3 Companies 6th Bn. Leic. Regt. remain in Camp "D" CHALONS LE VERGEUR as Divisional Reserve. State of readiness to move will be notified later.

All Nucleus parties are being organised into one Company under the command of the senior officer of the Nucleus parties. This officer will select four officers to do duty with the company, and will move his company to occupy Trench d'ESTERNAY between Boyau CHATILLON and Redruit NORD inclusive due West of CAUROY, as a reserve. This Company will be in position by 1 a.m., and the O.C. will report his arrival to O.C. 8th Bn. Leic. Rgt. under whose orders the Company will be, in case of necessity.

7th and 8th Bns. Leic. Rgt. will use the whole of their two companies West of the Canal for holding the main line of resistance, less those troops required as a line of outposts along the Eastern bank of the Canal, and for the defence of OUV de RIGA.

Officers to whom the method of destruction of Bridges over the marsh and Canal has been explained, will be given a party sufficient to destroy the Bridges if troops holding the Forward Zone are driven back over the Canal.

Prisoners state that the barrage is to commence at 1 a.m. and attack will be at 3 a.m.

G Whittick Captain,
Brigade Major,
110th Infantry Brigade.

26.5.18.

Issued at 8.45 to :-

6th Bn. Leic. Rgt.
7th " "
8th " "
All Nuclei.
110th T.M.Battery.
'A'.Coy. 21st M.G.Bn.
98th Fd. Coy. R.E.
Staff Captain.
B.T.O.
62nd Infantry Bde.
64th "
21st Division "G".
Signals.

Instructions regarding War Diaries and Intelligence Summaries are contained in F. S. Regs., Part II. and the Staff Manual respectively. Title pages will be prepared in manuscript.

WAR DIARY

~~or~~

~~INTELLIGENCE SUMMARY.~~

(*Erase heading not required.*)

Army Form C. 2118.

WO 33

Place	Date	Hour	Summary of Events and Information	Remarks and references to Appendices
			WAR DIARY OF THE 7th (S) Battalion The LEICESTERSHIRE REGIMENT JUNE 1918	

35 B

5 Schule

A7092). Wt. W12839/M1297 750,000. 1/17. D. D & L., Ltd. Forms/C2118/14.

Instructions regarding War Diaries and Intelligence Summaries are contained in F. S. Regs., Part II. and the Staff Manual respectively. Title pages will be prepared in manuscript.

Army Form C. 2118.

WAR DIARY

or

~~INTELLIGENCE SUMMARY.~~

(Erase heading not required.)

Place	Date	Hour	Summary of Events and Information	Remarks and references to Appendices
	June			
ETRECHY	1		Battalion in billets a composite company, consisting of 5 Officers and 111 other ranks, was formed from the battalion & sent to join 110th Composite Battn. Party embussed at 8 am.	H.W.
	2		Draft of 1 Officer (2nd Lieut. W.H.C. Cooper) and 20 other ranks joined battn	
	3		2/Lieut W.H.C. Cooper and 60 O.R's proceeded as first reinforcements to join 110th Composite Battn. Party embussed at Brigade H.Q at 9 am and proceeded to IGNY LE JARD.	
	"	9am	Remainder of battalion marched to COURJEONNET.	
COURJEONNET	4th – 8th.		Specialist training carried out as follows: Lewis Gunners, Signallers & Tactical Exercises for Officers and N.C.O's.	
	8th.		2/Lieut. A. J. KNIGHT and 28 other ranks proceeded as reinforcements to join 110th Composite Battalion. Party embussed at 1 pm.	
	9	10.30am	Remainder of battalion marched to MOEURS. Arrived 5.30 pm.	
MOEURS.	10th – 12th		Specialist training as for 4th – 8th June.	
	11th.		Lieut. Col. G.H. Sawyer, D.S.O. took over temporary command of 110th Infantry Brigade. Major T.C. Howitt, D.S.O assumed command of the battalion.	
	13th.		Lieut. M.C. McLAREN joined the battalion from England. Capt. J.C. Tanner, D.S.O., M.C. proceeded to take over command of Composite company with 110th Composite Battalion.	

A7092). Wt. W12839/M1293 750,000. 1/17. D. D & L., Ltd. Forms/C2118/14.

Instructions regarding War Diaries and Intelligence Summaries are contained in F. S. Regs., Part II. and the Staff Manual respectively. Title pages will be prepared in manuscript.

WAR DIARY

~~or~~

~~INTELLIGENCE SUMMARY.~~

(Erase heading not required.)

Army Form C. 2118.

Place	Date	Hour	Summary of Events and Information	Remarks and references to Appendices
MOEURS	June 13th	12 noon.	Transport proceeded by march route to SOMMESOUS	
	14		Remainder of battalion embussed at 1.30 pm. and proceeded to entraining station SOMMESOUS where transport rejoined the battn.	
HANGEST SUR SOMME	16	1.30am.	Detrained at HANGEST SUR SOMME & remained in rest camp outside the village	
			Transport proceeded direct by march route to FRAMICOURT.	
		9.30am.	Battalion embussed and arrived at FRAMICOURT at 1.30 pm.	
FRAMICOURT	17		Draft of three officers – 2/Lieut. J C Brammell, 2/Lieut. W.J. Linfield, 2/Lieut. L.A. Statham and 113 other ranks joined the battalion.	H.f. 10
	18		Draft of 9 O.R's joined the battalion.	
	17th–21st		Battn. training, including Lewis Gunners, Signallers, Musketry and Tactical Exercises.	
	20.		The Composite Company rejoined the battalion.	
			Draft of three officers – 2/Lieuts. G.A. Kirby, A.A.G. Allen & G.A. Hawkes joined battn.	
	22	9.50am.	Battalion marched to MONCHY SUR EV. Arrived at 6 pm.	

D. D. & L., London, E.C.
(A8co4) Wt W1771/M2031 750,000 5/17 Sch. 52 Forms/C2118/14

Army Form C. 2118.

Instructions regarding War Diaries and Intelligence Summaries are contained in F. S. Regs., Part II. and the Staff Manual respectively. Title pages will be prepared in manuscript.

WAR DIARY

or

~~INTELLIGENCE SUMMARY~~.

(Erase heading not required.)

Place	Date	Hour	Summary of Events and Information	Remarks and references to Appendices
MONCHY sur EU.	June 24th – 30th		Battalion training including close order drill P. & B. T., musketry, Lewis Gunners, Signallers and Tactical Exercises.	W/W
	26		Following Officers & O.R's joined from late 8th Battn. Leicestershire Regt.–	
			Lieut. A.E. Brodribb.	
			" R.W.G. Card	
			" G.W.C. Burrows.	
			" J.R. Warren.	
			" H.R. Gross.	
			2/Lieut. A.E. Ream.	
			" E. Hill.	
			" L.A. Fowke.	
			" W.H. Buckler.	
			" G.W. Beesley	
			" G.N. Hannis, M.M.	
			" T.H. Gostling	
			" C.S. Fletcher. and 309 other ranks.	
			Lieut. Col. G.H. Sawyer. D.S.O. rejoined from 110th Infantry Brigade.	
	29		Lieut. R.W.G. Card transferred to 110th Trench Mortar Battery	

A7092). Wt. W12839/M1293 750,000. 1/17. D. D & L., Ltd. Forms/C2118/14.

Instructions regarding War Diaries and Intelligence Summaries are contained in F. S. Regs., Part II. and the Staff Manual respectively. Title pages will be prepared in manuscript.

WAR DIARY
or
INTELLIGENCE SUMMARY.
(*Erase heading not required.*)

Army Form C. 2118.

Place	Date	Hour	Summary of Events and Information	Remarks and references to Appendices
MONCHY SUR EU.	29.		Lieut. Col. G. H. Sawyer, D.S.O. again assumed temporary command of 110th Infantry Brigade.	H/10
	30		Battn. standing by ready to move to new area.	
			Casualties in ~~to~~ composite company during the month.	
			5th June 2 O.R's. W in A	
			12th " 1 O.R. W in A.	
			15th " 5 O.R's. W in A	
			16th " 1 O.R. K. in A.	
			T. Clewitt Major. Comdg 7th Bn Leicestershire Regt	

A7092). Wt. W12839/M1293 750,000. 1/17. D. D & L., Ltd. Forms/C2118/14.

1.

Army Form C. 2118.

WAR DIARY
or
~~INTELLIGENCE SUMMARY.~~
(*Erase heading not required.*)

Instructions regarding War Diaries and Intelligence Summaries are contained in F. S. Regs., Part II. and the Staff Manual respectively. Title pages will be prepared in manuscript.

July 1918

7th Bn Leicester Regt

Vol 34

Place	Date	Hour	Summary of Events and Information	Remarks and references to Appendices
Monchy-sur Eu.	1 July	6.32 AM	Marched off from Monchy-sur-Eu. Arrived Eu Station 8.15 AM. Entrained 5.30 P.M.	Map Ref DIEPPE.
PUCHVILLERS	2 "	1.30 AM	Detrained. Marched to ARQUEVES, and went into billets at 4 A.M.	Map Ref ALBERT 51 D.S
ARQUEVES	3 "		Training - Battn programme - Platoon in attack, Musketry, Arm Drill B.F. on Consolidation. Specialists: Snipers, Stretcher-bearers, Signallers, L.G., Drums, N.C.O.s Class under Maj Tyler M.C. - Special training of L.Gs & complete double L.G. section per platoon. Hours of training 8.45 AM to 12.30 PM. Specialists 2pm to 4pm additional	WCM
	4		Do. 2Lt W.J.T. Peakman joined the battn from England. Capt. Gregory M.C joined from leave. (late 8th Leicr)	
	5		Do. Tactical tours for junior officers 2.30 - 5.30 pm. 2Lt W.H. Bone joined (Casualty)	
	6		Do. Visit of Army & Corps Commander - Battn on Range during visit 2-3 pm	
	7		~~D~~ Church Parade 10 AM. Rifle Shooting Competition - won by 3 Platoon. Transport 2nd. 2Lt A.C.C. Nunn joined from Hospital (late 8th Leicr)	

36 B

Gaskell

2

Army Form C. 2118.

Instructions regarding War Diaries and Intelligence Summaries are contained in F. S. Regs., Part II. and the Staff Manual respectively. Title pages will be prepared in manuscript.

WAR DIARY
or
~~INTELLIGENCE SUMMARY.~~
(*Erase heading not required.*)

Place	Date	Hour	Summary of Events and Information	Remarks and references to Appendices
ARQUEVES	July 8		Training as detailed. General idea - platoon commander to have 2 hrs with his platoon. All ranks to have 1 hr training in S.B.R. B Coy on Range. Practices - Grouping 100x Application 200x	Map Ref 41B E 9 - 54 D
	9		Training - N.C.O's Class breaks up. Examination [illegible] A Coy on Range with B Coy	
	10	"	Hours - 8.40 to 11 AM - Range for Coys detailed 2 pm to 4 pm. D Coy under B Coy. "B & C" Coys on [illegible] Range 600x Application 200x (5 rds) Rapid 200x (5 rds)	[illegible]
	11	"	A Coy on Range Grouping 100x Application 200x - Wet weather interfered with shooting	
	12	"	B Coy on Range - Snapshooting practice @ 200x	
	13		C & D Coys on Range do	
	14		Church Parade - Officers Rifle Shooting Competition.	

D. D. & L., London, E.C. (A8004) Wt. W1771/M2731 750,000 5/17 Sch. 52 Forms/C2118/14

3.

Army Form C. 2118.

Instructions regarding War Diaries and Intelligence Summaries are contained in F. S. Regs., Part II. and the Staff Manual respectively. Title pages will be prepared in manuscript.

WAR DIARY
~~or~~
~~INTELLIGENCE~~ ~~SUMMARY.~~
(Erase heading not required.)

Place	Date	Hour	Summary of Events and Information	Remarks and references to Appendices
ARQUEVES	July 15	10.30AM 2PM	Battalion inspected by Lt Gen Shute Comdg 5th Corps Presentation of Medals Battn Transport inspected A Coy on Range – Snapshooting practice at 200x	Map Ref ALBERT 57D
	16	2.30PM	Battalion moved @ 2.30pm to ACHEUX WOOD HQ P.7.a.a.3 – arrived 4.15pm – bivouacked – intention to relieve 2nd R.W. Fus. E. of ENGLEBEMER on night of 17th Orders cancelled 7PM	Map Ref ALBERT Sheet 57 D SE
ACHEUX WOOD	17	8AM	Battn moved back to ARQUEVES – Training 2pm to 4pm. C Coy on Range – Practice 10rds Rapid @ 300x with 1 sighting shot.	
ARQUEVES	18		Battalion moved N.E of ACHEUX WOOD & occupied BROWN LINE P.10.b.4.a. HQ P.9.b.6 (relieving parts of 190th & 113 Inf Bde) Battn relieved 4th R Fus. Arrived BROWN LINE 9PM	do
Nr ACHEUX	19		Battalion moved back to ACHEUX WOOD and bivouacked. D Coy to ACHEUX & Bn HQ – (6PM) Training:– L.Gs & Snipers on 30x Range – Reserve battn to Brigade.	
ACHEUX	20	9AM	Training: under Platoon Commanders. 9–11 – L.Gs & Snipers under Specialist Officers Parade hours 9–11 AM	
	21	10AM	Church Parade ACHEUX WOOD.	

D. D. & L., London, E.C. (A8004) Wt. W1771/M2731 750,000 5/17 Sch. 52 Forms/C2118/14

84

Army Form C. 2118.

WAR DIARY
or
INTELLIGENCE SUMMARY.
(Erase heading not required.)

Instructions regarding War Diaries and Intelligence Summaries are contained in F. S. Regs., Part II. and the Staff Manual respectively. Title pages will be prepared in manuscript.

Place	Date	Hour	Summary of Events and Information	Remarks and references to Appendices
ACHEUX	July 22	9AM	Training. Platoons under Commanders – Special gas + practical musketry. B Coy on Range W of FORCEVILLE – practice fire + movement scheme – Special lessons – fire orders + control by section leaders – B Coy 9–11 AM – Snipers + Signallers 6–8 pm. C.O. Maj [illegible] Div B HQ [illegible] + Adj. [illegible] Purple Line E. of ENGLEBELMER. – 2/Lt L.A. Fowke joined Battn from leave.	Map Ref Sheet 57D S.E. ALBERT
	23	9AM	Training – A Coy on Range as for B 22nd – 2nd C Coy. 2/Lt W.H. TYLER M.C. "A" + "C" Coy Comdrs, and C.O. reconnoitre Purple Line as above.	
	24	9AM	Training – Platoon Commanders [illegible] Hours 9–11 AM. Battn moved to ENGLEBELMER 9.30 pm. 3 Coys in Purple Line – A in Reserve Bn HQ P.19.a.8.4. Relieve 1st Bn ARTISTS RIFLES 63rd Div – Reserve Battn – Relief complete 1 AM 25th. Unloading party shelled. Casualties 2 K. 4 W. – Calibre 77mm – instantaneous fuze. Q.20.A.	
ENGLEBELMER	25		Quiet. Bn HQ shelled – target battery close by – between 1 pm + 2 pm – 2 150 mm H.E.	
	26		Quiet. Purple Line – C Coy – Q.20.c. shelled 105 mm H.E. – 10–10.30 pm approx 12 rds.	

D. D. & L., London, E.C.
(A8004) Wt. W1771/M2 31 750,000 5/17 Sch. 52 Forms/C2118/14

Instructions regarding War Diaries and Intelligence Summaries are contained in F. S. Regs., Part II. and the Staff Manual respectively. Title pages will be prepared in manuscript.

WAR DIARY
or
INTELLIGENCE SUMMARY.
(Erase heading not required.)

Army Form C

Place	Date	Hour	Summary of Events and Information	Remarks and references to Appendices
~~July~~ ENGLEBELMER	July	27	Normal. Change of Dispositions. Divisions approx 1 battn in Front, Intermediate & Reserve Zones respectively. Now - Two battns holding Front line and distributed in depth to Intermediate Zone inclusive with 1 Coy from each battn in Purple or Reserve line. One battn plus 2 Coys in support in Purple line. Front & Intermediate Left - 12th Bn [illegible] Right - 6th Bn Leics reserve 7th Bn Leics - Lt A G G. Mann to hospital with Spanish Flu.	Map Ref ALBERT 57D SE 1/20,000
	28	12.45 AM	Valley Q13 Cent & P24 Cent drenched with gas - Mustard - shells chiefly 77 mm. Time 12.45 am to 3 AM. Intermittent shelling area Q19 A & B - 150 mm at same time. No casualties or few, until sun got up when approx 30 O.R. reported sick - temporary blindness & sickness - morning of 29th.	[illegible]
	29		Normal - Total ~~[illegible]~~ evacuated 15. Special baths at ACHEUX 30 O.R. [illegible] valley shelled shelled strongly. Lt Gross evacuated nervous debility. Companies affected A & D occupying Reserve trench P24.c and Q19a. Repetition of gas shelling 11.30 pm to 1.30 AM. - same calibres but 150 mm continued until 4 AM being mixed H.E. & Mustard Gas. - Yellow Cross between M.N. & 2.30 A.M.	
	30		Casualties - Total evacuated up to morning of 31st 142 O.R. & 3 officers - eyes chiefly affected & sickness. Companies affected D mainly A & B. [illegible] Q [illegible]	

D. D. & L., London, E.C.
(A8004) Wt. W1771/M2-31 750,000 5/17 Sch. 52 Forms/C2118/14

Army Form C. 2118.

Instructions regarding War Diaries and Intelligence Summaries are contained in F. S. Regs., Part II. and the Staff Manual respectively. Title pages will be prepared in manuscript.

WAR DIARY
or
INTELLIGENCE SUMMARY.

(Erase heading not required.)

Place	Date	Hour	Summary of Events and Information	Remarks and references to Appendices
ENGLEBELMER	July 30 (Contd)		Battn relieved 6th Bn [illegible] R – [illegible] zone – Bn H Q – Q26 [illegible] 6.2. Relief complete 12.30 AM. Night quiet. D Coy strength Officers nil – OR 16. Two of our Corps aeroplanes brought down near Bn HQ 11.30 AM & 8 E.A. [illegible]	Ref. ALBERT [illegible] 1/20000
SSE of ENGLEBELMER	31		Quiet. B Coy in Front Line Q23 c 05.15 to Q29 c 95.70. C Coy Hill 142 Intermediate – A Coy Counter attack Coy at Bn HQ – 1 Coy 6th [illegible] taking over from D Coy in Purple Line. [illegible] Lt Col. [illegible] DSO [illegible] on [illegible] returned from leave [illegible] Maj. [illegible] DSO proceeded [illegible] 20th July [illegible] Maj. [illegible] MC taking over that date.	

Strength Summary

Increase				Increase	Decrease
20	OR	3rd July	from 6th Bn	2Lt [illegible]	2Lt [illegible]
5	"	"		[illegible]	2Lt [illegible]
11	"	13 "			2Lt [illegible]
2	"	9 "			6 OR [illegible]
23	"	12 "			12 OR [illegible]
15	"	20 "			
13	"	22 "			
18	"	30 "			
107					

[illegible] Lt Col
Comdg [illegible]

D. D. & L., London, E.C. (A8004) Wt. W1771/M2 31 750,000 5/17 Sch. 52 Forms/C2118/14

Confidential.

110/21

War Diary

August 1918.

7th Bn Leicestershire Regt.

Instructions regarding War Diaries and Intelligence Summaries are contained in F. S. Regs., Part II. and the Staff Manual respectively. Title pages will be prepared in manuscript.

Army Form C. 2118.

WAR DIARY
or
~~INTELLIGENCE~~ SUMMARY.
(Erase heading not required.)

Place	Date	Hour	Summary of Events and Information	Remarks and references to Appendices
ENGLEBELMER	Aug 1		Situation quiet. Forward Zone trenches in a bad state in spite of dry weather - Work begun on Intermediate Zone system. 2/Lt Peakman took out patrol from HAMEL OUTPOSTS to ascertain if enemy post on Road - end of CAT TRENCH - was occupied & [illegible] done - no [illegible]. Post found to be unoccupied - no enemy seen. Patrol 1 off & 15 O.R.	Sketch Maps 2 showing dispositions. Map Ref ALBERT 57D S E 1/20000. Operation Order & Battalion Relief B.O. 28 [illegible]
	2		Artillery activity on both sides. Enemy shelled HAMEL OUTPOSTS [illegible] about 11.30 AM. 2/Lt Peakman took out patrol to same post as previous and proceeded Road N to HAMEL. Quantities of wire were encountered on road - no sign of enemy. - 1 off & 15 O.R.	
	3		Enemy reported to have vacated HAMEL - 2 battle patrols under 2/Lt Knight and 2/Lt Peakman were sent out at 10 PM. HAMEL village was thoroughly explored - contact should have been established with patrol of Wiltshire Regt but that patrol appeared to be held up on N side of village - M.G. fire being heavy there. 18 pdr section heavily shelled from 9 AM to 11.30 AM - 150 mm H.E. - position close to Bn H Q - Q26 C. Two guns were damaged. Inter-company relief - D Coy relieved B in Forward Zone - A Coy relieving C & B in Reserve	Map Ref ALBERT Sh 57 D SE 1/20000
	4		I.O. sent 2 snipers to reconnoitre CHURCH TRENCH at 11.30 AM - patrol reached point 200x N of CAT TRENCH when fire by sniper was opened on them from E side of R ANCRE. No trace of enemy occupation evident - CHURCH TRENCH in bad condition.	[illegible]

D. D. & L., London, E.C.
(A8004) Wt. W1771/M2 31 750,000 5/17 Sch. 52 Forms/C2118/14

Army Form C. 2118.

WAR DIARY
or
~~INTELLIGENCE SUMMARY.~~
(Erase heading not required.)

Instructions regarding War Diaries and Intelligence Summaries are contained in F. S. Regs., Part II. and the Staff Manual respectively. Title pages will be prepared in manuscript.

Place	Date	Hour	Summary of Events and Information	Remarks and references to Appendices
ENGLEBELMER	Aug 4 (Contd)	1 PM	Enemy withdrawals near ALBERT and AVELUY WOOD reported. Two battle patrols were sent out under 2/Lt Yorke and 2/Lt Hawkes. The former exploring HAMEL village & dug-outs and the latter DRAKE ALLEY - RAVINE - N along Road and Railway to level crossing Q23 d 4 5 and ascertaining state of Bridge over R ANCRE at Q30 a 4 9. Former patrol encountering no enemy - MG fire was heard at N end of village - dug-outs found in bad state & unoccupied. The latter patrol reached Rly level crossing but found further progress E impossible owing to marshy state of ground. This patrol was sniped at & MG fire directed from direction E. Road running N parallel to Railway very much strewn with obstacles wire [illegible].	1 Offr 10 OR Map Ref ALBERT Sh 57D SE 1/20000
do.	5		Weather broken with heavy showers. - Trenches in sodden condition - some parts 2 & 3' of water. 2/Lt Allen took out patrol leaving Sunken Road Q29 a 7 4 & proceeded to Q23 d 4 0 (Road Junction). Progress E to R ANCRE was hindered by marshy ground and dark night and failed to find bridge Q30 a 4 9. No enemy were seen.	1 Offr 10 OR McW
	6		Quiet. Patrol under 2/Lt Hawkes went out by Sunken Road Q29 a 4 4 along Railway Road to level crossing Q23 d 4 3 & thence E to bridge Q30 a 4 9. Traces of a wooden bridge were found but in a damaged condition & track leading to bridge was impassable progress being made with great difficulty. No traces of enemy using track were found. 3 German rifles were [illegible] one being brought in in fair condition. Patrol returned [illegible]	

D. D. & L., London, E.C. (A8002) Wt. W1771/M2 31 750,000 5/17 Sch. 52 Forms/C2118/14

Instructions regarding War Diaries and Intelligence Summaries are contained in F. S. Regs., Part II. and the Staff Manual respectively. Title pages will be prepared in manuscript.

WAR DIARY
or
~~INTELLIGENCE SUMMARY.~~
(*Erase heading not required.*)

Army Form C. 2118.

Place	Date	Hour	Summary of Events and Information	Remarks and references to Appendices
ENGLEBELMER	Aug 7	1 AM	News reached expected attack by enemy on division on our left – 40th Div – Counter measures taken by our artillery – no enemy action followed	Map Ref. ALBERT 57D SE 1/20000
		12 noon	Lt Col. Sawyer D.S.O. left to take command of 62nd Inf Bde ([illegible]) – Maj [illegible] took command of battalion	
		10 PM	2/Lt Knight took out patrol (1 off + 10 OR) with the object of [illegible] of bridges over R ANCRE at Q 29 c 8 1 and Q 29 d 7 5. Patrol reported [illegible] of bridges at points mentioned [illegible] track leading to them from our lines. Ground in vicinity reported impassable to infantry owing to marshes	
Aug	8	2 AM	Company relief as per attached. Front line support [illegible] vicinity of [illegible] shelled – 300 rds 77 & 105 mm from 2 PM to 6 PM and from 3 AM to 3.40 AM – 5 men killed – S.O.S rocket appeared apparently from division on left at 3 AM – put up in error by 6th Bn	B.O.O. No 29 [illegible]
		10 PM	Battle patrol of 6th [illegible] of 2 off & 20 OR to secure identification – result 3 enemy killed, but, owing to M G fire & danger of being surrounded, no prisoners	
	9		Change in dispositions of battalion as per appendix. Battle patrol under [illegible] & 2Lt Vice reconnoitred HAMEL village – Enemy Sentry Group surprised but escaped in darkness at Q23 b 8.5 Enemy dispositions N and E of HAMEL discovered.	B.O.O. No 30

D. D. & L., London, E.C. (A8004) Wt. W1771/M2031 750,000 5/17 Sch. 52 Forms/C2118/14

WAR DIARY
or
INTELLIGENCE SUMMARY.
(Erase heading not required.)

Army Form C. 2118.

Instructions regarding War Diaries and Intelligence Summaries are contained in F. S. Regs., Part II. and the Staff Manual respectively. Title pages will be prepared in manuscript.

Place	Date August	Hour	Summary of Events and Information	Remarks and references to Appendices
ENGLEBELMER	10		Quiet. Patrol under 2/Lts FOWKE and PERKINS went out to same locality as previous night Q23 b 8.4 to rush enemy sentry post there. Enemy were found Q23 b 8.3 & fired at part of patrol under 2/Lt Perkins, who withdrew engaging enemy & sent runner to 2/Lt Fowke with news. 2/Lt Fowke also withdrew. – Strength of enemy estimated 12 in good position. Report attached.	Patrol Report [illegible]
	11.		Quiet. Battalion relieved by 1st Bn Wiltshire Regt. Relief complete 2 AM. Battalion disposition as per Sketch Map No 2 – Battalion in support Purple Line.	O.O. No 31
	12		Working Parties found. Vicinity of Battn H.Q. shelled during the day. – No casualties	
	13		Re-organisation of "D" Coy. Work on Purple Line – C Company [illegible] as Raiding Company – changed over with A Coy near FORCEVILLE. Battn H.Q. shelled 9-30 AM to 11 A.M. Our artillery active.	
	14		Raiding party returns to Battalion. News received of withdrawal of enemy to line of THIEPVAL RIDGE. Battalion under orders to push through 6th Battn and 1st Bn Wilts. when they establish line Q24 to Q30. approx	
	15	Dawn	Battn moves forward occupying line of Forward Zone Bn H.Q. Q22 d 3.3. B Coy to establish position Bridge Head Q24 a 5 2. B Coy in position	

D. D. & L., London, E.C. (A8004) Wt. W1771/M2731 750,000 5/17 Sch. 52 Forms/C2118/14

Instructions regarding War Diaries and Intelligence Summaries are contained in F. S. Regs., Part II. and the Staff Manual respectively. Title pages will be prepared in manuscript.

WAR DIARY
or
INTELLIGENCE SUMMARY.
(Erase heading not required.)

Army Form C. 2118.

Place	Date August	Hour	Summary of Events and Information	Remarks and references to Appendices
FORWARD ZONE BARN Support	15	(Contd)	at Bridge HEAD Q24 a 52 at 10.15 A.M. Patrol pushed over R ANCRE under 2Lt BOSS and encountered enemy on road Q24 d 74. Patrol fought rear guard action in good order making their way over R ANCRE to Bridge Head. Formation of ground afforded good view of fight from our old line, and patrol was very favourably commented on. 1st Bn Wilts pushed patrols CHICKWEED TRENCH Q30 Cent & [illegible] R25 a Cent. Former patrol captured by enemy — enemy in strength [illegible]. Latter patrol established at dawn 16th [illegible] 24 c 2 4. Bridge Head shelled heavily during the night	
	16		Quiet. Bridge HEAD visited during morning C.O. — and [illegible] by [illegible] — enemy very inactive. Battalion withdrawn to ENGLEBELMER 9pm taking up positions as on 14th inst except no company FORCEVILLE	
	17		Quiet. Battalion relieves 6th Battalion LEFT SECTOR. [illegible] Disposition map as per Appendix. Relief complete 2.15 am [illegible]	BO No 32

D. D. & L., London, E.C. (A8024) Wt. W1771/M2731 750,000 5/17 Sch. 52 Forms/C2118/14

Instructions regarding War Diaries and Intelligence Summaries are contained in F. S. Regs., Part II. and the Staff Manual respectively. Title pages will be prepared in manuscript.

WAR DIARY
or
INTELLIGENCE SUMMARY.
(Erase heading not required.)

Army Form C. 2118.

Place	Date	Hour	Summary of Events and Information	Remarks and references to Appendices
Q16a33	AUGUST 18		Extremely quiet.	57 d SE 1:20,000.
do.	19th		Day & Night were extremely quiet. A conference was held at Bde HQ at 9.30 PM. 2 Coys of the Bn were attached to 6th Bn for operations on the following day.	
do	20th		The Bn sector up to and including QUAKER ALLEY was handed over to 14th WELCH REGT (38 DW). Dispositions were then as follows. C Coy HAMEL OUTPOSTS. A Coy. OLD FRONT LINE. B & D Coys under command of 6th Bn in and about CHURCH ALLEY.	H.W.N.T.
do	21st		At dawn patrols of B & D went forward to establish themselves in COMMON LANE & LOGGING SUPPORT supported by their Coys. The crossing was made at the MILLBRIDGE Q 24 a 5.3. There was a thick ground mist. When over the bridge both Coys came under heavy enemy M.G. fire, holding up operations. Lt HACKETT was killed.	

D. D. & L., London, E.C. (A8004) Wt. W1771/M2-31 750,000 5/17 Sch. 52 Forms/C2118/14

Instructions regarding War Diaries and Intelligence Summaries are contained in F. S. Regs., Part II. and the Staff Manual respectively. Title pages will be prepared in manuscript.

WAR DIARY
or
INTELLIGENCE SUMMARY.
(Erase heading not required.)

Army Form C. 2118.

Place	Date AUG:	Hour	Summary of Events and Information	Remarks and references to Appendices
Q16a.3.3.	21.		B. D Coys were withdrawn to W of River ANCRE. A barrage of 105mm + 150mm Hows: was put down by the enemy during the withdrawal. Both Coys had a few casualties.	57 d SE 1:20000.
	22.		The whole day was quiet. Coys remained in their positions of 21st	
MAILLY MAILLET.	23.	4AM	The Battn was relieved by 6th Bn. and arrived in PURPLE SYSTEM E MAILLY MAILLET at 6AM.	
			The day was spent resting. Brigade conference 1.30 PM to discuss offensive arrangements for the following day.	H.W.H. Tyler Maj
		9PM.	Battn move to assembly position in LUMINOUS ~~TRENCH~~ AVENUE. Q12. Bde conference at 11. PM.	
	24.	2AM	Battn moved in single file following 6th Bn over the ANCRE making the crossing R8 c. and arriving in LITTLE TRENCH R14a about 4AM. A halt was made here until Coys of 6th Bn had established themselves in BATTERY VALLEY.	
		5.30AM	Battn moved to BATTERY VALLEY. R14d A + C Coys were sent forward to gain touch with 1st WILTS	

D. D. & L., London, E.C. (A8004) Wt. W1771/M2731 750,000 5/17 Sch. 52 Forms/C2118/14

Instructions regarding War Diaries and Intelligence Summaries are contained in F. S. Regs., Part II. and the Staff Manual respectively. Title pages will be prepared in manuscript.

WAR DIARY
or
INTELLIGENCE SUMMARY.

(*Erase heading not required.*)

Army Form C. 2118.

Place	Date	Hour	Summary of Events and Information	Remarks and references to Appendices
R16.c.	AUG 24th.		who were supposed to be in front. B & D Coys moved up in support. Touch with 1st WILTS was not made & B & D Coys took up a position on the line of road R22a & R16c.	57c SW. 1.20000
			Attached is a report of operations carried out by A & C Coys. Touch was lost with these 2 Coys until 10AM AUG 25th	
		7PM.	Except for intermittent enemy MG fire the day was very quiet. Enemy shelling was very weak.	[illegible]
			Bde conference at 5PM. The 110th Bde was ordered to make a night march to LE SARS & establish itself on the line DESTREMONT FM – LITTLE WOOD, 1st WILTS Right, 6th Bn Left, 7th in support.	
M 8 a.		8.30 PM	Bn assembled in BOOM RAVINE, & following in rear of 1st WILTS arrived in SUPPORT at 2AM in trenches M 8 a & c. The night was quiet, & the Bn was not engaged with the enemy.	

D. D. & L., London, E.C. (A8004) Wt. W1771/M2 31 750,000 5/17 Sch. 52 Forms/C2118/14

Instructions regarding War Diaries and Intelligence Summaries are contained in F. S. Regs., Part II. and the Staff Manual respectively. Title pages will be prepared in manuscript.

WAR DIARY
or
INTELLIGENCE SUMMARY.
(Erase heading not required.)

Army Form C. 2118.

Place	Date	Hour	Summary of Events and Information	Remarks and references to Appendices
M 8 a.	AUG 25.		The ~~day~~ morning was spent resting.	57C. SW 1:20 000
		1PM.	The Brigade was ordered to advance. The Battn moved to assembly positions near BUTTE de WARLENCOURT. During the march word came through that 62 Bde ~~[illegible]~~ were being counter attacked on the right E. LE SARS. A position was taken up as follows. A Coy on road W. EAUCOURT L'ABBAYE with Rt flank joining 6th Bn M 23 c 2.8. – B Coy in centre in trenches M 23 a. C Coy on left about M 23 a 6.9 joining up with 62nd Bde – D Coy in Support	H.W.N.T.
M 22 b 9.5.	..	..	The counter attack was repulsed, the Bn having a few casualties including CAPT. VANNER DSO. MC. & Lt FOWKE. The Bn remained in ~~its~~ the same position during the night. Enemy artillery & MGs were active, & some casualties were suffered including Lt BURROWS killed in action, & 2Lt BOWE wounded.	

D. D. & L., London, E.C.
(A8004) Wt. W1771/M231 750,000 5/17 Sch. 52 Forms/C2118/14

Instructions regarding War Diaries and Intelligence Summaries are contained in F. S. Regs., Part II. and the Staff Manual respectively. Title pages will be prepared in manuscript.

WAR DIARY
or
INTELLIGENCE SUMMARY.
(*Erase heading not required.*)

Army Form C. 2118.

Place	Date	Hour	Summary of Events and Information	Remarks and references to Appendices
M 22 b.	Aug: 26.		The day was quiet in the Bn Sector.	57 c SW. 1/20000.
		8PM.	A readjustment of the front was made. The Bn extending its front to M 28 a 8.5. and joining on to 17th DIV at this point. During the night there was considerable enemy artillery activity on EAUCOURT L'ABBAYE. C Coy had some casualties.	
	27	10AM	The Bn was ordered to advance & moved to assembly position M 17 c. The advance was cancelled & the Bn moved back to M 8 c. trenches to rest.	H.W.H.T.
	28.		Lt. Col. G.H. SAWYER. DSO. rejoined the Battn.	
		830 PM	Bn relieved 12/13 N.F. in YELLOW CUT M 18 b. M 12 d. B Coy Right front Coy D. left. with A & C in support in BLUE CUT. The night was fairly quiet.	
	29	10.30 AM	B & D Coys sent patrols to LUSENHOF FM - LIGNY TILLOY RD no enemy were seen.	
		11.30 AM	Bn moved forward occupying LUSENHOF FM - LIGNY TILLOY RD,	

D. D. & L., London, E.C.
(A8004) Wt. W1771/M2-31 750,000 5/17 Sch. 52 Forms/C2118/14

Instructions regarding War Diaries and Intelligence Summaries are contained in F. S. Regs., Part II. and the Staff Manual respectively. Title pages will be prepared in manuscript.

WAR DIARY
or
INTELLIGENCE SUMMARY.
(*Erase heading not required.*)

Army Form C. 2118.

Place	Date	Hour	Summary of Events and Information	Remarks and references to Appendices
N.14a.	AUG 29		thence to line N21a to N9a. Small parties of the enemy encountered were driven back.	57C S.W. 1/20,000
		5PM.	Bn was established as follows. D & C Coys in trenches W. BEUGNY-BEULENCOURT. N.16 a.5.0 to N.9a 7.0. with B & A Coys in support. The valley N9c was heavily shelled with 77mm, & considerable MG fire was directed from BEULENCOURT.	
		6PM	Instructions were received to keep in touch with the enemy, & patrols were sent forward to BEULENCOURT which was found to be strongly held. There was intermittent shelling of our positions during the night. Touch was made with 42 Div on the right.	HMT.
	30.	11.30 AM	BEULENCOURT was heavily shelled by our artillery. There was some retaliation on our front positions. Constant patrols were sent to BEULENCOURT which was still found to be held by the enemy.	

D. D. & L., London, E.C. (A8004) Wt. W1771/M2631 750,000 5/17 Sch. 52 Forms/C2118/14

Army Form C. 2118.

WAR DIARY
or
INTELLIGENCE SUMMARY.
(*Erase heading not required.*)

Instructions regarding War Diaries and Intelligence Summaries are contained in F. S. Regs., Part II. and the Staff Manual respectively. Title pages will be prepared in manuscript.

Place	Date	Hour	Summary of Events and Information	Remarks and references to Appendices
N 14 a.	AUG 31.		Bde conference 10 AM, 2 PM.—	57 C SW 1/20,000.
			The Bn received orders to attack SUGAR FACTORY N 24 d.	
			The 6th & 1st WILTS were to attack BEAULENCOURT from North.	H.W.H.T.
			Zero 2 AM. 1st SEPT. ~~[illegible]~~ BEAULENCOURT was captured.	
			The SUGAR FACTORY was not taken.	
			—	
	AUG 1 to AUG 31st		CASUALTIES. OFFICERS.	
			Lt. GWC. BURROWS K in A. CAPT V.C. VANNER DSO. MC. W in A	
			Lt BFM HACKETT K in A. " EA. GREGORY MC "	
			Lt W.R WARREN "	
			LA. FOWKE "	
			2Lt A. PERKINS "	
			" F.A. VOCE "	
			" LA. STATHAM "	
			" W.H. BONE "	
			" CQ CONNOLD. "	
			" W.H. BUCKLER "	
			" TH GOSTLING "	
	do		do O.Rs.	
			9 k in A. — 246 w in A. — 10 missing. — — —	Total 278.
			DRAFTS. Officers	
			2Lts A. PERKINS,— F.A. VOCE.— EQ CONNOLD.— HR RADFORD. EW BOSS.— W.H. BUCKLER.	
			ORs. 157 5/8/18 21 10/8/18. 10 17/8/18. 22 24/8/18	H.W.H.T.

G H Barker Lt Col
Comdg. 7 Leicestershire Regt

D. D. & L., London, E.C. (A8004) Wt. W1771/M2831 750,000 5/17 Sch. 52 Forms/C2118/14

JONE Operation Order No 28. Copy No..........

S E C R E T. 2nd August 1918.

1. Inter-Coy reliefs will take place tomorrow night, 3rd inst.

"C" Coy will relieve "B" Coy.
"A" Coy will relieve "C" Coy.
"B" Coy will relieve "A" Coy.

2. After relief, dispositions will be as follows:-

"C" Coy. - FORWARD ZONE Coy.
"A" Coy. - INTERMEDIATE ZONE Coy.
"B" Coy. - Counter-attack Coy.

3. "C" Coy will not move off before 9.39.p.m. Intervals of 200 yards will be maintained between Platoons.

4. GUIDES.

O.C. "B" Coy will arrange for platoon guides to be at ~~prsnt~~ present "B" Coy H.Q. at 9.45.p.m.

"A" and "B" Coys will arrange for advance parties to act as guides. Rendezvous will be fixed under Coy arrangements.

5. ADVANCE PARTIES.

1 Officer per Coy and 1 N.C.O. per Platoon will take over during the day.

6. TRENCH STORES.

All trench stores will be carefully checked, and receipts sent to Battn H.Q. by 12 noon 4th inst.

List of trench stores taken over is attached. All deficiencies will be explained.

7. PROTECTIVE PATROLLING.

O.C. "B" Coy will be responsible for protective patrolling along the front to 12 midnight, after which hour "C" Coy will take over.

8. RELIEF COMPLETE.

"A" and "B" Coys will report relief complete by runner. "C" Coy will report by Fullerphone, code word "HORNE"

H. J. W[illegible]

Capt & Adjt.
JONE

Copy No 1.....O.C."A" Coy.
" " 2.....O.C."B" "
" " 3.....O.C."C" Coy.
" " 4.....Q.M. and T.O.
" " 5.....War Diary.
" " 6.....File.

JONE Operation Order No 29. Copy No...5.......

SECRET. 6th August 1918.

1. Inter Coy reliefs will take place tomorrow 7th inst as follows:-

"A" Coy will relieve "C" Coy.
"C" Coy will relieve "B" Coy.
"B" Coy will relieve "A" Coy.

2. After relief, dispositions will be as follows:-

"A" Coy. - FORWARD ZONE.
"B" Coy. - INTERMEDIATE ZONE.
"C" Coy. - COUNTER ATTACK COY.

3. "A" Coy will not move off before 9.30.p.m. Intervals of 200 yards will be maintained between Platoons.

4. GUIDES.

O.C. "C" Coy will arrange for Platoon Guides to be at forward Coy H.Q. at 9.45.p.m.

"B" and "C" Coys will arrange for advance parties to act as guides. Rendezvous will be fixed under Coy arrangements.

5. ADVANCE PARTIES.

1 Officer per Coy and 1 N.C.O. per Platoon will take over during the day.

6. TRENCH STORES.

Officers Commanding Companies will ensure that the greatest care is exercised in the checking of Trench Stores. All trench Stores should be in Platoon and Company ~~posts~~ dumps.

A list of trench stores now in possession of Coys is attached. All deficiencies will be explained.

Receipts will be sent to Battn H.Q. by 12 noon 8th inst.

7. RELIEF COMPLETE.

"B" and "C" Coys will report relief complete by runner. "A" Coy will report by Fullerphone, code word "VANSER"

8. ACKNOWLEDGE.

[signature]

Capt & Adjt.
JONE

Copy No 1....O.C. "A" Coy.
" " 2....O.C. "B" Coy.
" " 3....O.C. "C" Coy.
" " 4....Q.M. and T.O.
" " 5....War Diary.
" " 6....File.

[illegible] Order No. [illegible]

S E C R E T. Reference [illegible] 57D.S.E. 1/20,000. 8.3.18.

1. [illegible] its front N. to [illegible] following troops of [illegible]

2. [illegible] Coys will relieve Coys of 6th Battn Leicestershire Regiment and 15th [illegible] Light Infantry as follows:-

Coy.	Position	Relieving
"C" Coy.	INTERMEDIATE SYSTEM.	1 Coy (less 1 Platoon) 6th Battn Leicestershire Regt
"D" Coy.	PURPLE LINE. [illegible]	1 Coy 15th Battn D.L.I.

3. All details of relief, times etc will be arranged between Company Commanders concerned.

4. [illegible] showing new [illegible] positions will be forwarded to Battn H.Q. as soon as possible after relief.

5. Details of work in hand, [illegible] photographs, maps and Trench stores will be taken over. List will be sent to Battn H.Q. by 12 noon tomorrow [illegible] inst.

6. BATTN GUIDES.
1 Guide per Coy will report to the Adjutant at [illegible] to guide [illegible] to new Coy H.Q.

7. RELIEF COMPLETE.
Relief complete will be reported to Battn H.Q. by runner. Code word "[illegible]."

8. ACKNOWLEDGE.

[illegible] Capt & Adjt.
[illegible]

Copy No 1.....O.C. "A" Coy.
" " 2.....O.C. "B" Coy.
" " 3.....O.C. "C" Coy.
" " 4.....O.C. "D" Coy.
" " 5.....T.O. and Q.M.
" " 6.....6th Battn Leicestershire Regt.
" " 7.....15th Battn D.L.I.
" " 8.....War Diary.
" " 9.....File.

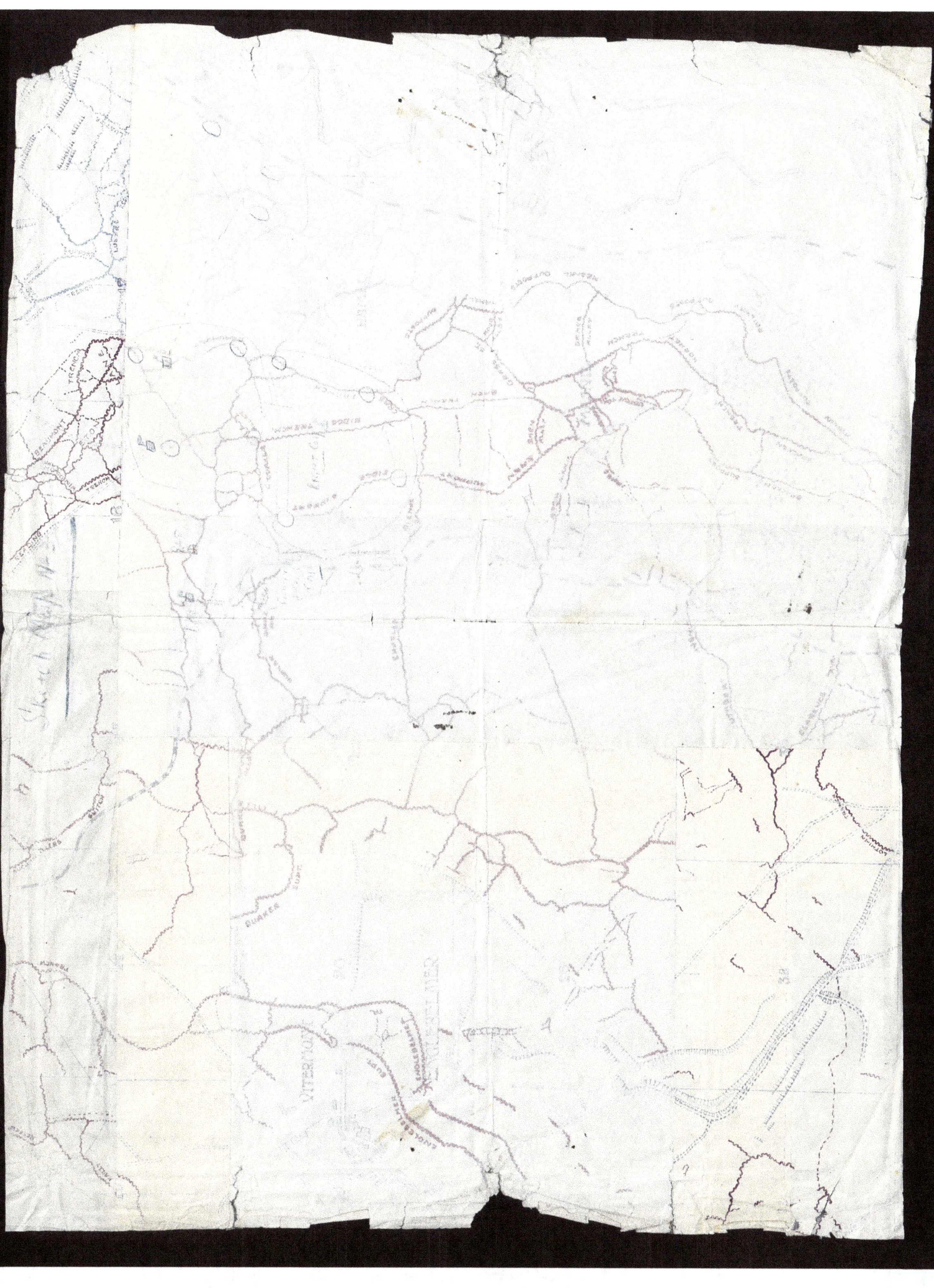

Lesby

PATROL REPORT

UNIT VOKE

DATE 9/10 Aug

Strength of Patrol. Orders given to. Patrol Leader's Name (in Block Letters)	Time of (a) Departure (b) Return	Point of (a) Departure (b) Return	ACTION OF PATROL (giving map co-ordinates of any posts located, work, patrols encountered etc.)
2 off + 25 OR Lt. LA FORKE and 2Lt Voce for instruction	(a) 9.15 (b) 2 am.	a&b Q29a 4.5	Patrol moved down Sunken Road and secured 1st & 2nd Objectives without incident. On proceeding N up Road at Q23 b 8 4 a barricade was met with. 2Lt Voce jumped this & was immediately challenged by enemy sentry, who fired his rifle, dropped a bomb & fled in direction of LUSTRE TRENCH Q23.b.8.8 together with remainder of sentry group, estimated at 5 men – 2Lt Voce fired two rounds from his revolver, and patrol mounted bank on W side of road, which was very steep, by which time the enemy had disappeared in darkness. At this time a brilliant floating light was dropped from an aeroplane (presumably ours) & numerous Verey lights were fired from LUSTRE Tr. Patrol posted L.G. on top of bank (position of enemy S.G.) & proceeded W. toward CHURCH Tr to intercept any patrol enemy might send down & to avoid being cut off. ½ hour was spent there and patrol returned way it had come. No hostile M.G. fire was directed at patrol

LUSTRE

TRENCH

CHURCH

CHURCH

TRENCH

BRITISH

D Objective

Enemy S.G.
[illegible] posts

Barrier

P Objective

Hostile S.P.

Note
dotted line ------
marks route of patrol

- REFERENCE -

German Wire

German Trenches derelict

Do Good Condition

Do Showing signs of recent work

Cellars

Dug-outs

28.7.18

PATROL REPORT

UNIT .... DATE

Strength of Patrol, Orders given to Patrol, & Patrol Leader's Name (in Block Letters)	Time of (a) Departure (b) Return	Point of (a) Departure (b) Return
2 Off 15 OR	9·15 pm	(a) Q29a 75
	1 – am	(b) Q29a 75

ACTION OF PATROL (Give map co-ordinates of any posts found, work, patrols encountered etc)

Patrol moved down sunken road to Q23·51 here lights were observed at Q29 b56, a party of 1 off & 5 men went to investigate but no enemy were found.

The whole patrol then moved north along road to Q23 b5.2 Here the patrol split into two parties, one under Lieut FOWKE moving to Q23. b55

The second party under 2nd Lt PERKINS moved further along road to Q23 b8.4; here a volley was fired on them by the enemy (estimated 12 strong) & bombs thrown. Our party opened fire & threw bombs, but as the enemy were behind bank they continued firing & we were forced to withdraw.

One man went to Lieut FOWKE & reported that 2nd Lieut PERKINS party had withdrawn, the enemy were in strength & his party had suffered casualties. Lieut FOWKE party then withdrew to our own line

Casualties 1 man missing believed killed & 1 man wounded

L A Fowke Lt

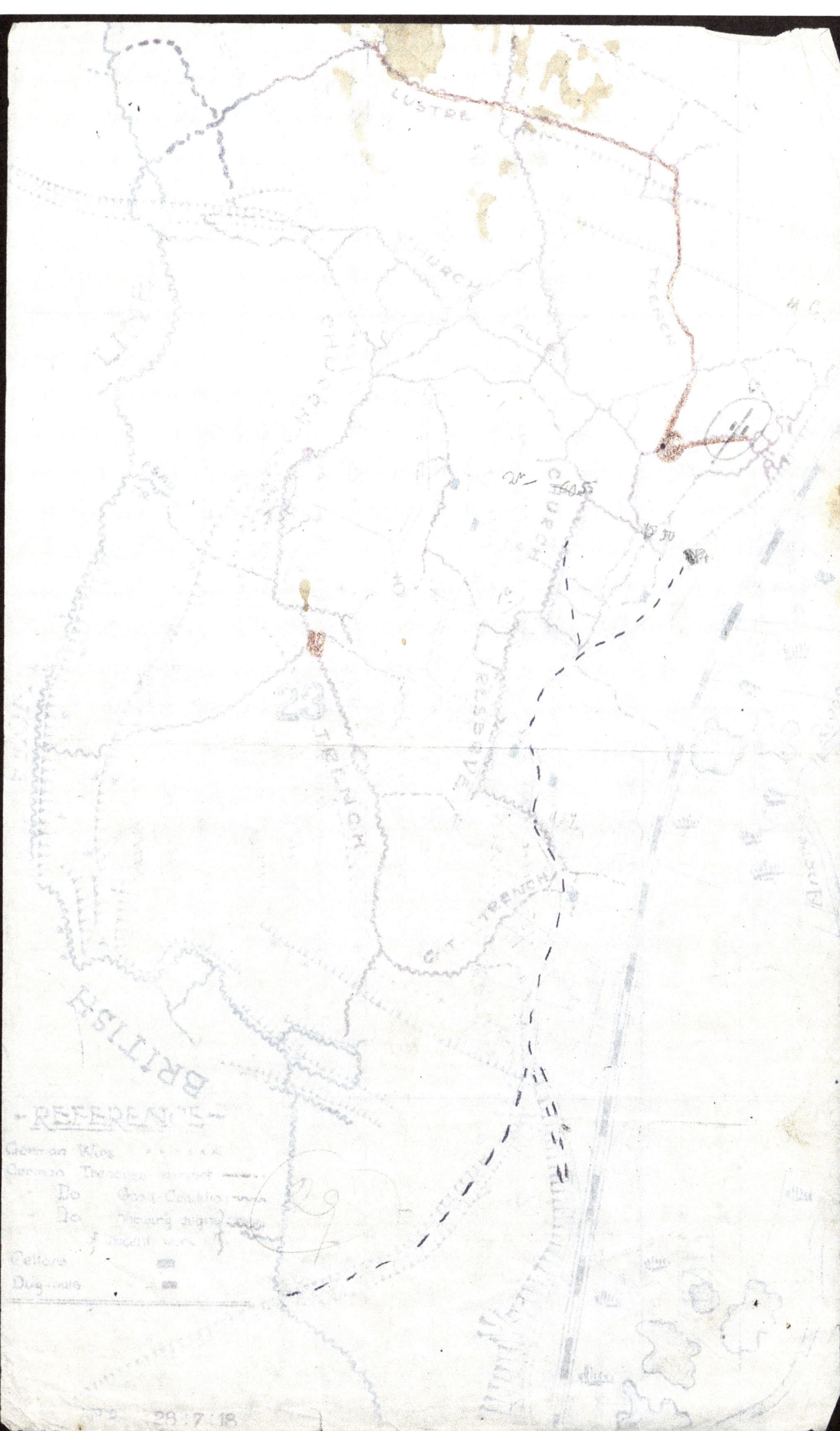

BRITISH
CHURCH TRENCH
23 TRENCH
RESERVE
LUSTRE
REFERENCE
German Wire
Cellars
Dug-outs
28.7.18

Sketch Map No. 2

Enemy encountered 10/8/18

Hamel

AREA - PATROLLED -

Our LINE

Co. H.Q.

No bridge

No bridge

No bridge

Ung 1 & Ung 17th

Sketch Map No 1

Purple Line Dispositions

Shewn – 1 Coy B.HQ

B.H.Q. –
Coy H.Q. –
Dispositions ... Posts
... H.Q.

Right Battn

Change in Dispositions – Platoons –

BRIGADE NORTHERN BOUNDARY

INTER – BATTN BOUNDARY

BRIGADE SOUTHERN BOUNDARY

1 Coy

1 Coy

1 Coy

1 Coy

1 Coy

– ½ Forceville 12"/12th Can.

C

2 Plts

2 Plts

O.P

unchanged 3 Plts

1 Plt

Sketch Map No. 1

Lt Mc[illegible]

8. GUIDES.

Guides (1 per Coy H.Q. and 1 per Platoon) from 1st Wilts Regt will report at present "B" Coy H.Q. at 11.p.m. for "A" "B" and "C" Coys.

O.C. "D" Coy will arrange for his advance party to act as guides.

9. ADVANCE PARTIES.

1 Officer Coy and 1 N.C.O. per Platoon will report to the Adjutant 1st Bn Wilts Regt at 2.30.p.m.

2/Lieut STU[illegible] M.G. will take over for Battn H.Q. 2/Lt [illegible]

10. TRENCH STORES.

All Trench Stores maps etc will be taken over.

11. RECEIPTS.

Receipts for Trench Stores taken over and handed over will be sent to Battn H.Q. by 12 noon 12th inst.

12. RATIONS.

Rations will be handed over to advance parties in new positions. Officers i/c advance parties will arrange to have gu[illegible] at [illegible] H.Q. [illegible]

13. WORKING PARTIES.

Details of working parties will be issued under separate cover.

14. RELIEF COMPLETE.

Relief complete will be reported by runner as Companies move out.

15. ACKNOWLEDGE.

[illegible signature]

Capt & Adjt.
JOKE.

Copy No 1....O.C. "A" Coy.
2.....O.C. "B" Coy.
3.....O.C. "C" Coy.
4.....O.C. "D" Coy.
5.....1st Battn Wilts Regt.
6.....T.O. and Q.M.
7.....War Diary.
8.....Office and File.

O.O. Operation Order No 51. Copy No..../....

SE C R E T. Reference Map 57D.S.E. 10th August 1918.

1. The Battn will be relieved by 1st Battn Wiltshire Regiment tomorrow 11th inst.

Coys will be relieved as follows:-

7th Leic.Regt.		1st Wilts Regt.
"A" Coy will be relieved by		"C" Coy.
"B" " " " " "		"B" Coy.
"C" " " " " "		"A" Coy.
"D" " " " " "		"D" Coy.

2. GUIDES.

Guides to the scale of 1 per Coy H.Q. and 1 per Platoon will be provided as follows:-

7th Leic Regt.	Time.	Rendezvous.
"A" Coy.	10.15.p.m.	"A" Coy H.Q. (old Left Bn H.Q.)
"B" Coy.	10.15.p.m.	-do-

Guides from "C" and "D" Coys will not be required. Each guide will be in possession of a slip of paper showing Coy and No of Platoon.

3. ADVANCE PARTIES.

Advance parties of 1 Officer per Coy and 1 N.C.O. per Platoon. [illegible] from 1st Battn Wilts Regt will report at Coy H.Q. at 2.30.p.m.

4. TRENCH STORES, MAPS etc.

Trench Stores will be carefully checked and handed over, and receipts obtained.

A list of stores in possession of Coys is attached. All deficiencies will be explained.

Details of work in hand, aeroplane photographs, maps etc will be handed over.

5. WATER TINS.

All water tins will be collected and sent out on limbers.

6. LIMBERS.

One limber per ~~Coy~~ Coy's kit, Officers' Trench kit and Mess kit will report at each Coy H.Q. at 9.30. p.m.

Transport Officer will arrange to send one limber to Battn H.Q. at 9.p.m. for canteen stores, mess kit etc.

7. On relief, Battn will move to positions occupied by 1st Wilts Regt. Dispositions will be as follows:-

7th Leic Regt.		1st Wilts Regt.	Position.
"A" Coy	relieves	"D" Coy	FORCEVILLE.
"D" Coy	"	"A" Coy.	PURPLE LINE (LEFT)
"B" Coy	"	"B" Coy	-do- (central)
"C" Coy.	"	"C" Coy.	-do- (RIGHT)

Battn H.Q. - Q.19.b.60.55.

P.T.O.

O.C. "A" Coy.
2/Lieut L.A.FOWKE.
Intelligence Officer.
T.45.

PATROL ORDER. NIGHT 9/10th.

STRENGTH. 1 Officer (2/Lieut FOWKE) and one Platoon strength not to exceed 25 men and one Officer for instructio (2/Lieut VOCE)

OBJECT. To encounter enemy patrols, obtain identifications, and to reconnoitre enemy posts.

TIME. 9.15.p.m.

ROUTE INSTRUCTIONS.

OBJECTIVE 1.
Road Junction 23.d.4.90. clearing CHURCH RESERVE with a detached section.

OBJECTIVE 2.
Communication Trench running E.S.E. from CHURCH RESERVE 23.[illegible].b.60.60 via CHURCH RESERVE and ROAD.

OBJECTIVE 3.
Reconnoitre Trench Junction 23.b.70.70 and CUTTING 23.b.45.50.

The patrol should wait at points mentioned in Objectives 1 and 2 in order to ambush any enemy patrols that may be out.
If no enemy are found points in objective 3 will be reconnoitred
Return by same route.

PASSWORD "SUGAR.

6th Battn Password. TIGER.

9.8.18.

Major.
Cmmdg 7th Battn Leic Regt.

The Battalion will move to [illegible] positions in the Support Line today, movement [illegible] will be by sections at [illegible] interval.

"C" Coy. First section will move at 1-30 pm.

"A" Coy. First section will move at 2 pm.

D Coy. First section will move at 4-30 pm.

Hqrs. First section will move at 3 pm.

ROUTE.

CHARLES AVENUE – 4 Stks.
Thence East to Support Line by ground or trackway parallel to road.

All movement in front of 4 Stks will be by CHARLES AVENUE.

Section Commanders must be warned that they must keep to the trench and no man must be allowed on the track under any circumstances.

(7) [illegible] could be secured
with [illegible] a position [illegible] TNE
Further particulars will be [illegible]
later.

DIXIES [illegible] to be carried by the
[illegible] the remainder [illegible]
dumped at a point [illegible] CHURCH
AVENUE [illegible] the [illegible]

The Battalion Intelligence Officer will
arrange for [illegible] the [illegible]
and for placing [illegible] at [illegible]
points on the [illegible].

H. [illegible]
Capt. Adjt.
[illegible]

August 16/18

Instructions regarding War Diaries and Intelligence Summaries are contained in F. S. Regs., Part II. and the Staff Manual respectively. Title pages will be prepared in manuscript.

110/51

WAR DIARY or ~~INTELLIGENCE SUMMARY.~~

(Erase heading not required.)

Army Form C. 2118.

Vol 36

Place	Date	Hour	Summary of Events and Information	Remarks and references to Appendices
W of BEAULENCOURT	Sep 1	–	Quiet – A and D Coys moved to N16d for attack on SUGAR FACTORY – B and C Coys to N19a to support 6th Leic R and 1st Wilts W of BEAULENCOURT in case of enemy counter attack. Bn HQ moved to N15b – Attack on SUGAR FACTORY postponed.	Map Ref 57c SE
	2	3AM	A and D Coys attacked SUGAR FACTORY from North. Assembly position S edge of BEAULENCOURT astride BAUPAUME – LE TRANSLOY Rd. Attack successful.	
		4.30AM	Enemy counter attacked – Companies driven back to line of Assembly positions	
		7AM	SUGAR FACTORY re-taken – 17th DIV went through on S. of FACTORY – enemy evacuated – 3 MGs and approx 40 prisoners taken by Battn. Lt WARREN 2Lt STATHAM – W in A	
		4PM	Battn HQ moved to N24a close to SUGAR FACTORY with Companies in reserve – line LABDA COPSE – O13c to SUGAR FACTORY – N24 A & B – Slight enemy shelling	
	3	4PM	Battn withdrawn into Corps Reserve in Huts N18c. Piano captured & in use	
	4		Battn did not move – Baths, Change of Clothing &c	
	5	5PM	Battn moved to SAILLY SAILLISEL to bivouacks N8c – Corps Reserve	

D. D. & L., London, E.C. (A7883) Wt. W803/M1672 350,000 4/17 Sch. 52a Forms/C2118/14

Instructions regarding War Diaries and Intelligence Summaries are contained in F. S. Regs., Part II. and the Staff Manual respectively. Title pages will be prepared in manuscript.

WAR DIARY
or
~~INTELLIGENCE~~ SUMMARY.
(*Erase heading not required.*)

Army Form C. 2118.

Place	Date	Hour	Summary of Events and Information	Remarks and references to Appendices
SAILLY-SAILLISEL	Sept. 6		Batt^n resting - baths &c Training - moving in Artillery formation - Officers compass march in evening	Map Ref 57^D SE
	7		Training - 6PM - Batt^n moved to MANANCOURT to billets arriving 8PM	
MANANCOURT	8		Training - Hostile H.V. 77 mm shells at intervals on CANAL du NORD & village	Map Ref 57^C S E
	9	5AM	Batt^n moved to ELSOM COPSE in support to attack on HEUDICOURT by 62nd Bde	
		8PM	Batt^n moved to HEUDICOURT to relieve 12/13th N.F in line & to attack at dawn. Night very dark with heavy rain - Hostile shelling on area of village - 2 coys 12/13th N.F unrelieved at 9 AM following day - Attack cancelled.	
HEUDICOURT	10		Situation cleared up as follows. D Coy W.22C. A B & C Coy Railway Cutting W23 a B^n HQ Brickyard HEUDICOURT Two coys 12/13 N.F relieved 8PM - Preparation for attack on line from CHAPEL REDOUBT to R 23d - part of ~~GREEN~~ YELLOW LINE	

D. D. & L., London, E.C. (A7883) Wt. W807/M1672 350,000 4/17 Sch. 52a Forms/C/2118/14

Instructions regarding War Diaries and Intelligence Summaries are contained in F. S. Regs., Part II. and the Staff Manual respectively. Title pages will be prepared in manuscript.

WAR DIARY
or
INTELLIGENCE SUMMARY.
(Erase heading not required.)

Army Form C. 2118.

Place	Date	Hour	Summary of Events and Information	Remarks and references to Appendices
HEUDICOURT	Sept 11	3 AM	Battn attacked ~~GREEN~~ YELLOW LINE successfully - 50 prisoners and 6 M.G.s taken - Touch on S obtained with LONDON Regt. - Touch with N - WILTS Regt established following night. Casualties - 2Lt HAWKES D. of W. - 2Lt BEESLEY, 2Lt WEST - W - in A - OR K. W & M 50.	Map. Ref. 57c S.E.
	12		Battn in line captured. 9 PM Relieved by 6th [illegible] R and moved to SUPPORT position BROWN LINE - Battn HQ W.8.d.8.0 - good relief.	
	13		Enemy attacked 1st [illegible] - flammenwerfer used - attack failed - 11 prisoners taken. Artillery activity on both sides - Dispositions D Coy - REVELON Fm. A Coy - close support C Coy reserve W9c B Coy - in reserve to 6th [illegible] R W22c	[illegible]
	14		Quiet day - M.O. - Capt FISCHELL K - in - A - Hostile bombing activity on back areas.	
	15		Battn relieved by 1st Cameronians - 33rd Div. - Battn moved to ~~[illegible]~~ EQUANCOURT. ~~[illegible]~~ bivouacs Hostile bombing & shelling on back areas unusually active.	

D. D. & L., London, E.C. (A7883) Wt. W803/M1672 350,000 4/17 Sch. 52a Forms/C/2118/14

Army Form C. 2118.

WAR DIARY
or
~~INTELLIGENCE SUMMARY.~~
(*Erase heading not required.*)

Instructions regarding War Diaries and Intelligence Summaries are contained in F. S. Regs., Part II, and the Staff Manual respectively. Title pages will be prepared in manuscript.

Place	Date	Hour	Summary of Events and Information	Remarks and references to Appendices
N. EQUANCOURT	Sep 16		Battn resting - baths &c 8.30 PM. Long range H.V. direct hit on A Coy's K 3 W.in A 7 2 OR	Map Ref 57c SE
	17	1 AM	Cyclone burst on camp - all tents &c blown away - torrential rain - thunder & lightning	
		7 AM	Sun shining. Bn receives orders to take part in attack on 18th Sept. Battn moved to Sunken Rd. W 22 C - assembly position	
	18	3 AM	Battn W22 C in support to 1st Wilts & 6th Lan. R Zero 7.20 AM - Objective line VILLERS GUISLAN - E of EPEHY. From W22 C. battn moved in artillery formation towards reaching RAILWAY TRIANGLE N. of EPEHY at 9 AM - Enemy barrage very close at first but eased off. 64 Bde in CRICKET Tr X19 cent - battn passed through encountering heavy M.G. fire from direction of EPEHY - H.Q established "14 Willows Road" X20 C at 10 AM - battalion in their objective position in same vicinity - Situation obscure - A Coy sent to re-inforce 1st Wilts on ridge X21 a D Coy to get in touch with 62nd Bde on left X14 d - B & C Coys in "14 Willows Road"	

W.C.M.

D. D. & L., London, E.C.
(A7883) Wt. W593/M1672 350,000 4/17 Sch. 52a Forms/C/2118/14

Instructions regarding War Diaries and Intelligence Summaries are contained in F. S. Regs., Part II. and the Staff Manual respectively. Title pages will be prepared in manuscript.

WAR DIARY

~~or~~

~~INTELLIGENCE~~ SUMMARY.

(*Erase heading not required.*)

Army Form C. 2118.

Place	Date	Hour	Summary of Events and Information	Remarks and references to Appendices
14 Willows Rd	Sept 18 Contd	2 PM	Situation on Right obscure - Poplar Tr held by enemy - two battns 58th Div attacking that area - on left 62 Bde held ridge W of VILLERS GUISLAN	Map Ref. 57c SE
		3 AM	A Coy is attacked - enemy driven off - A Coy inflicting heavy casualties on enemy throughout the day - enemy half hearted bombing attacks easily beaten off.	
		6 PM	Battn to attack MEATH POST - attack cancelled - 1st Welsh form defensive flank W & NW of MEATH POST - Intense artillery activity on both sides - 9.5 p.m. supply tank arrived	
	19		Enemy counter attack anticipated but no enemy action follows - artillery activity. Battn relieved by 1st Cameronians - Relief complete 12 M.N. - Battn moved to MANANCOURT to billets	[illegible]
MANANCOURT	20		Rest - Draft 160 O.R. joined battn composed of combed out miners, recruits (19 yrs) and our own gas casualties from ENGLEBELMER 30/7/18	
	21		Rest - Baths & re-formation of Companies.	

D. D. & L., London, E.C. (A7883) Wt. W803/M1672 350,000 4/17 Sch. 52a Forms/C2118/14

Instructions regarding War Diaries and Intelligence Summaries are contained in F. S. Regs., Part II. and the Staff Manual respectively. Title pages will be prepared in manuscript.

WAR DIARY
or
~~INTELLIGENCE SUMMARY.~~
(Erase heading not required.)

Army Form C. 2118.

Place	Date	Hour	Summary of Events and Information	Remarks and references to Appendices
MANANCOURT	Sep 22	10AM	Divine Service - address by Lt Col. Sawyer DSO.	Map Ref 57c SE
	23.		Address by Brig. Gen. Cummings DSO - News received battn to relieve 17th Div in line.	
	24		Address by Maj Gen Campbell CB. DSO - Battn. Congratulated on fine work.	
SOREL.		4PM.	Battn moved to SOREL LE GRAND to billets and bivouacs - night quiet	
	25	7.15PM	Relieved 7th Lincolns & 2 Coys 7th Borders S. of GOUZEAUCOURT in line	
S. of GOUZEAUCOURT	26		Dispositions. BHQ W6d.60. - C Coy QUENTIN REDOUBT - A B & D Coy line of Sunken Road & Rly W.6 b & d. Enemy artillery active on that area.	
	27		No change. Sunken Road W.6 d in filthy state - Many enemy dead unburied. Traverse built to prevent enemy M G fire from GOUZEAUCOURT - No activity shown by enemy from GOUZEAUCOURT since 25th.	
	28	2PM	Battn moved forward - C Coy clearing up QUENTIN REDOUBT - Capturing 1 M G & 7 prisoners - B Coy extending N of C Coy Capturing 2 M. Gs A + D Coys moving N of B Coy - GREEN SWITCH and KENNEL SUPPORT - Casualties slight 2Lt Walker W. & A	

A5834 Wt. W4973/M687 750,000 8/16 D. D. & L. Ltd. Forms/C.2118/13.

Army Form C. 2118.

Instructions regarding War Diaries and Intelligence Summaries are contained in F. S. Regs., Part II. and the Staff Manual respectively. Title pages will be prepared in manuscript.

WAR DIARY
or
INTELLIGENCE SUMMARY.

(*Erase heading not required.*)

Place	Date	Hour	Summary of Events and Information	Remarks and references to Appendices
S of GOUZEACOURT	Sept 29	3AM	Battn held in readiness to attack. B Coy in reserve to 1st Wilts & 6th Leic R. remainder of Battn in support. Attack held up by heavy M.G. fire, but subsequently fairly successful - artillery activity on both sides. Battn in same positions.	Map. Ref 57c S.E.
	30	2PM	Battn pushed through 6th Leic R. A & B Coys in front occupied Green Line from R 34 cent to X 5 a encountering no opposition with exception of light artillery. Patrols pushed forward to CANAL - no enemy encountered on W side of CANAL - QUENTIN -, but all bridges found to be destroyed - one bridge blew up as patrol reached it. Active patrolling during the night - two prisoners captured. Battn. disposed:- Bn H.Q. KITCHEN CRATER R 33 c 7.6 - A C & B Coys in line of trenches R 34 b 9.0 to X 5 c 3 5 with D Coy in support - ROSE SUPPORT.	[signature]

A5834 Wt. W4973/M687 750,000 8/16 D. D. & L. Ltd. Forms/C.2118/13.

Instructions regarding War Diaries and Intelligence Summaries are contained in F. S. Regs., Part II. and the Staff Manual respectively. Title pages will be prepared in manuscript.

WAR DIARY
or
~~INTELLIGENCE~~ SUMMARY.
(Erase heading not required.)

Army Form C. 2118.

Place	Date	Hour	Summary of Events and Information	Remarks and references to Appendices
September			**Drafts**	
			3rd Sept. OR 78	
			16 " 28	
			21 " 160	
			23 " 20	
			286	
			Officers Lt Gabble C.C. 2Lts F.W. Walker, M. Brown, J.C.R. White	
			2Lts J.R. Marshall, C.W. Sheldon, F.L. Chandler, H.D. Varney	
			2Lt A.E. Garner - 17 Sept	
			Capt W.G. Rigby - N. Fus 20th	
			2Lts D.A. Rynie, G.W. Teasdale, L.G. Fisher	
			Casualties.	
			D. of W. 2Lt J.A. HAWKES - 11th Sept	
			W.in.A. Lt WARREN, T.J.R. 2 "	
			" 2Lt L.A. STATHAM 2 "	
			" 2Lt F.A. VOCE 2 "	
			" 2Lt W.H. WEST. 11 "	
			" 2Lt G.W. BEESLEY 11 "	
			" 2Lt W.H. BUCKLER 18 "	
			To Base Lt H.R. GROSS. - W.in.A 2Lt F.W. WALKER	
			OR Killed 34	
			Wounded 231	
			Missing 18	
			283	
			G. Hawes Lt Col Comdg. 1/7th Leic R	

A5834 Wt. W4973/M687 750,000 8/16 D. D. & L. Ltd. Forms/C.2118/13.

110/31

C O N F I D E N T I A L.

Vol 37

WAR DIARY

7th Bn Leicestershire Regiment.

October 1st - 31st 1918.

Army Form C. 2118.

Instructions regarding War Diaries and Intelligence Summaries are contained in F. S. Regs., Part II. and the Staff Manual respectively. Title pages will be prepared in manuscript.

WAR DIARY
or
INTELLIGENCE SUMMARY.
(Erase heading not required.)

Place	Date	Hour	Summary of Events and Information	Remarks and references to Appendices
	Oct 1.		Bn. remained in position of Green Line from TURNSROW to GEORGE ST i.e. R34c to X5a. A C & B Coys in trench R32 b 90 to X5 c 35 with D Coy in support ROSS SUPPORT & Bn HQ KITCHEN CRATER R33 b 76.	Map Ref. 57C SE
	Oct 2		Relieved at night by 1st WILTS & the Bn relieved the 6th LEICS in support Bn HQ being at POPPY POST X2 b 44.	
	Oct 3		Relieved the 1st & 2nd LINCOLNS in line opposite BANTEUX the disposition of the Bn being HQ R27 b 32. B Coy in trenches in southern outskirts of BANTEUX & HQ R30 c 24, D & A in support with their HQ in GONNELIEU BANTEUX road. C in reserve in RIBBLE TRENCH with their HQ R32 d 88.	
	Oct 4		No change. B Coy report enemy mortaring the village; active patrolling.	
	Oct 5		Enemy reported to have withdrawn, so B Coy order to cross canal & occupy HINDENBURG LINE at M33 b 60 to M33 a 89; D Coy M33 a 89 to M27 b 16; A Coy from M27 b 16 to M26 b 58; C Coy 2 platoons in M26 a & 2 platoons in M26 c. Bn HQ R30 b 72	57 B SW

(A7092). Wt. W12839/M1293 75,000. 1/17. D. D. & L., Ltd. Forms/C.2118/14.

Army Form C. 2118.

WAR DIARY
or
~~INTELLIGENCE SUMMARY.~~
(Erase heading not required.)

Instructions regarding War Diaries and Intelligence Summaries are contained in F. S. Regs., Part II. and the Staff Manual respectively. Title pages will be prepared in manuscript.

Place	Date	Hour	Summary of Events and Information	Remarks and references to Appendices
	Oct 6		The 64 Bde having passed through us the Bn remained in the same positions. The Commanding Officer left the Bn for Paris leave Major Sopper MC taking over the Bn during his absence.	
	Oct 7		Bn moved at 10 pm to M 36 a in preparation for attack on BEAUREVOIR LINE.	
	Oct 8	0100	The 1st Wilts attacked at 0100 taking their objective	
		0236	Bn moved off to assembly position in trench running east & west in N 32 a. Hostile machine gun fire was encountered on approaching assembly position & wire found to be uncut.	
		0445	Bn ultimately assembled in trenches running N & S in N 32 a south of C.T. in N 32 a	
		0515	Bn attacked objective with barrage as laid down	
		0730	Bn reached final objective from line running E & W in N 19 c to CT in N 32 a. Prisoners taken over 150 & many machine guns, Casualties fairly light. Bn HQ N 31 a 25 (Sunken road)	
		0800	62nd Bde pushed through 110th Bde. Hostile Artillery very active	
		1200	Bn ordered to concentrate in N 14 a. Bn HQ moved to N 13 d 75	
		1830	Bn moved to sunken road in N 21 a. HQ N 21 a 27. C & B Coys in sunken road. A & D in trench running N & S in N 21 a. Slight gas shelling during the night.	

(A7092). Wt. W12839/M1293. 75,000. 1/17. D. D. & L., Ltd. Forms/C.2118/14.

Army Form C. 2118.

Instructions regarding War Diaries and Intelligence Summaries are contained in F. S. Regs., Part II. and the Staff Manual respectively. Title pages will be prepared in manuscript.

WAR DIARY
or
INTELLIGENCE SUMMARY.
(Erase heading not required.)

Place	Date	Hour	Summary of Events and Information	Remarks and references to Appendices
	Oct 9		Bn remained in same position of H21a Draft of 2 Officers + 49 O.R. arrived	
	Oct 10		Bn moved to & were billeted in CAULLERY for rest and training.	
	Oct 11		Bn Resting, baths & clean clothes for men.	
	Oct 12		Training commenced 2 hrs arms drill, close order drill, Platoon inspections march past. Commencement of special Lewis Gun Class consisting of 32 untrained men under L.G.O. the best 16 to be left on Nucleus, when Bn goes into the line again, for further training. Draft of 1 Off & 26 O.R. arrived	
	Oct 13		Brigade Church Parade	
	Oct 14		Training (2 hrs) Companies under Coy Commanders. Coy Lewis gunners under Coy arrangements. (1 hour) Platoons under Platoon commanders for 1 hour. Subalterns under R.S.M. on Guard mounting.	

(A7092) Wt. W12839/M1293 750,000. 1/17. D. D. & L., Ltd. Forms/C.2118/14.

Instructions regarding War Diaries and Intelligence Summaries are contained in F. S. Regs., Part II. and the Staff Manual respectively. Title pages will be prepared in manuscript.

WAR DIARY
or
INTELLIGENCE SUMMARY.
(Erase heading not required.)

Army Form C. 2118.

Place	Date	Hour	Summary of Events and Information	Remarks and references to Appendices
	Oct 15.		Training 2 hrs 1st period Coys under Coy Commanders Arms drill close order drill. 2nd period Platoons under Platoon commanders. Lecture by Coy Commander to Platoon & Section commanders on Fire control etc.	
	Oct 16		Training 2 hrs. 1st period Coys under Coy Commanders. Practice moving into Artillery formation & open order from column of route. 2nd Period 2 Coys musketry on range (preliminary practice) 2 Coys under Platoon commanders. Major Piper returned & takes over Bn. Major Hopper takes over 6th Bn	
	Oct 17		Bn Parade Advance guard to a Brigade — March past. Officers riding school 2pm to 3pm	
	Oct 19		Bn Parade. Short route march with fighting transport march discipline, March past. Commanding Officer returns from leave.	
	Oct 20		Brigade Church Parade cancelled owing to wet weather	
	Oct 21st		Continuation of training under Coy arrangements.	
			C.O Adjt. and Coy Commanders reconnoitre the line.	
	Oct 22nd		moved up to INCHY in preparation to attack on the 23rd inst later moved up to NEVILLY.	

(A7092). Wt W12839/M1293 75,000. 1/17. D. D. & L., Ltd. Forms/C.2118/14.

Army Form C. 2118.

Instructions regarding War Diaries and Intelligence Summaries are contained in F. S. Regs., Part II. and the Staff Manual respectively. Title pages will be prepared in manuscript.

WAR DIARY
or
INTELLIGENCE SUMMARY.
(Erase heading not required.)

Place	Date	Hour	Summary of Events and Information	Remarks and references to Appendices
	~~Nov~~ Oct. 23rd		Bn: attacked. Capt MacLaren killed.	
			Stayed in OVILLERS the night.	
			Coys concentrated.	
	~~Nov~~ Oct 24th		moved up in Support of 62nd & 64th Bdes	
			Stopped in GREEN LINE F.2.c – F.8.b about 4 hrs then moved	
			forward again to N.W. of POIX du NORD where we stayed until	
			5.30 [illegible] but withdrew to GREEN LINE owing to	Ref Map
			62. Bde being held up. Stayed the night.	51A S.E.
	Oct 25th		B Coy: moved to X 28 a at 0530 hrs to carry on advance	
			guard if enemy had gone. Enemy had not gone.	
			B.H.Q at F.7.a 8.6.	
			Late. Bde moved up to relieve 62nd & 64th Bdes in line.	
			6th Leic: and 1st Wilts in front 7th Leic: in support.	
			B.H.Q at F 7. a 7.5.	
	Oct 26th		Relieved by ⓓ of NS 17th Div: move to camp near	
			AMERVAL. Very good, early relief no shelling.	

(A7092). Wt. W12859/M1293. 75,000. 1/17. D. D. & L., Ltd. Forms/C.2118/14.

Instructions regarding War Diaries and Intelligence Summaries are contained in F. S. Regs., Part II. and the Staff Manual respectively. Title pages will be prepared in manuscript.

WAR DIARY
or
~~INTELLIGENCE SUMMARY.~~
(Erase heading not required.)

Army Form C. 2118.

Place	Date	Hour	Summary of Events and Information	Remarks and references to Appendices
	Oct 27th		Cleaning up and reorganising in camp at AMERVAL.	
	Oct 28th		Cleaning up etc. Draft of 4 Off. & 60 O.R. all old men.	
	Oct 29th		Relieved 11th Div. in line. Relief complete rather late owing to guides getting late, Village heavily shelled from 2300 hrs onwards, also forward areas a little. B.H.Q. at X 28. b. 2. 3.	
	Oct 30th		0400 hrs to 0530 forward areas badly shelled particularly between front and support Coys. no casualties. Village shelled again at night also Bn. H.Q.	Ref Map 51A S.E.
	Oct 31st		Heavy shelling in the early morning owing to attack on right. Bn. H.Q shelled again and moved to X. 28. d. 2. 4 where R.Es built shelter. Dispositions. D Coy along road running N.W & S.E. in X. 17. d. A Coy in same road in X 24. a. Each company with posts forward C in support to D about 300x behind.	

(A7092). Wt W12839/M1293 75,000. 1/17. D. D. & L., Ltd. Forms/C.2118/14.

Army Form C. 2118.

WAR DIARY
or
~~INTELLIGENCE SUMMARY.~~
(Erase heading not required.)

Instructions regarding War Diaries and Intelligence Summaries are contained in F. S. Regs., Part II. and the Staff Manual respectively. Title pages will be prepared in manuscript.

Place	Date	Hour	Summary of Events and Information	Remarks and references to Appendices
	Oct	31st	B Coy in support to A Coy about 400x behind. much quieter night. 2nd Lt. Stubbs wounded.	[illegible]
				[illegible]
			Drafts	
	Oct	6	Lt V C Hales	
		14	2/Lt E G Connold	
		28	Capt E Pearce + 59 O Ranks	
			Lt D Hugh Jones	
			2/Lt W J Dowell MC	
			W H West	
		31	2/Lt J W Walker	
		10	79 O Ranks	
		11	44 —"—	
		12	11 —"—	
			Casualties	
	Oct 1		2/Lt J E R Marshall W – A	
	8		" J R White W – A	
	15		A/Capt E Gribble D of W	
	23		A/Capt M C Maclaren K – A	
			2/Lt J G Winslade W – A	
	24		" C W Shelton W – A	
	25		" M Brown W – A	

O Ranks

Oct 8/9 103 OR (36 K. 46 W. 1 M)

23 120 OR (21 K 98 W 1 M)

G. [illegible] Lt Col
Comd 7th Leic Regt

(A7092). Wt. W12839/M1293 75,000. 1/17. D. D. & L., Ltd. Forms/C.2118/14.

C O N F I D E N T I A L.

WAR DIARY

OF

7th Bn Leicestershire Regiment.

FROM 1st November 1918. TO 30th November 1918.

Instructions regarding War Diaries and Intelligence Summaries are contained in F. S. Regs., Part II. and the Staff Manual respectively. Title pages will be prepared in manuscript.

WAR DIARY
or
~~INTELLIGENCE SUMMARY.~~
(Erase heading not required.)

Army Form C. 2118.

Place	Date	Hour	Summary of Events and Information	Remarks and references to Appendices
	NOV 1st		Bn in line near POIX du NORD.	
			Dispositions:-	
			'D' Coy along road running N.W. & S.E. in X 14. a.	
			'A' Coy same road in X 24. a.	
			Each coy with post forward.	
			'C' in support to 'D' about 300x behind.	
			'B' " " 'A' " 400x "	
		1430hrs	Bn sidesteps to the right, the dispositions then being:	
			'A' as before LEFT FRONT.	
			'D' move to CENTRE FRONT.	
			'C' move to RIGHT FRONT.	
			'B' as before in SUPPORT.	
			Day quiet. M.Gs active at night.	
	NOV 2nd		Day quiet in front. Bn H.Q. shelled.	
			Bn was relieved at night by the Manchester ~~Fus~~ Regt.	
			'B' Coy late owing to guides getting lost.	
			Move into billets at OVILLERS. Roads shelled during the relief.	
	NOV 3rd		Bn cleaning up etc: in billets at OVILLERS.	
			Receive orders to take part in attack through FOREST DE MORMAL.	

Instructions regarding War Diaries and Intelligence Summaries are contained in F. S. Regs., Part II. and the Staff Manual respectively. Title pages will be prepared in manuscript.

WAR DIARY
or
~~INTELLIGENCE SUMMARY.~~
(Erase heading not required.)

Army Form C. 2118.

Place	Date	Hour	Summary of Events and Information	Remarks and references to Appendices
	NOV. 4th	1300hrs	Bn: move to concentration area F.5.C. Order of march H.Q. A. B. C. D Coys.	
		1630hrs	Bn: move to billets in FUTOY. Stayed the night.	
	NOV 5th	0615hrs	Move up through FORET DE MORMAL to pass through the 62nd Bde and resume the attack on the BLACK LINE (near LA TETE NOIRE) 62 Bde: push on to BERLAIMONT and in consequence 110th Bde march into LA TETE NOIRE as a Bde: Order of march of Bn through FORET de MORMAL. A B C D Coys H.Q. Sect 110th T.M.B. Bn stayed the night at LA TETE NOIRE. Enemy shelled the village slightly. Reconnoitre the HIGH GROUND T 23 b. facing N.E. for positions in case enemy counter attacks.	Ref MAP SHEET 51 S.W.
	NOV 6th		110th Bde: resume attack over SAMBRE RIVER.	
		0415hrs	Bn: move from LA TETE NOIRE in support to 6th LEIC and 1st WILTS. To cross the RIVER SAMBRE by bridge head secured by 62nd Bde: at LOCK U. 21. c. 4. 2.	
		0550hrs	Two front Bns across RIVER followed by A Coy. Held up on EASTERN BANK by enemy M.G.S and ARTILLERY FIRE.	
		1130hrs	Attack planned to relieve situation. Bn: to cross RIVER SAMBRE by PONTOON BRIDGE U. 24. a. 2. 5. Object of attack HIGH GROUND in U. 22. b.	
		1215hrs	B. C. D Coys across RIVER and A Coy moved along RIVER BANK into following dispositions B LEFT FRONT — A RIGHT FRONT D LEFT SUPPORT — C RIGHT SUPPORT Bn H.Q at U.20.a.9.4.	

Instructions regarding War Diaries and Intelligence Summaries are contained in F. S. Regs., Part II. and the Staff Manual respectively. Title pages will be prepared in manuscript.

WAR DIARY
or
~~INTELLIGENCE SUMMARY.~~
(Erase heading not required.)

Army Form C. 2118.

Place	Date	Hour	Summary of Events and Information	Remarks and references to Appendices
	NOV 6 Cont.			
		1330 hrs	Coys: reported starting well.	
		1400 hrs	" GAMPIN ROAD PASSED.	Ref SHEET 51. S.W.
		1420 hrs	" LE BOUVIER ROAD PASSED.	
		1515 hrs	" HIGH GROUND U 23 central reached. Bn digging in.	
			Bn H.Q established at U. 24. b. 9.9.	
		1520 hrs	6th LEIC and 1st WILTS move up to this line.	
		1430 hrs	Bn withdrew into Support along road in U. 22 b.	
	NOV 7th	0545 hrs	Bn: resume attack on RED LINE (running through centre of Squares 9. 15 & 21) Passing through 6th LEIC and taking front line Bn: with 1st WILTS on LEFT. Enemy withdrew. Bn move up to RED LINE and dig in. Much artillery fire and M.G fire in new positions.	Ref MAP SHEET 51 1/40000
		0830 hrs	64th Bde pass through to attack BLUE LINE	
		0900	Bn H.Q opened near CHURCH. BACHANT. BACHANT shelled heavily during the day.	
		2015	Bn: withdrew to AULNOYE in billets.	
	NOV 8th	0815	Bn: moved to BERLAIMONT in billets. Day spent in cleaning up etc:	
	NOV 9th		Bn at BERLAIMONT. Cleaning up etc:	
	NOV 10th			

(A7092). Wt W12839/M1293 750,000. 1/17. D. D. & L., Ltd. Forms/C.2118/14.

Instructions regarding War Diaries and Intelligence Summaries are contained in F. S. Regs., Part II. and the Staff Manual respectively. Title pages will be prepared in manuscript.

Army Form C. 2118.

WAR DIARY
or
INTELLIGENCE SUMMARY.
(Erase heading not required.)

Place	Date	Hour	Summary of Events and Information	Remarks and references to Appendices
	NOV 11th	1100 hrs	ARMISTICE WITH GERMANY.	
		1300 hrs	Bn on march to BEAUFORT Order of march H.Q. 'A' 'B' 'C' 'D' Coys.	
	NOV 12th		Bn at BEAUFORT. Day spent in cleaning up.	
	NOV 13th		" " " 2 hours parade under coy arrangements.	
	NOV 14th		" " " do	
		0900 TO 0945	Physical Training Close order and Saluting drill.	
		0945 TO 1030	Coys under Coy Commanders Close order drill.	
		1045 TO 1145	Specialist Training under Coy Commanders.	
		1200 TO 1300	Battalion Drill.	
		1430 TO 1600	Recreational Training Inter-Platoon Football Competition	

(A7092). Wt. W12839/M1293. 75,000. 1/17. D. D. & L., Ltd. Forms/C.2118/14.

Army Form C. 2118.

WAR DIARY
or
~~INTELLIGENCE SUMMARY.~~
(Erase heading not required.)

Instructions regarding War Diaries and Intelligence Summaries are contained in F. S. Regs., Part II. and the Staff Manual respectively. Title pages will be prepared in manuscript.

Place	Date	Hour	Summary of Events and Information	Remarks and references to Appendices
BEAUFORT	Nov 15th		Bn. still at BEAUFORT. Training as on the 14th inst:	
"	Nov 16th	0900 to 1230	The Bn: took part in Brigade Ceremonial Parade on Bde Parade Ground at V. 15. d. 6. 4. Dress. belt, sidearms and rifles. Caps	SHEET 51 / 1/40000.
"	Nov 17th	1030.	The Bn: took part in Brigade Divine Service on the Square BEAUFORT.	
"	Nov 18th		Bn took part in Brigade Route March. Start 0900 hrs. Dress. Fighting order - i.e. Pack to contain jerkin, waterproof sheet, iron rations, 1 pair of socks and cleaning kit. Caps. Route. Road junction W. 16. c. - Road junction W. 23. c. 9. 8. - Road junction W. 23. b. 25. 25. - Cross tracks W. 24. a. 25. 00. - Road junction W. 15. d. 6. 6. - DAMOUSIES - Cross Roads O. 36. c. 25. 50. - Cross Roads W. 4. b. 6. 4. - MARLUERE - Road junction W. 9. c. - BILLETS. Afternoon. Inter Company football matches.	"
"	Nov 19th		Training as on the 14th inst. 0900 hrs TO 1300 hrs. Tactical Exercises. Junior Officers and N.C.Os under Coy: Com: 1430 hrs TO 1600 hrs.	
"	Nov 20th		Training as on the 14th. Afternoon inter-company cross country run.	
		0900 to 1145	Coys: at disposal of Coy. Com:	
		1200 to 1300	As per programme. C Coy D. Coy B. H Q Afternoon cross country run.	

(A7092). Wt. W12839/M1293. 75,000. 1/17. D. D. & L., Ltd. Forms/C.2118/14.

Army Form C. 2118.

Instructions regarding War Diaries and Intelligence Summaries are contained in F. S. Regs., Part II. and the Staff Manual respectively. Title pages will be prepared in manuscript.

WAR DIARY
or
INTELLIGENCE SUMMARY.
(Erase heading not required.)

Place	Date	Hour	Summary of Events and Information	Remarks and references to Appendices
BEAUFORT	NOV 21st	0900 TO 1300	Bn training as before. Afternoon inter-platoon football match.	
"	NOV 22nd	0900 TO 1000	Platoons & Coys at disposal of Coy: Com:	
		1000 TO 1245	Coys under Coy: Com: in attack formation in small units.	
		1100 TO 1145	Specialists training under Coy: Com: S.Bs. under M.O.	
		1200 TO 1300	Bn: Ceremonial Drill. Football and Cross Country Run in the afternoon.	
	NOV 23	0930 TO 1230	Brigade Ceremonial Drill.	
			Church Parade in Concert Hall.	
	NOV 24th		Brigade Route march Cancelled owing to bad weather.	
	NOV 25		Coys at disposal of Coy Com:	
			Captain H. R. Horne M.C. appointed Imprest Holder for the Bn:	
	NOV 26th	0900 TO 1200	Bn: carried out a route march. Dress full marching order. Order of march. Drums 'B' 'C' 'D' 'A' Coys:	
			MAJOR T. C. HOWITT. D.S.O awarded CROIX de CHEVALIER de LEGION d'HONNEUR.	
			NO 5 PLATOON WON BN INTER PLATOON CHAMPIONSHIP BEATING NO 10. 4 goals to 0.	

A7092 Wt. W128 9/M1293 750,000. 1/17. D. D & I. Ltd. Forms/C2118/14.

Army Form C. 2118.

Instructions regarding War Diaries and Intelligence Summaries are contained in F. S. Regs., Part II. and the Staff Manual respectively. Title pages will be prepared in manuscript.

WAR DIARY
or
~~INTELLIGENCE~~ SUMMARY.

(*Erase heading not required.*)

Place	Date	Hour	Summary of Events and Information	Remarks and references to Appendices
BEAUFORT	NOV 24th	0900 to 1130	Bn: training as per programme.	
		1200 to 1300	Company Drill under Coy: Com:	
"	NOV 28th	0900 to 1045	Inspection of Companies by Commanding Officer.	
		1100 to 1145	Specialist training under Coy: Com:	
		1200 to 1300	R. S. M's Parade. Bn: Close Order Drill.	
			2nd LIEUT: BONE and Billeting Party left for new area.	
	NOV 29th	0930 to 1230	Bn carried out a route march. Full marching order. leather jerkins carried outside pack, under waterproof sheet.	
"	NOV 30th	1000 to 1130	Bn took part in a Brigade Close Order Drill Parade on Bn Parade Ground. Dress. Belt and Sidearms, with rifles. Steel Helmets. The weather was very unfavourable for drill, being very cold and misty.	

G. H. Sawyer Lt. Col.
Comdg 7th Leic: Rgt.

A7092 Wt. W123.9/M1293 750,000. 1/17. D. D & L. Ltd. Forms/C2118/14.

Instructions regarding War Diaries and Intelligence Summaries are contained in F. S. Regs., Part II. and the Staff Manual respectively. Title pages will be prepared in manuscript.

WAR DIARY
or
~~INTELLIGENCE SUMMARY.~~
(Erase heading not required.)

Army Form C. 2118.

Place	Date	Hour	Summary of Events and Information	Remarks and references to Appendices
			NOVEMBER 1918.	
			DRAFTS.	
			52 O.R. 3/11/18. 92 O.R 10/11/18 30 O.R. 19/11/18. 65 O.R. 25/11/18.	
			Lt. H. C. DAVIS 2Lt. T. H. GRIFFITHS. " R. S. POOLE. " F. A. VOCE. " E. L. RAE. " L. G. COLEMAN. } 25/11/18.	
			" J. BEARSMORE. 30/11/18. " H CLARKE. 29/11/18.	
			CASUALTIES.	
			2 O.R. W. in A. 2/11/18 44 O.R. (10 K. 34 W. in A.) 4/11/18. Lt. V. C. HALES. W in A. 4/11/18. 2Lt. PEAKMAN. TO ENG: (S) 3/11/18. 2nd LT STUBBS W in " 3/11/18.	
			G. H. Sawyer [?] Lt. Col. Commanding 4th Lac: Regt:	

(A7092). Wt. W12839/M1293. 75,000. 1/17. D. D. & L., Ltd. Forms/C.2118/14.

CONFIDENTIAL.

WAR DIARY

OF

7th Bn Leicestershire Regiment.

FROM:- 1st December 1918. TO:- 31st December 1918.

Army Form C. 2118.

Instructions regarding War Diaries and Intelligence Summaries are contained in F. S. Regs., Part II. and the Staff Manual respectively. Title pages will be prepared in manuscript.

WAR DIARY
or
INTELLIGENCE SUMMARY.
(Erase heading not required.)

Place	Date	Hour	Summary of Events and Information	Remarks and references to Appendices
BEAUFORT.	DEC. 1st		BATTALION IN REST BILLETS.	SHEET 51
			Church Parade.	
		1100.	Companies marched to Theatre, BEAUFORT independantly for Church Service at 1100 hours. C. of E. Nonconformists also in the Theatre at 1000 hours.	1/40000.
	2nd	0925	Battn took part in Bde Route March. Passed Starting Point at 09.25 hours. Arrived back in billets 1300 hours. Order of March. Drums. A.B.C.D. Dress : Full Marching Order. ROUTE. LE PAYE - X roads Q.20,a, - FERRIERE LE GRAND - X roads Q.23c50.45 - LE CHAMP DE LOUP - MARLIERE - BEAUFORT.	
			Afternoon devoted to Recreational Training - Div. Concert appeared in Theatre.	
	3rd	0700	HIS MAJESTY THE KING visited the area passing PONT SUR SAMBRE at 10.15.hours. The Battalion left Beaufort at 0700 hours in order to be present and cheer the King.	
	4th	0900.	Battalion Training.	
		0900-1045	Platoon and Company Drill.	
		1100-1145	Specialist Training under Company arrangements.	
		1200-1300.	Battalion Drill Parade.	
	5th		Battalion carried out a Route March. Time09.30 hrs. Order of March C.D.Drms A.B. Dress Full marching order. Route: MARLIERE - LE CHAMP DE LOUP - X rds Q23c50.45 FERREIERE LE GRAND - X rds Q20a - LE PAYE - BEAUFORT.	
	6th		Battalion Training as for December 4th.	
	7th		Battn took part in Bde Ceremonial Parade on 7th Battn Parade Ground W7b at 1000 hours. Dress: Belt and Side Arms, Rifle and Steel Helmets.	
	8th		Church Parade. C of E at 11.15 hrs in the Theatre BEAUFORT. Companies marched there independently. Nonconformists at 1030 hours.	
		1415	Battn played the 1st Wilts Regt at Football. Battn won 4 - 2.	

(A7092). Wt. W12839/M1293. 75,000. 1/17. D. D. & L., Ltd. Forms/C.2118/14.

Army Form C. 2118.

Instructions regarding War Diaries and Intelligence Summaries are contained in F. S. Regs., Part II. and the Staff Manual respectively. Title pages will be prepared in manuscript.

WAR DIARY
or
INTELLIGENCE SUMMARY.
(Erase heading not required.)

Place	Date	Hour	Summary of Events and Information	Remarks and references to Appendices
BEAUFORT	9th		Bde Route March.- Battalion took part in Brigade Route March. Time 09.30 hrs. Dress - Fighting Order with Steel Helmets. Order of March Drums C.D.A.B.	
			Officers Class commenced.	
	10th		Battalion Training.	
		0900-1045	Platoon and Company Training.	
		1100-1145	Specialists under O. C. Coys.	
		1200-1300	Adjutants Drill Parade on Battn Parade Ground.	
	11th		Battalion Training as for 10th only alteration R.S.M.s Parade from 1200-1300 h Battalion bathed.	
	12th		Battalion Training as for 11th only alteration Battn Drill 1200-1300 hrs by C.O.	
	13th	0900-1100	Companies inspected in Full Marching Order by O. C. Coys. Remainder of Parades as for 12th.	
BERLIAMENT	14th		The 110th Inf. Bde commenced to move to the CAVILLON area by march route and bus. The 7th Battn marched to BERLIAMENT. Starting Point Hd of Column BEAUFORT CHURCH - Time 0945 hours. Order of March HQ A.B.C.D. - Dress Full Marching Order. Route. LIMONT FONTAINE - rd running through 2nd N in Limont Fontaine - rd running S.W. through BACHANT to rd junction 500 yds S.E. of E in AULNOYE thence W through AULNOYE crossing river by Bridge 300 yds W of C in lock - Transport in rear of the Battalion - 2/Lt A.J. Knight i/c Billeting Party. The Men had a hot meal on arrival in Billets, which were quitegoodMen marched well, and it was quite interesting coming back through our old Battlefields BACHANT - AULNOYE -BERLIAMENT.	
VENDEGIES	15th		The Battalion continued the march to VENDEGIES. Starting Point, Berliament Church - Time 0900 hours - Order of March A.B.C.D.HQ Dress as on 14th inst. ROUTE,-OVILLERS,-AMERVAL, thence NEUVILLY,-INCHY. NOTES. Short march, roads very bad also weather, Billets none toogood, Once again we knew the country quite well. On arrival at INCHY we marched past the BRIGADIER.	

W1293 75,000. 1/17. D. D. & L., Ltd. Forms/C.2118/14.

Instructions regarding War Diaries and Intelligence Summaries are contained in F. S. Regs., Part II. and the Staff Manual respectively. Title pages will be prepared in manuscript.

WAR DIARY
or
INTELLIGENCE SUMMARY.
(Erase heading not required.)

Army Form C. 2118.

Place	Date	Hour	Summary of Events and Information	Remarks and references to Appendices
VENDEGIES.	15th		The Battalion continued the move to VENDEGIES. Starting Point - Berliament Church - time 0900 hours - Order of March A.B.C.D.HQ. Dress as on 14th inst. Route - LOCQUIGNOL - X roads 5/8 mile N of Q in LOCQUIGNOL thence W to Road junction 1/2 mile N.E. of last E in ENGLEFONTAINE - POIX DI NORD - Road junction 5/8 mile E of last E of NEUVILLE thence S to VENDEGIES. NOTES: It was a long march - no men fell out - The Battalion march Past by the Commanding Officer was very good. Billets were not very good. Roads were in a bad state. Again it was a very interesting march especially through the FORET DE MORMAL.	SHEET 51 1/40000
INCHY	16th		The Battalion continued the march to INCHY. Starting Point: Head of Column B.H.Q. 09.55 hours - Order of March B.C.Drums D.HQ.A. Dress as for 14th. Route : OVILLERS -AMERVAL &thence NEUVILLY - INCHY. NOTES. Short march - roads very bad also weather; billets were none too good. and again we knew the country quite well. On arrival at INCHY we marched past the Brigadier	

(A7092). Wt W12839/M1293 750,000. 1/17. D. D. & L., Ltd. Forms/C.2118/14.

Instructions regarding War Diaries and Intelligence Summaries are contained in F. S. Regs., Part II. and the Staff Manual respectively. Title pages will be prepared in manuscript.

WAR DIARY
or
INTELLIGENCE SUMMARY.
(Erase heading not required.)

Army Form C. 2118.

Place	Date	Hour	Summary of Events and Information	Remarks and references to Appendices
INCHY	16th		For the three days marching the 6th. and 7th. massed "Drums".	SHEET 51
FERRIERES	17th		The Battalion continued to move to FERRIERES (Cavillon Area) by bus. Starting Point INCHY CHURCH - Order of March HQ.A.B.C.D. Dress as for 14th. Rationsfor 2 days. Route & CAMBRAI - BOIS - LATEAU - GOUZEAUCOURT - METZ - BAPAUME - ALBERT -AMIENS -FERRIERES. The Battalion was embussed by 06.15 hours and moved off at 06.35 hours. It was intensely cold. A number of busses broke down, however the Battalion was reported present at 2200 hours. Billets very poor on the whole, "C" & "D" Coys in the Chateau, HQ, "A"&"B" in Barns.	1/40,000. AMIENS 1/100,000
	18th		One hours P.T. during the morning and a lecture by Doctor to all Companies on Sanitation.	
	19th		One hours P.T. during the morning, remainder spent in cleaning equipment,etc. Lecture to all companies by the Medical Officer.	
	20th		Training as for 19th.- Recreational Traing in the Afternoon. Troops allowed to use the School in the evening for letter writing. etc.	
	21st		Training as for December 20th. 1918.	
	22nd		Church Parades in the School - The Battalion bathed and clean clothing issued. Inter-Company League resumed "A" v "C" "C" won. Sports Meeting held at Estaminet MOREL at 17.30 hours. Major. H.W.H. Tyler. M.C. - President.	
	23rd	0900-1000. 1045-1145	Physical Training. Battalion Drill Parade - Ground (Battn) Just E of the AILLY -SUR-SOMME Road - Northern outskirts of the village.	
	24th		Companies carried out 1 hours P.T.	
	25th		<u>CHRISTMAS DAY.</u> Voluntary Church Services in the School at 09.45 hours. R.C. Mass in Ferrieres Church at 0900 hours. Football Match - Officers v Sergts. Result : 4 - 1.	

(A7092). Wt. W12839/M1293 75,000. 1/17. D. D. & L., Ltd. Forms/C.2118/14.

Instructions regarding War Diaries and Intelligence Summaries are contained in F. S. Regs., Part II. and the Staff Manual respectively. Title pages will be prepared in manuscript.

WAR DIARY
or
~~INTELLIGENCE SUMMARY.~~
(Erase heading not required.)

Army Form C. 2118.

Place	Date	Hour	Summary of Events and Information	Remarks and references to Appendices
FERRIERES	Dec. 25th		Christmas Dinner for all Troops - The afternoon Football Match 50 aside. Sergts had their dinner in the Sergts Mess.	AMIENS, 1/100,000
	26th		General Holiday. Officers Dinner.	
	27th		Route March ordered but cancelled owing to the weather.	
	28th		Companies under Company arrangements - 1 hours Physocal Training carried out.	
	29th	1000 1100	Voluntary Church Services in the School. Voluntary Church services (Noncomformist) in the School. FOOTBALL- LEAGUE. "C" v "B" Result "C" won.	
	30th	1000	Battn. Paper chase from Battn. Parade GRound. Officers acting as HARES with 5 minutes start - 10 Francs for any N.C.O. or Man catching a HARE. All HARES were caught with the exception of two,	
	31st		Companies under Comoany arrangements - 1 hours P.T. to be carried out. Football "C" v"D" - "C" Coy won 7 - 2.	

(A7092). Wt. W12839/M1293. 75,000. 1/17. D. D. & L., Ltd. Forms/C.2118/14.

Army Form C. 2118.

Instructions regarding War Diaries and Intelligence Summaries are contained in F. S. Regs., Part II. and the Staff Manual respectively. Title Pages will be prepared in manuscript.

WAR DIARY
or
~~INTELLIGENCE SUMMARY~~
(Erase heading not required.)

Place	Date	Hour	Summary of Events and Information	Remarks and references to Appendices
FERRIERES			DECEMBER 1918	
			DRAFTS 25 O.R. 8/12/18 2Lt W.H. Lobb 4/12/18 2Lt C.W. Shelton 14/12/18	
			DEPARTURE 50 O.R. (MINERS) to ENGLAND 4-12-18 101 " " " " 6-12-18	
			J.W.H. Tyler Major Commanding 7th Leic Regt	

2449 Wt. W14957/M90 750,000 1/16 J.B.C. & A. Forms/C.2118/12.

C O N F I D E N T I A L.

WAR DIARY

OF

7th Batt. Leicestershire Regiment.

FROM:- 1st January 1919. TO:- 31st January 1919.

Instructions regarding War Diaries and Intelligence Summaries are contained in F. S. Regs., Part II. and the Staff Manual respectively. Title pages will be prepared in manuscript.

WAR DIARY
or
INTELLIGENCE SUMMARY.
(Erase heading not required.)

Army Form C. 2118.

Place	Date	Hour	Summary of Events and Information	Remarks and references to Appendices
			War Diary	
			7th Battn Leicestershire Regiment	
			January 1919	

D. D. & L., London, E.C.
(A8001) Wt. W1771/M2031 750,000 5/17 Sch. 52 Forms C2118/14

Instructions regarding War Diaries and Intelligence Summaries are contained in F. S. Regs., Part II: and the Staff Manual respectively. Title pages will be prepared in manuscript.

WAR DIARY
or
~~INTELLIGENCE SUMMARY.~~
(Erase heading not required.)

Army Form C. 2118.

Place	Date	Hour	Summary of Events and Information	Remarks and references to Appendices
Ferrieres	Jan 1st		A General Holiday was observed.	
	Jan 2.	9.00 10 10–	Spent cleaning up.	
		10–10.30	Company Inspection	
		11.30	Batt Drill Parade	
			Batt v. 1st Wilts at Soccer was a draw 1 goal each.	
	Jan 3.	1000	Company Cmdrs inspected companies, inspection followed by 3/4 hrs P.T.	
		8.45	A working party of 2 Officers + 60 Other Ranks reported to OC 147 Coy RE. at Concentration Camp E of Saveuse on Saveuse – Amiens Road, for unloading etc. C Coy played D Coy at Soccer. 'D' Coy 1. 'C' Coy nil.	
	Jan 4.	9.00	The Batt. marched to ground near Aeroplane Hangars near Bovelles for inspection by G.O.C. 21st Division.	

D. D. & L., London, E.C.
(A8001) Wt. W1771/M2031 750,000 5/17 Sch. 52 Forms C2118/14

Instructions regarding War Diaries and Intelligence Summaries are contained in F. S. Regs., Part II. and the Staff Manual respectively. Title pages will be prepared in manuscript.

WAR DIARY
or
INTELLIGENCE SUMMARY.
(Erase heading not required.)

Army Form C. 2118.

Place	Date	Hour	Summary of Events and Information	Remarks and references to Appendices
Ferriers	Jan 5.		Church Parade	
		10.00	C. of E. Voluntary Service in the school at Ferrieres	
		10.30	R.C. In Church at Boveller	
		11.00	N. Con. In School at Ferrieres	
	Jan 6	10.00	A working party found by "C" Coy, of 2 Officers + 60 O.Rs reported to O.C. 147 Coy R.E at Concentration Camp.	
		9.30 to 12.00	Education.	
		9.30	Officers Class for week 6.1.1919 – 11.1.19 commenced.	
	Jan 7.	9.30	Education.	
			"B" Coy. found working party for Concentration Camp as for the 6th inst	
		9.00	"A" Coy found party for Salvage of barbed wire + stakes in Ferrieres Area	
		9.30–10.00	"C" + "D" Coys. Company Inspection	
		10.00–10.45	P.T.	
		11.00–12.00	Coy. Ceremonial drill on Coy. parade grounds.	

D. D. & L., London, E.C.
(A8001) Wt. W1771/M2031 750,000 5/17 Sch. 52 Forms C2118/14

Instructions regarding War Diaries and Intelligence Summaries are contained in F. S. Regs., Part II. and the Staff Manual respectively. Title pages will be prepared in manuscript.

WAR DIARY
or
INTELLIGENCE SUMMARY.
(Erase heading not required.)

Army Form C. 2118.

Place	Date	Hour	Summary of Events and Information	Remarks and references to Appendices
Ferrieres	Jan 7. Contd	14.15	Rugby Football Officers of 110th Brigade played N.C.O's + men of 6th + 7th Batts Leics R. on 7th Batt ground	
		14.15	Association Football Replay "C" Coy 1 v. "B" Coy nil. Brigade League 7th Bat. Leicestershire R, 5 goals. 6th Bat Leic. 1 goal.	
	Jan 8.	9.30 to 1200	Education.	
			"A" Coy. found working party of 1 Officer + 40 ORs. for Concentration Camp.	
		9.00	"B" Coy found Salvage party of 1 Officer + 50 O.R's, "A" Coy found Salvage party of 1 Officer and 20 O.R's.	
			Ass Football 4 Six aside inter platoon matches were played. Inter Coy. League Final. "C" Coy 1. D. Coy nil.	
	Jan 9	~~Jan 9~~	Education. "D" Coy. found working part for Concentration Camp as previously. "C" Coy found Salvage party of 1 Officer + 20 O.R's "D" Coy found 10 O.R's. Batt played 1st Wilts away	

D. D. & L., London, E.C. (A8001) Wt. W1171/M2031 750,000 5/17 Sch. 52 Forms C2118/14

Instructions regarding War Diaries and Intelligence Summaries are contained in F. S. Regs., Part II. and the Staff Manual respectively. Title pages will be prepared in manuscript.

WAR DIARY
or
INTELLIGENCE SUMMARY.
(Erase heading not required.)

Army Form C. 2118.

Place	Date	Hour	Summary of Events and Information	Remarks and references to Appendices
Ferriers	Jan 10.		Education.	
		10.00	"A" Coy. found working party for Concentration Camp	
			A Coy found 20 O.Rs, "B" Coy found 40 O.R's. for Salvage party. Plat. Comdrs accompanied their platoons.	
	Jan 11	10.00	Education. – Bookkeeping.	
			"C" Coy. found working party for Concentration Camp	
			"B" Coy. found working party for Officers Mess. of 1 officer + 40 O.R.	
			"A + B" Coys found party ~~for~~ for Salvage.	
		14.15	Football. 4 Six a side inter Platoon match. were played.	
			Boxing Brigade Finals were fought.	
	Jan. 12	10.45	Church Parade. Non Conformists. Voluntary C of E. parade in the school.	
			Inter-Coy. Rugby. "D" Coy 16 points "B" Coy. 3 points	

D. D. & L., London, E.C.
(A8001) Wt. W1771/M2031 750,000 5/17 Sch. 52 Forms C2118/14

Instructions regarding War Diaries and Intelligence Summaries are contained in F. S. Regs., Part II. and the Staff Manual respectively. Title pages will be prepared in manuscript.

WAR DIARY
or
INTELLIGENCE SUMMARY.
(*Erase heading not required.*)

Army Form C. 2118.

Place	Date	Hour	Summary of Events and Information	Remarks and references to Appendices
Ferriers	Jan 13.	10.15	A representative company marched to Aerodrome for full rehearsal of the consecration of the colours.	
			"A" Coy found working party for Concentration Camps.	
		9.30.	Education.	
		14.15	Rugby Football 110th Bry. played 64th Bde.	
	Jan 14	11.00	The "Colours" were consecrated at the Aerodrome near Boucles, by the Bishop of ~~[illegible]~~ Leicester, and presented to Colour Party by G.O.C. 21st Divn.	
			"C" Coy found the working party for Concentration Camps. "A" Coy found party for salvage.	
	Jan 15	9.30	Education, "C D" Coy, found working party for Concentration Camps.	
			"D" Company found working party to assist Engineers at Borehole at Ferriers.	
		9.30	Officers' Class	
			<u>Soccer</u> H Q + Transport 3 goals. "B" Coy nil.	
			<u>Rugby</u> "A" 33 points. "C" Coy nil.	

D. D. & L., London, E.C.
(A8011) Wt. W1771/M2031 750,000 5/17 Sch. 52 Forms C2118/14

Army Form C. 2118.

Instructions regarding War Diaries and Intelligence Summaries are contained in F. S. Regs., Part II. and the Staff Manual respectively. Title pages will be prepared in manuscript.

WAR DIARY
or
INTELLIGENCE SUMMARY.
(*Erase heading not required.*)

Place	Date	Hour	Summary of Events and Information	Remarks and references to Appendices
Ferrieres	Jan 16	9.30	Education "A" Coy found working party for Concentration Camp. "B" Coy found working party for "bore hole" Ferrieres. The Batt. Baths were opened. The Batt played the 6th Battn on Company ground.	
	Jan 17	10.00	Education. "A" Coy found working party for Concentration Camp.	France Sheet 62E. 1/40,000
		9.30.	Batt. Route March:– Ailly-sur-Somme, Rd junction S.W. of B. in Breilly – Cross Roads ¼ 1/8 miles S of Picquigny – Ferrieres. Order of march – Drums, "B" C. D Coys. Soccer: Sergts v Officers on Company ground.	
	Jan 18	9.50	Batt. marched to Bovelles for lecture by the Brigadier. Those not parading with their Coys. went on working party to Concentration Camp. Rugby 110th Bty. 14 points 64th Bty. nil	

D. D. & L., London, E.C.
(A8001) Wt. W1771/M2031 750,000 5/17 Sch. 52 Forms C2118/14

Instructions regarding War Diaries and Intelligence Summaries are contained in F. S. Regs., Part II. and the Staff Manual respectively. Title pages will be prepared in manuscript.

WAR DIARY
or
INTELLIGENCE SUMMARY.
(Erase heading not required.)

Army Form C. 2118.

Place	Date	Hour	Summary of Events and Information	Remarks and references to Appendices
Ferriers	Jan 19	1000	Church Parades. Nonconformists parade at 9.20 hrs for service at [illegible] at 10.00 hrs C of E Voluntary Service in School.	
	Jan 20		"D" Coy. found working party for Concentration Camp. "C" Coy. " Salvage party.	
		9.30	Education	
		1700	Lecture by Capt Wilson on Demobilization.	
			Soccer. "B" 10 goals. "D" Coy. 1 goal	
	Jan 21	9.30	Education. "A" Coy. found working party for concentration camp. "B" Coy found salvage party.	
		17.00	Captain Sawbridge gave lecture to officers on "Empire after the War".	
	Jan 22	9.30	Education. "C" Coy found working party for concentration camp. "D" Coy found salvage party.	
		14.30	Soccer. Batt. played 21st Div Art. — Arty [illegible] Bat nil	

D. D. & L., London, E.C.
(A8001) Wt. W1771/M2031 750,000 5/17 Sch. 52 Forms C2118/14

Instructions regarding War Diaries and Intelligence Summaries are contained in F. S. Regs., Part II. and the Staff Manual respectively. Title pages will be prepared in manuscript.

WAR DIARY
or
INTELLIGENCE SUMMARY.
(Erase heading not required.)

Army Form C. 2118.

Place	Date	Hour	Summary of Events and Information	Remarks and references to Appendices
Ferriers.	Jan 23	9.30	Education. "B" Coy found party for concentration camp. "A" Coy found Salvage party.	
		1700	Capt Wilson gave lecture to all ranks in School on Demobilization.	
		1415.	"A" Coy. played "D" Coy at Rugby.	
	Jan 24.	1000.	Education. "D" Coy. found working party for Concentration Camp.	
		9.30.	Batt. Route March. Route:- X. Rds. Q.1.A. - Rd. junct. K.21.d. - Rd jun. K.35.c. Sorrance	
		14.15	Soccer. Batt. v. 110th Bry. T.M.B. at Bovelles.	
	J. 25	1000	Education.	
		9.00.	Coy. Kit Inspection by R.Q.M.	
		10.00	Coy. Inspection by Coy. Cmdrs.	
	Jan. 26.	1000	Church Parades. Non Conformists at Guignemicourt C of E Voluntary services in School.	

D. D. & L., London, E.C.
(A8001) Wt. W1771/M2031 750,000 5/17 Sch. 52 Forms C2118/14

Instructions regarding War Diaries and Intelligence Summaries are contained in F. S. Regs., Part II. and the Staff Manual respectively. Title pages will be prepared in manuscript.

WAR DIARY
or
INTELLIGENCE SUMMARY.
(Erase heading not required.)

Army Form C. 2118.

Place	Date	Hour	Summary of Events and Information	Remarks and references to Appendices
Ferrien.	Jan 27	9.30	Education. "C" Coy found Salvage Coy.	
		14.15	Soccer. H.Q + Transport v "D" Coy on Coy. ground.	
	J. 28	9.30	Education. "B" Coy. found Salvage party	
	J. 29	9.30	Education. "D" Coy found Salvage party	
		14.15	Soccer. A. Coy. v. "B" Coy.	
	Jan 30	9.30	Education. "A." Coy found Salvage party. Weather too bad for sports.	
	Jan 31.	9.30	Education.	
		9.30	Batt. Route March. Route:- X Rds P.9.a. - Saissoal. X X Rds 5.30.a	

D. D. & L., London, E.C. (A8091) Wt. W1771/M2031 750,000 5/17 Sch. 52 Forms C2118/14

Instructions regarding War Diaries and Intelligence Summaries are contained in F. S. Regs., Part II. and the Staff Manual respectively. Title pages will be prepared in manuscript.

WAR DIARY
or
INTELLIGENCE SUMMARY.
(Erase heading not required.)

Army Form C. 2118.

Place	Date	Hour	Summary of Events and Information	Remarks and references to Appendices
Ferriers			January. 1919.	
			Arrivals	
			Drafts 2nd 118 O.R.	
			6th 10 O.R.	
			8th 17. O.R.	
			Departures	
			1st 1 O.R. Demobilized	
			5th 2 O.R. "	
			11th 17 O.R. "	
			13th 13 O.R. "	
			14th 2/Lt Turner "	
			6 O.R.	
			19th 8 O.R. "	
			22nd 2/Lt Lane [illegible]	
			Hill [illegible]	
			36 O.R.	
			26th 2/Lt Fisher [illegible] "	
			25 O.R.	
			29th 2/Lt Garner [illegible]	
			Lott [illegible]	
			56 O.R.	

G. H. Sawyer Lieut Col
Commanding 7th Leices. Regt

D. D. & L., London, E.C.
(A8001) Wt. W1771/M2031 750,000 5/17 Sch. 52 Forms C2118/14

2'

War Diary.

7th Battn Leicestershire Regiment

February 1919

Army Form C. 2118.

Instructions regarding War Diaries and Intelligence Summaries are contained in F. S. Regs., Part II. and the Staff Manual respectively. Title pages will be prepared in manuscript.

WAR DIARY
or
~~INTELLIGENCE SUMMARY.~~
(Erase heading not required.)

Place	Date	Hour	Summary of Events and Information	Remarks and references to Appendices
Ferrieres	1/2 Feb. 1.	9.50	Kit + Coy Stores Inspection by Coy Commanders	
	2	11.00	Church Parades - Nonconformists in School, Ferrieres; C of E voluntary services	
	7.	9.30	Batt Route March was carried out. Route: Chateau Gates, x Rds. P 9 a, Saissval, x Rds 30 a.	
	8.	9.30	Coy Kit Inspections.	
			The remainder of the week ending 8 2 19 was occupied by Salvage Parties, Education classes, and Sports.	
	9.	9.00 10.00	Church Parades; Nonconformists for service at Guyencourt. C of E in School, Ferrieres	
	12.		A Batt. Route March was carried out. Route: Chateau Gates, ~~Pissy~~ Bovelles, Pissy, Revelles, Clairy, Guignemicourt	
			The remainder of week ending 15 2 19 was occupied by Salvage Parties, Education + Sports.	

D. D. & L., London, E.C.
(A8001) Wt. W1771/M2031 750,000 5/17 Sch. 52 Forms/C2118/14

Army Form C. 2118.

Instructions regarding War Diaries and Intelligence Summaries are contained in F. S. Regs., Part II. and the Staff Manual respectively. Title pages will be prepared in manuscript.

WAR DIARY
or
INTELLIGENCE SUMMARY.
(*Erase heading not required.*)

Place	Date	Hour	Summary of Events and Information	Remarks and references to Appendices
Ferrieres.	Feb. 16	1000	Church Services in the School, Ferrieres.	
	19.		A Batt. Route March was carried out. Route - Chateau Gate, Pugmemcourt, Rd. junct. Q22 c. 5-3. X Rds Q13 b. 8-9. Saveuse.	Map. Ref Sheet: No. M62E. 1/40000
			The remainder of the week ending 22.2.19. was occupied by Salvage Parties, Working Parties, + Sports.	
	23.	1000	Church Parades. Services in the School, Ferrieres.	
		1500	110th Brigade Race Meeting.	
	26.		A Batt. Route March was carried out. Route: Chateau Gates, Saveuse, X Rds. K30.c.5.5. Ailly sur Somme, X Rds. Q1 a 2.9. Ferrieres.	Map. Ref Sh. M62E. 1/40000
			The remainder of the week was occupied by Salvage Parties, Working Parties, + Sports.	

D. D. & L., London, E.C.
(A8001) Wt. W1771/M2031 750,000 5/17 Sch. 52 Forms/C2118/14

Instructions regarding War Diaries and Intelligence Summaries are contained in F. S. Regs., Part II. and the Staff Manual respectively. Title pages will be prepared in manuscript.

WAR DIARY
or
INTELLIGENCE SUMMARY.
(Erase heading not required.)

Army Form C. 2118.

Place	Date	Hour	Summary of Events and Information	Remarks and references to Appendices
			February 1919.	
			Arrivals — Nil	
			Departures	
			Feb. 2. 2nd Lt Ward J. A.	
			3 " Skelton C. W.	
			Roe E. L.	
			7 Capt Horn H. R. M.C.	
			8 2nd Lt Connold C. Q.	
			Coleman L. G.	
			Feb. 10th Capt Goodwin B.	
			14 2nd Lt Teasdale G. W.	
			14 Boss G. W.	
			2nd 19 O.R.	
			3. 32	
			7 27	
			8 47	
			10 20	
			12. 6	
			14 4	
			15. 18 "	
			20. 20	
			27. 16	

G. H. Dawson
Lieut. Colonel, Commanding
7th Bn. Leicestershire Regt.

D. D. & L., London, E.C.
(A8001) Wt. W1771/M2031 750,000 5/17 Sch. 52 Forms C2118/14

WAR DIARY
or
INTELLIGENCE SUMMARY.
(Erase heading not required.)

7th Leic. Regt

Army Form C. 2118.

Instructions regarding War Diaries and Intelligence Summaries are contained in F. S. Regs., Part II. and the Staff Manual respectively. Title pages will be prepared in manuscript.

Place	Date	Hour	Summary of Events and Information	Remarks and references to Appendices
FERRIERES.	Mar 2nd	1130 hrs.	Church Parades:- Nonconformists in School, FERRIERES. C. of E. Voluntary Services.	
	Mar 5th.	0930 hrs.	Batt. Route March was carried out. Route:- Chateau Gates - Saveuse - X Cross Roads K30.c.5.5 - Ailly-sur-Somme X Roads Q1.a.2.9. - Ferrieres.	
	Mar 8th.	0930 hrs.	Coy Stores and Kit Inspections.	
			The remainder of the week-ending 8.3.19. was occupied by Sports, Training and Education Classes.	
	Mar 9th.	1130 hrs.	Church Parades:- Nonconformists in School FERRIERES. C.ofE. Voluntary Services.	
	Mar 12th.	0930 hrs.	Batt. Route march was carried out. Route:- Chateau Gates - X Roads Q1.a.2.1. X Roads J23.a.7.1. - X Roads J22.d.3.0. X Roads P9.a.4.1. - FERRIERES.	
	Mar 15th.	0930 hrs.	Coy Stores and Kit Inspections.	
			The remainder of the week-ending 15.3.19. was occupied by Training, Sports and Education Classes.	
	Mar 16th.	1130 hrs.	Church Parades:- Nonconformists in School, FERRIERES. C.ofE. Voluntary Services.	
	Mar 19th	0930 hrs.	Batt. Route march was carried out. Route:- Chateau Gates - X Roads P12.c.1.9. X Roads P9.a.4.1. - BEUX - BOVELLES - FERRIERES.	
	Mar 22nd.	0930 hrs.	Coy Stores and Kit Inspections.	
			The remainder of the week-ending 22.3.19. was occupied by Training, Sports and Education Classes.	

D. D. & L., London, E.C.
(A8001) Wt. W1771/M2031 750,000 5/17 Sch. 52 Forms/C2118/14

Army Form C. 2118.

WAR DIARY
or
INTELLIGENCE SUMMARY.
(Erase heading not required.)

Instructions regarding War Diaries and Intelligence Summaries are contained in F. S. Regs., Part II. and the Staff Manual respectively. Title pages will be prepared in manuscript.

Place	Date	Hour	Summary of Events and Information	Remarks and references to Appendices

MARCH

ARRIVALS

Mar.4th. 1.O.R.
Mar.14th. 2.O.R.
Mar.22nd. 1.O.R.
Mar.25th. 1.O.R.

DEPARTURES.

Mar.1[illegible]th. A/Capt. W.A. CHAPMAN.
Mar.27th. Lieut. W.T. DOWLELL.
Mar.27th. 2/Lieut. E.R. BERWICK.
Mar.24th. Lieut. H.C. DAVIS.
Mar.24th. 2/Lieut. E.W. RICHARDS. MM.
Mar.24th. 2/Lieut. A.H. GRIMLEY.
Mar.30th. 2/Lieut. C.S. FLETCHER.
Mar.30th. 2/Lieut. H.R. RADFORD.
Mar.30th. 2/Lieut. H. CLARKE.
Mar31st. Capt. H.J. WALSH. MC.
Mar.31st. Major. G.E.T. DIXON. M.C.
Mar.31st. Capt. E. Pascoe.
Mar.3rd. 2.O.R.
6th. 14.O.R.
5th. 1.O.R.
13th. 28.O.R.
4th. 1.O.R.
8th. 1.O.R.
20th. 8.O.R.
27th. 8.O.R.
Mar. 31st 80.O.R.
Mar. 31st 4.O.R.

****

[signature]
Lieut-Colonel, Commdg.
7th Bn. The Leicestershire Regiment.

D. D. & L., London, E.C.
(A8001) Wt. W1771/M2031 750,000 5/17 Sch. 52 Forms/C2118/14

Instructions regarding War Diaries and Intelligence Summaries are contained in F. S. Regs., Part II. and the Staff Manual respectively. Title pages will be prepared in manuscript.

WAR DIARY for the month of ~~MARCH~~ APRIL.

or

~~INTELLIGENCE SUMMARY.~~

(Erase heading not required.)

Army Form C. 2118.

Place	Date	Hour	Summary of Events and Information	Remarks and references to Appendices
FERRIERES.	APRIL 1st.		The Battalion was reorganised into one Company under the command of Captain W.H.RIGBY.	
FERRIERES.	APRIL 2nd.		A Battalion Route march was carried out at 0930 hours. Route:- CHATEAU GATES - X ROADS P.3.a.4.1. - SEUX - BOVELLES - FERRIERES.	
FERRIERES.	APRIL 3rd.		Captain W.H.RIGBY took over command of the Battalion, vice Lieut- Col G.H. SAWYER, D.S.O. who proceeded to take over command of the 10th Queens (R.W.S.)	
BOUCHON.	APRIL 5th.		The Battalion proceeded to BOUCHON by march route, moving off at 0930 hours and arriving in billets 1430 hours. The march discipline was good. ROUTE:- PICQUIGNY - HANGEST-sur-SOMME - LONGPRE les CORPS SAINTS - L'ETOILE - BOUCHON.	
BOUCHON.	APRIL 6th.		Voluntary Services in the School. (Church of England)	
BOUCHON.	APRIL 7th.		A Working Party of 2 Sergts and 22 O.R. proceeded to the Cadre Park LONGPRE for work under 2/Lieut J.BEARDSHORE and returned at 1600 hours. Remainder of Battalion paraded on the Football field for Training under 2/Lieut E.W.COX.	
BOUCHON.	APRIL 8th.		Parades as for the 7th. A Cricket Match was played, The Battalion V 1st Bn. Wilts Regt, the Battalion losing.	
BOUCHON.	APRIL 9th.		Parades as for the 8th.	
BOUCHON.	APRIL 10th.		Parades as for the 9th.	
BOUCHON.	APRIL 11th.		A party of 1 Officer and 46 Other Ranks proceeded to the 349.P. of W. Coy, DUNKIRK, moving off at 1000 hours. The remainder of the Battalion paraded for baths at 1430 hours.	
BOUCHON.	APRIL 13th.		Voluntary Church of England Services in the School.	

D. D. & L., London, E.C. (A8001) Wt. W1771/M2031 750,000 5/17 Sch. 52 Forms/C2118/14

Army Form C. 2118.

Instructions regarding War Diaries and Intelligence Summaries are contained in F. S. Regs., Part II. and the Staff Manual respectively. Title pages will be prepared in manuscript.

WAR DIARY

or

INTELLIGENCE SUMMARY.

(*Erase heading not required.*)

Place	Date	Hour	Summary of Events and Information	Remarks and references to Appendices
BOUCHON.	APRIL	20th.	Voluntary Church of England Services in the School.	
BOUCHON.	APRIL	22nd.	A Cricket Match was played, Battalion V 1st Bn. The Wilts Regt, the Battn winning.	
BOUCHON.	APRIL	23rd.	A Cricket Match was played, Battalion V 21st Divisional Signal Coy, the Battalion winning.	
BOUCHON.	APRIL	27th.	Voluntary Church of England Services in the School.	

D. D. & L., London, E.C.
(A8001) Wt. W1771/M2031 750,000 5/17 Sch. 52 Forms C2118/14

Army Form C. 2118.

Instructions regarding War Diaries and Intelligence Summaries are contained in F. S. Regs., Part II. and the Staff Manual respectively. Title pages will be prepared in manuscript.

WAR DIARY
or
INTELLIGENCE SUMMARY.

(*Erase heading not required.*)

Place	Date	Hour	Summary of Events and Information	Remarks and references to Appendices
			ARRIVALS and DEPARTURES.	

Arrivals.

April 16th. 1.Other Rank.
April 24th. Captain W.W.MAWSON.
Captain A.LEAKE.
Lieut G.B.C.NOEL.
2/Lieut A.E.ESDIN.
2/Lieut J.S.WEAVING.
1.Other Rank.

Departures.

April 3rd. Lt-Col G.H.SAWYER.D.S.O.
April 5th. Lieut A.J.KNIGHT.
2/Lieut F.W.WALKER.
16.Other Ranks.
April 6th. 2.Other Ranks.
April 11th. 2/Lieut L.G.BURSTALL.
63.Other Ranks.
April 13th. 10.Other Ranks.
April 17th. Major H.W.H.TYLER.M.C.

W H Rigby Captain.,
7th Bn. The Leicestershire Regiment.

D. D. & L., London, E.C.
(A8001) Wt. W1771/M2031 750,000 5/17 Sch. 52 Forms C2118/14

Instructions regarding War Diaries and Intelligence Summaries are contained in F. S. Regs., Part II. and the Staff Manual respectively. Title pages will be prepared in manuscript.

WAR DIARY
or
INTELLIGENCE SUMMARY.
(Erase heading not required.)

Army Form C. 2118.

Place	Date	Hour	Summary of Events and Information	Remarks and references to Appendices
FERRIERES.	Mar 28th.	0930 hrs.	Batt. Route March was carried out. Route:- Chateau Gates - X Roads Q1.a.2.9. X Roads J25.a7.1. - X Roads J22.a.5.9. - X Roads P9.a.4.1. - FERRIERES.	
	Mar 29th.	0930 hrs.	Coy Stores and Kit Inspection.	

****

D. D. & L., London, E.C.
(A8001) Wt. W1771/M2031 750,000 5/17 Sch. 52 Forms C2118/14

www.ingramcontent.com/pod-product-compliance
Lightning Source LLC
Chambersburg PA
CBHW080845010526
44114CB00017B/2372
* 9 7 8 1 4 7 4 5 1 2 3 5 0 *